Electric Bluesman

The Life and Times of Jimi Hendrix

Wylie Graham McLallen

Mechanicsburg, PA USA

Published by Sunbury Press, Inc.
Mechanicsburg, PA USA

www.sunburypress.com

For information about special discounts for bulk purchases, please contact Sunbury Press Orders Dept. at (855) 338-8359 or orders@sunburypress.com.

To request one of our authors for speaking engagements or book signings, please contact Sunbury Press Publicity Dept. at publicity@sunburypress.com.

FIRST SUNBURY PRESS EDITION: February 2026

Set in Adobe Garamond | Interior design by Crystal Devine | Cover by Lawrence Knorr | Edited by Sarah Peachey.

Publisher's Cataloging-in-Publication Data
Names: McLallen, Wylie Graham, author.
Title: Electric bluesman : the life and times of Jimi Hendrix / Wylie Graham McLallen.
Description: First trade paperback edition. | Mechanicsburg, PA : Sunbury Press, 2026.
Summary: Storming London as a black guitarist in a world of white musicians, Jimi Hendrix reclaimed rock and roll as true American music. For rock and roll, though brilliantly interpreted by great English bands like the Beatles, had its roots in the small grimy dance halls and roadhouses in the heartland of America where Jimi had grown up poor and destitute.
Identifiers: ISBN : 979-8-88819-391-4 (softcover).
Subjects: BIOGRAPHY & AUTOBIOGRAPHY / African American & Black | BIOGRAPHY & AUTOBIOGRAPHY / Music | HISTORY / Social History.

Designed in the USA
0 1 1 2 3 5 8 13 21 34 55

For the Love of Books!

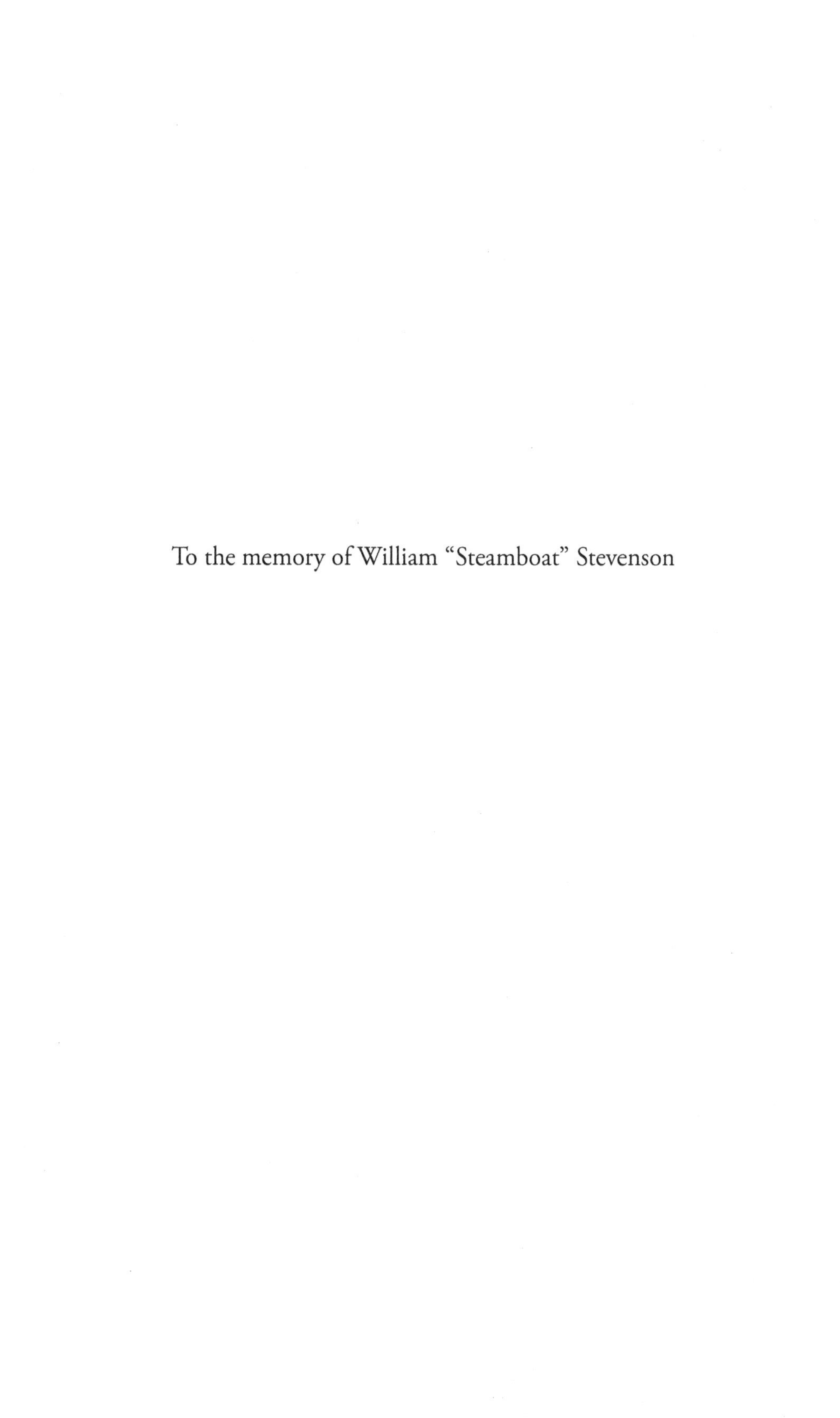

To the memory of William "Steamboat" Stevenson

Contents

Hendrix believed in improvisation when he played in public,
and that way, being free and creative,
something new can happen.

Acknowledgments

Through the long course of research into the life of Jimi Hendrix there were many people who stepped forth to encourage and give aid and insight into this precise and critical endeavor. I wish to thank the staff of the main branch of the Vancouver Public Library; they are always courteous and helpful and interested as I searched for books to further and complete my research. I would like to thank Henri Brown and his sister Faith Hendrix, who were open and kind and gave factual and in-depth insight from first-hand knowledge of their cousin, Jimi Hendrix, through years of growing up together. Steve Cropper, guitarist of Booker T. and the MGs, shared the extraordinary and positive encounter of a personal visit by Jimi Hendrix at Stax Records in Memphis long before he was touched by fame: it was Steve's son, Stephen, who kindly forward my request to his father. The *Sunbury Press* creative team of Sarah Peachey and Crystal Devine, who helped to edit and build the book. Tom Gettelfinger, who, in addition to being an outstanding ophthalmologist, has a keen interest in rock 'n' roll and found and forwarded a journal with a rare and unique interpretation of Jimi Hendrix. Webster McDonald and Calvin Turley, both old friends and musicians who provided insight into Hendrix's playing style. Rob Frith of Neptoon Records on Main Street, shared not only his encyclopedic knowledge of rock music, particularly of Hendrix sites in Vancouver, but also material from his vast collection of rock memorabilia, which became very useful as I wrote this story. My brothers, Lyman and John, were encouraging and interested throughout this long effort of research and writing. Lastly, and perhaps most importantly, my family for their understanding through the long and undisturbed hours of concentration.

Crossroads

One night, in the spring of 1966, a beautiful, young English woman named Linda Keith watched an electric blues guitarist, going by the name of Jimmy James, perform on a large stage before a paucity of patrons in the huge ballroom of a Midtown Manhattan nightclub. She could hardly believe the sound and sight of the man, nor why he was playing with such a mediocre and forgettable band. "He was clearly a star," remembered Linda, "though he was such an odd-looking star, and it was such an odd place, it didn't seem right."[1] During the break between sets, she invited him to the table where she sat with friends. Smitten with his physical beauty, a polite, soft-spoken demeanor, and the depth of his musical knowledge, she became determined to bring this brilliant young man the recognition due. As the girlfriend of Keith Richards, the lead guitarist of the Rolling Stones, Linda had connections. When she heard that Chas Chandler, the bassist of the Animals, was looking for an act to manage, Linda told him about her obscure electric bluesman. Chas came to see him play in the dim cavern of Cafe Wha? in Greenwich Village and could hardly believe his eyes and ears as he watched this bluesman create remarkable sounds from an electric guitar. Chandler decided to take this young black musician to England, where his skills would be much more noticed than in America, where Jimi Hendrix almost starved on the streets.

The British, through a vibrant interpretation of the black rhythm and blues mainstream America neglected, were enthralling the world with small rock and roll bands that surpassed the fame of all but Elvis Presley.

Great black bluesmen had played in England before Hendrix. Muddy Waters (at whose feet Jimi once sat on a quick visit to Chicago during his poor, itinerant years), whose rich, chesty baritone and piercing, keening slide guitar had transformed the Delta Blues, traditionally the music of loners and transients, into a collective rooted experience, received a harsh reception on his first British tour in 1958, driving influential jazz critics from the halls with his fierce electric guitar, only to return six years later—this time with an acoustic guitar and a well-rehearsed repertoire of old-time Delta tunes—to find the country crawling with groups like the Rolling Stones, the Mojos, and David Bowie's Manish Boys, who had taken their names from his songs.

When the great R&B veterans came to England in the early sixties, they played in places packed with "mods" and art students screaming for the songs they'd heard from the Stones, Manfred Mann, and the Yardbirds (named for jazzman Charlie "Bird" Parker), and except for Muddy Waters, who transcended what these "white kids" thought his music should be, they did not fare well. John Lee Hooker doing cabaret in his checkered jacket almost looked pathetic. Sonny Boy Williamson, Jimmy Reed, and others who rode the English vogue for rhythm and blues looked old and lost before the drastically different interpretation of their music by the young English bands. Jimi Hendrix followed in their wake, but he was young, ready, supremely gifted, and guided by a savvy young English bassist who knew the London music scene. The English guitarists who had captured the world—Jeff Beck, Eric Clapton, Keith Richards, and a few extraordinary others—were the musical sons of Muddy Waters, but Hendrix, who, as Howlin' Wolf once said of Elvis Presley, "made his pull from the blues,"[2] was an authentic Delta Bluesman, and in England he reclaimed rock and roll as a preeminent American art form.

Blues has been around forever, following in the long wake of many strands of music and culture; perhaps its deepest root being Voodoo, the religious and mystical practices and philosophy crossing over on slave ships from West Africa. The practices were immediately incorporated into the brands of Christianity enforced upon black people by white slave-masters (when Hendrix recorded "Voodoo Child," he was making a statement of black identity by staking a claim to musical turf white bluesmen could never truly explore), but the emergence of blues happened around 1900, years after the arrival of the guitar in America and a few more years before the advent of recording. Blues was almost immediately divided into two strains: one urban, mostly performed by female singers accompanied by a piano and sometimes brass and reeds; the other rural, performed by male singers, either solo or duo, who played the guitar or harmonica.

The men who played the blues were often itinerant, poor, and considered unsophisticated and less respectable than the women, but it was country blues that transformed into the rockin' electric music that immediately followed World War II. The women of blues soon aligned themselves with the jazz world, where a loud, beautiful female voice could make a lot more money, while the male singers, following the lead of T-Bone Walker in the late 1930s, joined forces with the swing bands that featured instrumental soloists on piano or electric guitar and big brassy ensembles. From T-Bone came B. B. King, Clarence "Gatemouth" Brown, and other lead guitarists of the blues. By the fifties, Otis Rush and Buddy Guy, drawing heavily on more advanced harmonic variations on the traditional twelve-bar structures, merged the guitar styling of King and Walker into the Chicago idiom derived from Muddy Waters. The blues sounds easy: twelve bars divided into three lines of four bars each, the second bar generally a repetition of the first, and containing three chords—the first (tonic), fourth (sub-dominant), and fifth (dominant) of the scale. Anybody who can play a musical instrument can quickly learn something that sounds like the blues, but it would only *sound* like the blues. To play or sing something that *feels* like the blues can take a lifetime.

Blues came naturally to Jimi Hendrix. He felt it throughout the tragedies of a poverty-stricken childhood in Seattle, Washington. His feelings never strayed during a long, hard apprenticeship playing alongside the masters who defined the genres of rhythm and blues and rock and roll as he practiced and developed his sense of musical and performance skills in the shabby halls and joints in the Jim Crow South of the early 1960s. His mature work as an innovative leader spanned a mere four years, into which he crammed an astonishing amount of creative work that influenced a range of music as diverse as hard rock and jazz. And though the body of his work is complete, he died on the threshold of what could have been an entirely new musical phase, for he was ready to sort out the horrible tangles of his business affairs and was preparing to work with legendary arranger Gil Evans on an album which could have launched a fresh and innovative career in jazz. The truest reflection of Jimi Hendrix, which paths might he have taken on the crossroads, can be found in the lives of two earlier black musicians who also died young: one virtually invented the electric guitar as an amplified solo voice; the other was a shadowy Delta bluesman, who, according to legend, sold his soul to the devil in exchange for his musical gift.

The shadowy bluesman Robert Johnson lived obscurely until a talent scout named Ernie Oertle took a chance by summoning him to record for Don Law of ARC Records in San Antonio, Texas, where, in November 1936, he sang and played on his acoustic guitar a few dozen songs that would change American music. Johnson then returned to the Mississippi Delta, drifting further into dark obscurity. Two years later, music producer John Hammond, by virtue of the remarkable Texas recordings, wanted to present Johnson at Carnegie Hall in New York City only to discover his death. During his short life, before the wake of his great recordings and their ceaseless rhythmic repercussions, Robert Johnson was as unknown to the world as any other dark-skinned child in the long, flat land of the rich alluvial Mississippi Delta, where the blacks lived under such severe restrictions that after the harsh daily drudge of planting and picking cotton, they could only find their souls in music; and in country juke joints and on small town street corners throughout the Delta they certainly did play music.

Johnson was born out of wedlock into a large family of sharecroppers near Hazelhurst, Mississippi, in 1911. His biological father soon disappeared, and the man to whom his mother was married fled to Memphis after a dispute with white landowners. When Robert was about two, he joined this man and spent eight or nine years in Memphis, where he attended a Negro school on Carnes Avenue, learning geography, language, math, and music. It was in Memphis that he acquired his love of popular music along with an education that set him apart from most of his contemporary blues musicians. Still a boy, he returned to the Mississippi Delta, settling with his mother, who had married another sharecropper on a large plantation near Tunica, Mississippi. He played the harmonica well and, taking the surname of his biological father, a man named Noah Johnson, started hanging around the local juke joints, profuse throughout the Delta, where, encountering Son House, Willie Brown, and Charley Patton—all to become legendary—he grabbed their guitars during breaks and, according to Son House, made such a horrible racket that, derisively dubbing him "Little Robert," they would quickly snatch them back.

He briefly tried to settle down, marrying a fifteen-year-old girl who died in childbirth along with the baby, and then he disappeared. When he resurfaced about a year later at a joint near Robinsonville, Mississippi, Son House and Willie Brown were astounded. "He had a guitar swinging on his back," remembered Son House.

"What do you do with that thing," said Son House. "You can't do nothing with it."

Robert asked him to let him play.

"So he sat down there and finally got started. And, man, he was so good. When he finished all our mouths were standing open."[3]

How Robert Johnson became so good so quick, enough to shake a founding father of Delta Blues and leave an everlasting mark, is no longer open to speculation: Young Robert returned to his birthplace, Hazelhurst, searching for his biological father, and encountered, instead, a master blues guitarist named Ike Zimmerman, who mentored Johnson like a son, teaching all he knew on the gravestones of a local cemetery late at night where no one would disturb them. However, perhaps such a transformation is more understandable by leaving the realm of facts to reconsider his "pact with the devil at the crossroads" in accordance with the rituals of Voodoo worship.

Far from primitive superstition, Voodoo is a complex and sophisticated belief system from Africa that considers the "devil" a primal force in the universe, dispensing blessings and curses in equal measure. Reference to Voodoo symbols and charms resound throughout country and electric blues. Muddy Waters performed such songs as "Hoochie Coochie Man" and "Got My Mojo Working," as have many who sing and play the blues. Johnson was probably initiated in a Voodoo cult somewhere down in the bayous, where "the tradition of making a pact at the crossroads to obtain supernatural prowess" is a ritual of ancient Voodoo worship, and some of the lyrics of his songs could not have been written without this knowledge of initiation. Maybe Robert Johnson didn't actually encounter the big black deity Legba, mischief-maker and god of the crossroads, who took his guitar, tuned it, played a piece, and handed it back, but somehow this green kid was transformed into the most consummate artist of his tradition, which can hardly be attributed to playing on street corners for nickels.

Johnson's music consolidated the Delta tradition and extended it into new realms. Among the first bluesmen to have learned from listening to others' recordings; rather than rework the ideas of local bluesmen through the "folk" process, he could entertain at a dance by extending a song with improvised verses and keep the beat going as long as dancers stayed on their feet, but his music was mostly shaped from recordings. His songs were tightly constructed, virtually conceived for the three-minute format of the 78 rpm record, and from his records the blues were transformed into rock and roll by musicians as diverse as Cream, the Rolling Stones, Bob Dylan, and Jimi Hendrix. John Hammond wanted to bring Johnson to New York City, where the energy and sophistication could not have failed to further transform the shy, wild Delta wanderer. But he died before this could happen, and even his death is obscure and not without mystery. Alone in a small town near Greenwood, Mississippi, at the age of twenty-seven, he was poisoned by a jealous husband. A death certificate proves his existence, but his recordings reveal the magnitude of the value of his life.

Nearly all early bluesmen played anywhere they could, street corners and shacks, using an acoustic guitar. (When a young Muddy Waters encountered Robert Johnson playing on a hamlet corner near Stovall, Mississippi, so good was he with his guitar he frightened Muddy away.) Electric guitars took longer to take hold in country blues than in jazz and urban music because few homes among the Delta poor had electricity. The man who would bring the electric guitar into the spotlight was a young black man named Charlie Christian from Oklahoma, who had his hands in as many music genres as would Jimi Hendrix thirty years later. A good-humored country boy who loved to play music and party, Charlie found a national audience as a member of the Benny Goodman sextet in 1939 but died from tuberculosis almost three years later at the age of twenty-two.

Charlie grew up in Oklahoma City. His father played the trumpet, his mother played the piano, and together they accompanied silent films in local movie houses. Trying his parents' instruments, he at first preferred the piano and was good enough to gain local work. At the age of fourteen, he teamed up with T-Bone Walker, alternating on guitar and bass. Playing on the streets and passing the hat for coins, Charlie played string bass in an ornately funky and musically adventurous style that caught people's attention. In 1937 he was leading his own band when he met Eddie Durham, who played the electric guitar for the big band of Count Basie. Receiving formal instructions from Durham convinced Charlie to drop his other instruments. He bought a Gibson ES–150 and an amplifier and went to work.

John Hammond dropped in to catch his act at a club in Oklahoma City and was so impressed that he called Benny Goodman, who reluctantly agreed to fly Charlie to Los Angeles. Charlie, wearing a ten-gallon hat, purple shirt, narrow pointed yellow shoes, and lugging a guitar case and amplifier, made a less-than-auspicious impression. After the first set of an evening performance, Hammond and the bassist lugged Charlie's amplifier onto the stage and plugged it in. Goodman, an intimidating man, was not amused, but when the music started, Charlie cranked up his volume and played dazzling solo after dazzling solo, immediately becoming part of the band, earning $150 a week playing on national radio. Goodman remembered Charlie as "retiring and reserved, but, by gosh, when he sat down to play the guitar he was something."[4]

Like most jazz guitarists of the time whose experience was mostly with acoustic guitars, Charlie had cultivated speed of execution, necessary because of the short duration and fast decay of notes struck on an unamplified instrument, and a facility to play easily and fluently. The electric guitar enabled him to hold a note far longer than an acoustic guitar and gave him a greater degree of choice and flexibility in phrasing. (When Muddy Waters went to Chicago and found that his acoustic didn't cut it in the noisy taverns, he turned to the electric guitar and soon realized the amplifier didn't just make it louder, it also made it sound different.) The breakthrough year for the electric guitar was 1939. Among those recording were Les Paul, T-Bone Walker (Christian's old buddy from Oklahoma City), Les Hite, Eddie Durham, and leading the way was Charlie Christian. Yet for all his acclaim with the Goodman Sextet, it was in his extracurricular activities where his personal and artistic ambitions far outstripped his role with Goodman's band.

In New York City his second home was a Harlem nightclub on 118th named Minton's, which attracted the best young jazz musicians. Charlie would arrive late at night, still soaked with sweat from Goodman's shows, haul his guitar and amp up on the stand, and jam with the likes of pianist Thelonious Monk, saxophonist Charlie Parker, Dizzy Gillespie on trumpet, and drummer Kenny Clarke in after-hours sessions that brought forth the birth of bebop and laid the groundwork for most post-war jazz. Blowing over and improvising the standard popular songs of the time—"Stardust," "I Got Rhythm," "Heart And Soul," and others—Christian's extended solos vaulted off into harmonic realms with the voice of his guitar and amplifier as thick and distorted and rough-edged as that of T-Bone Walker and fifties guitarists B. B. King and Chuck Berry. Combined with the adventurous rhythms of Clarke, Monk, Parker, and Gillespie, it was intensely challenging music, both intimidating and exhilarating, much like that of Jimi Hendrix thirty years later.

As the influence of bop spread, Charlie Christian was the "boss" whenever he climbed on stage at Minton's. However, in the summer of 1940, he collapsed while coughing on stage in Chicago. An X-ray revealed a spot on the lung. He never told Goodman or Hammond about his tuberculosis and, against all medical advice, continued to fulfill his commitment to Goodman, showing up after hours to jam uptown. His refusal to slow down made matters worse. In the spring of 1941 he became a patient at a sanitarium on Staten Island, where loyal friends like Hammond regularly brought him chicken, chocolate cake, and new records (to his sorrow, he never heard from Goodman), but other friends brought him marijuana and booze and helped sneak him out to jams and parties where he continued to get high and bed women. That winter the tuberculosis became pneumonia, and in February 1942, at the age of twenty-two, Charlie Christian was gone.

Gifted people who die young can become a romantic memory at odds with the reality of life and obscuring their true lasting achievements. It's often said they were too beautiful or too sensitive to live in the world, and while they were beautiful and sensitive, they were also unlucky or made the wrong decisions. Robert Johnson died, not because he discarded his pact with the devil, but because he was too reckless and cocksure to care about proffered bottles of whiskey or which women he tried to bed. Charlie Christian died young because the lifestyle of a jazz musician was too demanding for a youth with tuberculosis, and he failed to heed the medical advice that probably would have saved his life. Jimi Hendrix, Brian Jones, Jim Morrison, and Janis Joplin died from drug overdoses; Buddy Holly and Otis Redding were just plain unlucky. They are all, however, very special, for death, no matter how it happened, cannot tarnish the glory of their achievements nor diminish the remembrance of their beauty. Robert Johnson played the most eloquent and evocative blues of his time, perhaps of any time, and Charlie Christian created a new and expressive voice for the electric guitar, an instrument then in its infancy. Jimi Hendrix embodied them both and extended their achievements in a few short years.

B. B. King

Charlie Christian

Muddy Waters

Robert Johnson

A Struggling Musical Family

Early in the twentieth century, Jimi's grandmother, Nora Moore, along with her sister Belle, left the family farm in Tennessee to join a traveling vaudeville troupe as chorus girls/dancers, touring the country and performing on stages in extravagant costumes. Bertran Philander Ross Hendrix (named by his black mother after his white father, who had once owned her, in the vain hope of receiving child support) was a stagehand in the same Dixieland Vaudeville troupe that broke up soon after reaching Seattle in 1909. Bertran and Nora married. It was hard for a black man to find work in Seattle, and so, on the advice of a friend, they moved north about 120 miles, crossing the Canadian border to Vancouver, British Columbia, where Ross found work as a steward in expensive private clubs. They started a family and began a new life, becoming active in a small black community that became known as Hogan's Alley.

Hogan's Alley, the lane between Union and Prior that ran for a few blocks east of Main Street, was just south of Chinatown, which lies east of downtown Vancouver. Then known as "the East End," it was the kind of place many wished to ignore. "To the average citizen, Hogan's Alley stands for three things—squalor, immorality, and crime," wrote a columnist in the *Daily Province* in 1939; "the name . . . conjures up images of bootleggers, canned heaters, prostitutes, and all types of criminals. Police records bear this out."[1] The nearby streets and residences were home to the city's small black community, which had established itself in the area by the early 1920s. The alley served food and music throughout all hours, attracting black musicians like Louis Armstrong and Fats Waller, who, when performing in town, often appeared there at night to eat chicken and cornbread and continue playing music in some of the clubs housed in the shacks. Black people settled in the neighborhood because of its proximity to The Great Northern Railway station, where many of the men worked as porters, and because housing was cheap and discrimination was less than in other parts of the city.

Bertran and Nora generally found Vancouver a good place to raise their children and were granted Canadian citizenship in 1922. Nora did laundry and other domestic work and helped to found the local chapter of the African Methodist Episcopal Church, which purchased an older church building at the end of Hogan's Alley on Jackson Avenue. The couple had four children, three sons and a daughter. The fourth child, James Allen Ross Hendrix, born June 10, 1919, would become the father of Jimi Hendrix. For a while the family lived in a house near the fairgrounds at Hastings Park in the northeast part of the city. Bertran was working as a steward at the Quilchena Golf Club on the west side of Vancouver. He woke up early each morning to take the streetcar across town to the golf course and return home in the evening, with the family awaiting his arrival for dinner.

The children remember their father's manner being as distinguished as the people he served at the private club by the wealthy neighborhood of Shaughnessy. He often dressed formally for dinner, and as they had seen "big rich folks" act this way in the movies, his children thought it was funny. Bertran was a literate man who enjoyed reading the *Vancouver Sun*, and was quiet and stern but patient, never giving his children whippings. Nora, always home, was affectionate and fun, and liked to listen to Jack Benny, Moms Mabley, and other comedians on the radio. Bertran was dark-skinned but had the sharp features of his white father, while Nora, whose great-grandmother was a full-blooded Cherokee, looked more Negro with a wide flat nose. In the summers the parents took their children to the fairgrounds, where they rode the rides at the fair.

Soon they moved near downtown Vancouver to a large wooden house on Richards Street that became a hangout for all the kids in the neighborhood, regardless of their ethnic background or the color of their skin. James Allen Ross, or "Al," played with his brother Frank, who was a year older and "was always cool-looking" with girls falling all over him. The family had picnics at Stanley Park and Kitsilano Beach, and the children attended school at Dawson Annex on Burrard Street. Al was smart and learned to read and write but never studied, and would drop out before finishing high school. Older brother Leon played the violin with his long, tapering fingers. There was a piano in the house and Leon could play that well, too. They sang spirituals at Christmas, and, at any other time throughout the year, would wind up an old gramophone and listen to Louis Armstrong. Bertran, who was much older than Nora, walked with a cane and sang in a jubilee choir. Sometimes he accompanied his wife to dances, where she would dance while he gabbed with other fellows.

They were a lively family, full of entertainment. As a child, Al picked up steps watching Frank and his sister, Pat, dance. Leon took it to a higher level with a regular partner, rehearsing at the house doing the waltz, tango, and an Apache dance where the guy tossed the girl around. Nora taught Al some tap, and a jazz step called "fall off the log;" he also learned the Charleston and Lindy Hop. But the Depression came along, and times became tough. Although Bertran had a stable job, life was precarious for black people in a city so overwhelmingly white, where, even with their sterling characters, blacks like Bertran and Nora felt like oddities. Death began to stalk the family when a little black girl in the neighborhood, Bernice, a close family friend who followed Al to school, died from what may have been an accidental poisoning. Then it happened closer.

In March 1932, Leon, diagnosed with appendicitis, died suddenly of a ruptured appendix in an ambulance on the way to the hospital. He was the oldest child, had graduated from high school, and the family took his death hard, especially Bertran, who had planned to send Leon to college. Two years later, Bertran passed away from heart failure at the age of sixty-eight. The family enrolled in and received Canadian relief, and Nora took in laundry and worked as a part-time cook at Jean Fuller's late-night café. They could no longer afford to rent the house on Richards Street, so the family moved in with Nora's boyfriend in a small house on East Georgia Street, not far from the docks where incoming boats gave away salmon before it would spoil, which Nora cooked for dinner. Here Al grew into manhood. This was also the house where Jimi and his younger brothers often stayed when visiting their grandmother during summers in the late forties and early fifties.

Al was small but strong and athletic, a good boxer, and a nightlife seeker. He decked out in a zoot suit with ballooning pants tapered tight to the ankle with a jacket that hung to his knees, and he danced at every dance in every ballroom when and where he could. But there were few available black women in Vancouver, and it was dangerous for a black man to date a white girl.

He also had trouble getting a job. He applied for a job as a railroad porter but was repeatedly rejected (maybe because he had such a feisty personality). Striking out for Seattle, where there were more opportunities for a black man, he searched for work. He had dual citizenship since both his parents were American on the day he was born.

There were thousands of black people in Seattle and nearly all of them lived in a large area east of downtown called the Central District. Extending to Lake Washington, it had started as a Jewish neighborhood with many synagogues and was still the center of Jewish life in the city. The houses were old and some of the streets looked like slums. This was where immigrants landed. The neighborhoods were home to Filipinos, Japanese, Chinese, Italians, Germans, and people from other parts of the world. Culturally diverse, Seattle was not as segregated as most of the country, but few people rented to Negroes outside of the Central District. Though, as in Vancouver, the only employment open to them were in factories or service jobs like cooks, maids, waiters, and porters, there were so many of them that they could make the most of it. The black community had its own newspapers, shops, restaurants, and, running along Jackson Street, one of the most vibrant entertainment districts in the United States, where black, white, and everyone else crowded its jazz clubs at night and spilled out onto the musical streets.

Al Hendrix reached Seattle in 1940. For a while he did odd jobs about the house of a family he had known in Vancouver. He cleaned, vacuumed, washed windows, mowed the lawn, and weeded. He was determined not to sponge off anybody and instead work his way through as his father had always taught him. His first regular job was at Ben Paris, a restaurant on Pike Street, where he cleaned, bussed tables, and shined shoes. From there he got a job as a laborer on the day shift at an iron foundry. Al was working at the foundry and living with friends from Canada when one night, as he was getting ready for a dance at Washington Hall, the landlady's oldest daughter brought in her friend from high school and said, "Al, I want you to meet Lucille."[2] Her name was Lucille Jeter, and she had just turned sixteen. At the daughter's suggestion, he took her to the dance where the featured act was legendary jazz pianist Fats Waller. Soon there were romantic feelings. When Al suffered a hernia working at the foundry, Lucille visited him in the hospital every day.

Born in 1925, Lucille was the youngest child of a poor family and was mostly raised by older sisters. Her father, Preston (whose mother had also been owned by his white father), was an invalid, and her mother, Clarice, worked as a domestic, caring for white babies while having eight children of her own. A friend recalled Lucille as a "nice-looking girl and a very good dancer," and "very light-skinned with pretty hair. She could have passed,"[3] which meant her complexion was light enough to pass in the world as white. She had musical talent, once winning a five-dollar prize at an amateur singing contest, and was slim but not frail. When she had the money to dress up, she did so with style. She was jovial and fun and loved dancing with a handsome partner like Al Hendrix, who could deftly swing her lithe body around the dance floor.

Lucille turned heads when she walked down the street and had so many friends that Al was jealous. "Al was a very muscular guy," recalled a friend. "Everyone stayed away from Lucille because of him. He had a temper and he wasn't afraid to use it. If anyone did run around with her, they certainly didn't do it in public because Al would have killed them."[4]

Al was working in a pool hall, racking balls, when he heard that the Japanese had bombed Pearl Harbor. Twenty-two years old and soon to be drafted, he drew tighter with Lucille. He visited her parents regularly, a requirement of the day. Lucille's parents liked Al but felt their daughter was too young to be deeply involved with a man.

By late February, Lucille was pregnant. Her parents were furious. "This was the last thing anyone expected," recalled her sister Delores.[5] They became more displeased, especially the father, when Al and Lucille married on March 31, 1942, at the King County Courthouse by the justice of the peace. The father's assessment was right, for beyond their physical attraction and love of dancing, they shared little else except poverty-stricken backgrounds. For only three days they lived together as husband and wife before Al shipped out to serve in the army. On the last night, they partied at the Rocking Chair Club on Fourteenth and Yesler (where a few years later, a teenaged pianist named Ray Charles, having fled the South on a Greyhound bus, was steered into a jam session on his first night in town). The groom left Seattle knowing he could do little to provide for his bride and baby while in the army.

Lucille Hendrix was ill-prepared to be a mother. For a few months she continued to live with her parents, who were on welfare and could not support an unemployed, pregnant daughter. She had hoped to finish the ninth grade, but with a child on the way and no means of support, she left school and found work as a waitress at the Bucket of Blood, a nightclub on Jackson Street, where she served drinks and sometimes provided entertainment. "She would sing," Delores Hall recalled, "and men would give her tips because she was such a good singer."[6] That Lucille was underage hardly mattered on "The Main Stem" of Seattle.

The Main Stem "was the term used to describe where everything was happening," remembered Bob Summerrise, one of Seattle's first black DJs. "It was a wild play there: pimps, whores, gamblers, drug dealers, some drug addicts, but also all the other successful business people of black life who went there to be entertained or have a drink." Spreading out from the corner of Fourteenth and Jackson, a colorful and rich alternative world existed in clubs like the Black & Tan, the Rocking Chair, and the Little Harlem Nightclub, unseen by most of white Seattle. "It was zoot suits, big hats, and patent leathers on up," recalled Jimmy Ogilvy, whose parents founded Seafair Records. "You weren't admitted unless you were dressed right. The clubs didn't care if you were white: they just wanted you to be dancing and happening. You had to be suave."[7]

To pretty, sixteen-year-old Lucille Jeter Hendrix, Jackson Street shattered every notion she had about life. It was a different, more exuberant side of life than the church-based community Lucille had grown up in, and she was quickly entranced by the exotic lure of Jackson Street's many clubs, the center of rhythm and blues in the city. The street became her social environment, where she knew people and they knew her. She would never feel completely comfortable again in the staid Central District of her parents, nor would she ever really fit into the traditional world of work and family represented by Al Hendrix, a marriage which already seemed like an odd and distant memory.

By the fall, Lucille was unemployed and living with Dorothy Harding, a close friend several years older, who was a single mother working in the Seattle shipyards. Though she attended church every Sunday, Dorothy loved music and men, and at night was often found on Jackson Street. Lucille, very pregnant, called Dorothy "auntie," and her friend took care of her. It was at Dorothy's house on a stormy night that Lucille's labor began. She was rushed to King County Hospital where, in the maternity ward on Friday morning, November 27, 1942, she gave birth to a healthy eight-pound, eleven-ounce boy. It was the day after Thanksgiving, and his arrival was seen by all as a true sign of thanksgiving from God. Al was a twenty-three-year-old private stationed at Fort Rucker, Alabama, when the congratulatory telegram arrived from his sister-in-law Delores Hall, who had nicknamed the child "Buster" from the comic strip *Buster Brown*, a name most of his neighbors and relatives in Seattle would call him throughout his life. The legal name his mother gave him at birth was Johnny Allen Hendrix, a name which no one, not even his mother, would ever call him.

Al Hendrix

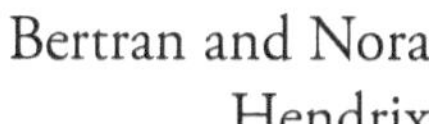

Bertran and Nora Hendrix

Lucille Jeter

Battered Childhood

AI was in the South Pacific, loading and unloading ships with the 903rd Airbase Security Battalion, when Lucille sent a picture of the baby sitting on her lap; both were photogenic and shared the same dark, almond-shaped eyes. He would not meet his first child until the boy was three years old. "I believed in what we were fighting for," he wrote many years later. "I just hated being in the service on account of it taking me away from my home life. Having a son made me more anxious to get home."[1] Lucille wrote often at first, then not much at all. A year passed before she received his army pay. Meanwhile, her life became complicated: Her father passed away in June 1943, and her mother, an emotionally fragile woman, suffered a nervous breakdown and was away when their house burned to the ground, the family losing everything.

Over the next year, Lucille and Buster lived a precarious life as she worked in clubs, while Dorothy, Delores, and her mother, Clarice, mostly looked after the child. There was occasional neglect. One cold night, Clarice appeared at the home of family friends with the baby in her arms. He was "icy cold, his little legs were blue," remembered Freddie Mae Gautier, and his diaper was frozen solid with urine.[2] Freddie's mother gave the child a warm bath, rubbed his skin with olive oil, and kept him until the mother came to retrieve him. When Lucille arrived, Mrs. Gautier gave her a lecture on infant care. Desperately poor and not knowing if or when her husband would return from the war, Lucille began going with other men. "Lucille held out a good long while, I guess, before she started running around with her girlfriends and other men," remembered Al.[3] His letters to Lucille were frequently returned, and the few letters she did write were addressed from seedy hotels. One of her men took her and the baby to Oregon, where relatives found her in a Portland hospital after a beating. "We got Jimi and her and took them home," recalled her sister Delores.[4] Since Lucille was only seventeen, the man was charged under the Mann Act and given a five-year prison term.

As the war ended, the baby was almost three when Lucille and Clarice took him along to a church convention in Berkeley, California, where, when Lucille returned to Seattle and Clarice visited relatives in Missouri, he was left in the temporary care of Mrs. Champ, a church friend, that stretched on until adoption was considered. Delores wrote to Mrs. Champ, telling her that she needed to write to Al to tell him the baby was in California. Mrs. Champ did so, and Al Hendrix, thousands of miles away in the Pacific, just weeks away from being released from the army, received a letter informing him that his child was under the care of a stranger. He then began divorce proceedings.

Discharged from the army, Al returned to Seattle on a troop transfer ship that sailed into Elliot Bay in September 1945. He first visited his family in Vancouver, then traveled to California, where Buster was living in a project in Berkeley with the Champ family. Al was nervous at first with "a feeling I'd never had before" when he walked into the apartment to meet his son. "A new, warm baby would have been different," he remembered. "Here he was, three years old, and able to look and judge for himself."[5] The bashful child looked very much like his mother, especially his eyes; even the boy's wide, flat smile reminded Al of Lucille. Al wrote to his mother in Vancouver that Buster is "a fine boy and he is sweet. He's over average in smartness for his age, and these people are just crazy about him—everybody is." Mrs. Champ was heartbroken to lose the boy. "But after all, he's my son, and I want him to know who his daddy is." Al ended the letter by saying that if he were to leave California without the boy, "I'd never forgive myself for it, so when I leave here, he'll be with me."[6]

Returning to Seattle, they first stayed at a little house on Jackson Street with his sister-in-law Delores and her daughters. When Delores moved to Yesler Terrace, Al and Buster moved with her. Yesler Terrace, the first integrated housing project in the United States, was a poor but tight-knit community of diverse cultures. "There weren't many blacks," Delores recalled, "but everyone there got along."[7] Their unit had a fenced-in backyard where Buster could play. Soon, to everyone's surprise, Lucille knocked on her sister's door. Now a beautiful young woman with a wild and independent air about her, Al was again smitten.

"Here I am," she said. He asked her about not taking care of Jimmy, and she replied, "Well, I was moving around too much," and then she asked, "Do you want to try to make it?"[8] The physical attraction between them was strong; she moved in as his wife. Al abandoned divorce proceedings.

The next several months went smoothly. Living with Delores, their expenses were minimal, and with Al still receiving small payments from the army, they could go out almost every night. Delores babysat Buster at night, and Al and Lucille watched Delores's children during the day while she worked at a Boeing factory. "They had their honeymoon then," Delores observed. "They'd go up and down Jackson Street."[9] They even took a road trip to Vancouver so Al could show off his wife and child to Nora. Buster loved his grandmother, and this was the first of many trips he made to Vancouver to visit her. Soon, however, their lives again turned bitter.

Delores became fed up with their drinking and wanted Al and Lucille to leave. "They would drink and party, and I was raising a family," she remembered.[10] When Lucille drank, she became emotional and overly affectionate. Al was the opposite: He became sour, and his temper flared.

Al found work in a slaughterhouse and moved his family to a transient hotel on Jackson Street. Their modest room had a single bed, which they all shared, a one-burner hot plate, and a chair. While they lived here, Al changed his son's legal name to James Marshall Hendrix: James being Al's legal first name and Marshall the middle name of his deceased brother, Leon. Lucille's popularity in the neighborhood made her husband jealous. "Al knew only Lucille's friends," Delores said. "He didn't have any friends of his own."[11]

When Al took a job on a freighter to Japan, upon his return several weeks later, Lucille, caught with another man in the room, had been evicted from the seedy hotel. Still, he took her back. "It was almost like a cycle," wrote Al. "Things would go along real nice for two or three months. After that I'd go, 'Uh-oh . . . something's going to happen.'"[12]

Jimi Hendrix, remembering his parents' fiery relationship, said, "My mother and father used to fall out a lot. I always had to be ready to go tippy-toeing off to Canada."[13] In Vancouver, he would briefly experience a stable continuity of life, staying with his grandmother or his aunt and uncle, Pearl and Frank Hendrix. But, more often, he was shunted off to relatives in Seattle.

In the spring of 1947, the reunited family moved into an apartment in the Rainier Vista project. Dorothy Harding also lived there and became a frequent babysitter. The Rainier Vista was three miles south of the Central District, bordering Lake Washington on the east, and had become home for an increasing number of African Americans. Buster slept in the bedroom closet, which became a retreat as his parents battled ever more frequently.

Most of Al's jobs were manual labor. He would come home from work exhausted, and Lucille would go out without him. "When she came home," Delores recalled, "he'd be sitting out there drinking, and he'd be mad." Neighbors heard fussing and fighting every night. Sometimes Lucille had bruises. Alcohol fueled most of their fights. "When they drank, they fought," observed Delores.[14] One of their fights was so bitter that Lucille left and lived for a month with a Filipino man. But whenever she left, Al seemed to want her more, and when she returned, he took her back.

Their apartment was a place to party. "When Lucille and I had alcohol at the house, we drank together and there would be other people there, too," remembered Al.[15] The parties were so raucous that both Delores and Dorothy Harding banned their children from the Hendrix home. Buster, having to either leave or sit in his closet and hear the racket, became withdrawn. When asked why he was so quiet, he frequently replied, "Momma and Daddy are always fighting."[16]

During the high times, Lucille was a decent mother. "Lucille did really good with Jimi," remembered Al. "She'd be cuddling him and talking to him, and he'd be hugging on her."[17] But when his parents began bickering, he sometimes retreated to Dorothy Harding's home. He was so quiet that Dorothy wondered if he had a medical condition.

"He barely said a word," she remembered.[18] When the boy did talk, he had a slight stutter. He created an inner life and could play by himself for hours. From age four to six, he had an imaginary friend named Sessa, who was his constant companion. Jimi Hendrix would get through a difficult, lonely childhood with imagination, love from his aunts, and the respites offered by his father's family in Vancouver.

Lucille became pregnant again and, on January 13, 1948, gave birth to a baby boy in Harborview Hospital (formerly known as King County Hospital). Al named him Leon after his deceased brother, and their lives seemed to improve. "Al had a better job for a while," recalled Delores, "and the fighting seemed to slow down."[19]

They moved into a larger unit in Rainier Vista, where the two boys had their own rooms. Buster started kindergarten that fall. After school in the afternoons, he played in the woods in the green belt just west of the project and pretended he was an Indian warrior like those of his Grandmother Nora's stories, fighting battles with imaginary cowboys. Eleven months after Leon was born, Lucille gave birth to another boy named Joseph Allen Hendrix, who was short and stocky and looked like Al. Now there were three children in a family that could barely survive with one.

Joe was born with a clubfoot, a cleft palate, had one leg shorter than the other, and two rows of teeth. His medical care became costly, which brought out Lucille's maternal instincts. She frequently took Joe to the Children's Hospital.

Al had finished an electronics course, but the only job he could find was as a night janitor at Pike Place Market, sweeping up after the farmers. Lucille discovered that though the family would bear some expenses, the state would pay for most of Joe's medical needs. Al didn't think there was enough money. He had distanced himself from this son and refused to pay for anything. With hardly enough money to feed the children, in the summer of 1949, and again in 1950, he sent all three sons to Canada to spend time with his mother.

Grandmother Nora was knowledgeable about herbs and full of old-fashioned remedies for illnesses. Buster loved to hear her tell of their Cherokee ancestors and her life in early minstrel shows. Some of their time was spent with Al's sister Pat and her husband, Joe Lashley, who lived in a house on Drake Street. As the summer of 1950 extended into fall, Buster was enrolled in the Dawson Street Elementary School, the same school his father had once attended. Wearing a green cloth vest with little tassels like a Spanish dancer's vest, one of Nora's stage outfits, Jimi would later remember, "The kids at school would laugh when I wore the shawls and poncho things she made. . . . I wore it to school every day in spite of what people might have thought, just because I liked it. I liked to be different."[20]

Their time in Vancouver with their grandmother, aunt and uncle, and cousins was a time of small, ordinary events of childhood in a peaceful, stable environment. Leon Hendrix remembered, "Grandma Nora lived down by Vancouver's Dockyards on Hastings Street, not far from Dad's brother, Uncle Frank, and his wife, Aunt Pearl, so Buster and I spent time staying between each house. . . . [We] were just happy to be eating breakfast regularly in Vancouver. Grandma Nora and Aunt Pearl made sure we were well taken care of. Compared to our life back in Seattle, we were in heaven up in Canada staying with our relatives."[21]

In the afternoons, along with their cousin Bobby Hendrix, the boys explored the neighborhood and played and walked along the docks along the inlet. Images of the beauty of Vancouver with the mountains rising above the sea remained with Jimi throughout his life and are reflected in the lyrics of his songs. But by October, the boys returned to Seattle to Al and Lucille, whose marriage was on the upswing again. However, the down cycle quickly followed, and when Buster started second grade at Horace Mann Elementary, he was living with Aunt Delores.

In the fall of 1950, Lucille gave birth to a daughter named Kathy Ira, born sixteen weeks premature and weighing just one pound, ten ounces. It was discovered she was blind: She became a ward of the state and was put into foster care. A second daughter, Pamela, was born in October 1951. She, too, had health complications and was placed in foster care. Both parents were struggling with drinking, and Al couldn't find steady work, but baby Joe's health issues were their undoing. In a cramped apartment with both parents fighting, Buster escaped into comic books, going to movies, and drawing pictures of cars on a notepad. He wrote a postcard to his grandmother Nora: "How have you been? I have been good. How is [my cousin] and them. Are they good too? We went to a picnic and I ate too much, but it was a good picnic. We had fun. Tweet. Tweet. Love, Buster."[22] Life soon became so hard and complicated that his tweets to his grandmother ended.

Lucille hoped Joe could live normally with the help of an operation on his leg, but Al kept refusing, saying he couldn't afford it. Having given away two girls, the idea of giving up Joe was more than Lucille could stand. She thought Al's decision came from meanness and miserliness, and in the fall of 1951, just after Buster turned nine, Lucille left Al again. They were officially divorced on December 17, 1951, but were soon back together, and just as quickly broke up again. Al was awarded custody of the boys—Buster, Leon, and Joe—but they were mostly raised by their grandmothers (Clarice Jeter in Seattle and Nora Hendrix in Vancouver), their aunt Delores Hall, close friend Dorothy Harding, and others in the neighborhood who often took care of each other.

Because Al refused to pay medical expenses, the only way Joe could get the care he needed was to become a ward of the state. The parents would have to give up rights to their three-year-old son. Lucille pleaded with Al to reconsider, Delores and Dorothy Harding both offered to adopt Joe, but Al vetoed these suggestions, and in the summer of 1952, he borrowed a car, packed up Joe's possessions, and, along with Lucille, took Joe to the hospital. Buster and Leon were old enough to feel deep sorrow as they waved goodbye to their brother. Joe remembered his mother holding him in her arms during the car ride. "She smelled so good," he recalled, "like flowers." At the hospital, Lucille carried Joe out of the car and handed him to a waiting nurse. Joe sat on the curb with the nurse and cried as his mother climbed back into the car. "My dad," he recalled, "never even got out of the car. He kept it running the whole time."[23]

Lucille briefly reunited with Al for Buster's tenth birthday on Thanksgiving Day, 1952. She was pregnant with their sixth child, Alfred Hendrix, who was born on February 14, 1953, with developmental disabilities and immediately put up for adoption. Lucille moved out not long after the birth and lived with her mother in an apartment near Jefferson Park. For a while she remained in their lives. The boys walked to see her, or sometimes Al sent them there if they did something he didn't like. The parents often fought at the handoff, with Al storming back to the project with the boys. They would sneak back to see their mother, but if Al found out, he'd beat them with a belt, though he rarely beat them when he wasn't drunk. As Buster grew larger, he grabbed the belt and tried to hold it, attempts that were usually futile. "My dad was strong," Leon remembered. "He'd hold us with one hand and whip us with the other."[24]

They were living downtown in a one-room unit on Terrace Street with the bathroom down the hall. Al found little time to watch the children. "The neighbors started to take over watching us," Leon said, "because they knew what was going to happen—that welfare was going to take us away."[25] Buster and Leon learned to watch for the green cars driven by welfare department workers and beat a retreat whenever they saw one. "They weren't bad kids," recalled a neighbor, "they were just a little wild and lost."[26] Al had menial jobs and could hardly feed them, and the home was dirty because Al could not, or would not, clean the apartment and wash clothes, which he considered a woman's work. Around dinnertime, the boys were usually at a neighbor's house.

Their lives got better in the spring of 1953, when the city's engineering department hired Al as a laborer, giving him enough income to purchase a small, two-bedroom house at 2604 South Washington Street that put them back in the Central District. Soon, Al's niece, Grace Hatcher, moved in with her husband, Frank. "Al asked us to come and live with him to take care of the children," recalled Frank. "He just couldn't do it himself. He was drinking a lot, and gambling, and a lot of times he didn't even come home."[27] Grace became one of the boys' many mother figures. Their real mother, Lucille, drifting from hotel to hotel, was no longer much of a presence. At last living in a home of their own, for the boys, even with their mother fading away, this was the most idyllic time of their childhood.

Buster attended Leschi Elementary, the most integrated primary school in the city, and made several good friends. The grandmother of one of his friends, Mae Jones, used to feed them breakfast. "We used to eat breakfast there every day before school," remembered Jimmy Williams, who came from a family of thirteen children and was Buster's closest friend.[28]

Buster occasionally joined Terry Johnson and his family at Grace Methodist Church. "I think it was one of the first times he'd been to church," recalled Johnson.[29] Hearing the choir moved Buster to an understanding of the power of live music.

During the summer, the boys swam in Lake Washington or watched a cheap matinee at the Atlas Theatre. Buster loved the *Flash Gordon* and *Prince Valiant* movies, and named their adopted dog Prince, after Prince Valiant. The brothers jousted at home with brooms, which Buster also pretended were imaginary guitars.

He began to follow the popular song charts. "We'd always listen to the Hit Parade Top Ten," remembered Jimmy Williams.[30] While listening to crooners like Frank Sinatra, Nat King Cole, and Dean Martin, Buster would strum the broom like a guitar and play along with the radio. Al didn't like him using the broom this way. "My dad would see straw from the broom on the bed and get mad," remembered Leon. The boys also worked in the fields south of Seattle in the summer, picking beans and strawberries for a piece rate. Once, while swimming in the Green River, Buster saved Leon from drowning. Some nights they splurged on ten-cent horse meat hamburgers. "We'd get two and that was the highlight of the day," said Leon. "Then we'd go home and wait for Dad, because, well, sometimes he didn't come home."[31]

Grace and Frank Hatcher became fed up with Al and moved out, leaving the boys alone again with their father. Al had the only key to the house, so when they returned and Al wasn't there, the boys searched the taverns to find their father. Many times they gave up and spent the night with friends. A welfare worker cornered Al and gave him two choices: send his sons to a foster home or put them up for adoption. Al argued that Buster, almost a teenager, needed less care and should stay; Leon, however, would have to enter foster care. The grim conditions at home were all the boys had ever known, but they loved their father and begged Al not to separate them. Al cried at this decision—the only time his boys saw him cry. On the last night they lived together, Al was uncharacteristically affectionate, softly rubbing his knuckles through their hair as a salve for their pain. The boys loved these moments of tender connection.

Luckily, Leon was placed in a foster home only six blocks away, so the brothers were hardly apart. The foster parents, with six children of their own, were church people who opened their house to needy children. "Jimi was at our house more than he was at his dad's," recalled Doug

Wheeler, one of the sons. "A lot of times Jimi would spend the night so he could have breakfast before going to school. Otherwise, he might not have anything to eat."[32] Despite such tense agitation, Buster's attendance at Leschi Elementary was consistent and his grades were good. He liked art and drew automobiles and flying saucers in his notebook. At his father's urging, he tried out for the football team. The coach was Booth Gardner, who later became governor of Washington. In contrast to the agility he later showed with the guitar, "He was no athlete," Gardner recalled. "He wasn't good enough to start; to tell the truth, he really wasn't good enough to play."[33] However, Buster's interest in music took another leap after watching Jimmy Williams sing in a Leschi talent show. "There was a lot of applause," remembered Jimmy.[34] That the stage could transform someone as shy as his friend into an esteemed performer was a lesson the boy never forgot.

Dorothy Harding was as much a mother to Buster as anyone in his life. During the day, she worked as a riveter at Boeing and then hurried home to feed her children before traveling to her second job as a domestic for a wealthy white family. Her family had a three-bedroom apartment in Rainier Vista, and she slept on the couch so the children could sleep in beds. When Dorothy hadn't seen Buster for a while, she tracked down Al and berated him. She was the only woman from whom Al would take such criticism. Raising nine children as a single mother, she kept her family fed and took them to St. Edward's Catholic Church on Sundays. Buster often accompanied them and felt like part of the family. The older Harding boys protected him. "There was a silent understanding that nobody would bother him because of us," Melvin Harding recalled. "He wasn't a fighter. He was quiet, and he had a ready smile."

But often he was unhappy. "He would never say he missed his mom or his dad," noted Ebony Harding, "but you knew he did. He cried a lot." One night he made a prescient statement. "He told me," Dorothy recalled, "'I'm going to leave here, and I'm going to go far, far away. I'm going to be rich and famous and everyone here will be jealous.'"[35]

On March 30, 1955, Al and Lucille appeared at a hearing in the King County Courthouse to give up parental rights to Joe, Kathy, Pamela, and Alfred. The hearing was only a formality. The children had been turned over, but by signing the court decree, Al and Lucille gave away "any and all parental rights and interests in, and to, the children." Lucille was destroyed by admitting in court her failure as a mother, and on this day, too, though Al Hendrix sometimes claimed otherwise, he admitted to fathering all four children. Falling farther through the cracks, Al lost his job and fell behind on mortgage payments. The house had so deteriorated that the aunts could not keep up with the filth and disrepair. When Booth Gardner stopped by one day, he said, "the power had been turned off" and Buster was sitting alone in the dark.[36]

Roaming the neighborhood at all hours of the day and night, many in the Central District came to know Buster as they would a recurrent stray dog. Yet through his wayward movements, he soon discovered every musician in the neighborhood by listening for the sounds of their playing. When he heard music from a house, he'd knock on the door. A friend recalled, "My brother played keyboards and Jimi heard and one day just stopped by."[37] But there were dangers in an itinerant lifestyle. Roaming nearby woods with friends one day, one of the boys lagged behind; Buster and the others found him just as he was about to be assaulted by an older man, who they scared away. In fact, in later life, Jimi Hendrix admitted to a girlfriend that he had been sexually assaulted in youth by a man who wore a uniform.

That summer, the welfare department again threatened foster care. Al agreed to a compromise to let Buster live with Frank, Al's brother, and his wife, Pearl, who became another strong matriarchal figure in Buster's life. Aunt Pearl had a beautiful singing voice much like her sister, the great Canadian jazz singer Eleanor Collins, and ran the house strict and orderly but was affectionate. "My mother explained to me that Jimi needed a place to stay because Al couldn't afford to take care of him," Faith Hendrix recalled.[38] Frank made a good income working at Boeing and could supply an extra plate at the table.

Al took in boarders Cornell and Ernestine Benson to help with bills. He still talked about Lucille. "He would call her a drunk," remembered Ernestine, who also remembered that Al's drinking was so out of control he would sometimes get lost coming home and mistakenly wander into other's homes.

Ernestine was a blues fan and had a large collection of 78 rpm records. Buster would hang around and listen to Muddy Waters, Lightnin'

Hopkins, Robert Johnson, Bessie Smith, and Howlin' Wolf. "I love my blues," Ernestine recalled, "and Jimi loved the same down-home stuff." As he listened, his air guitar, the broom, became more animated. Cornell remembered, "He would play that broom so hard, he would lose all the straw."[39]

When Frank and Pearl separated in February 1956, Buster returned to Al. The Bensons had departed and, for a time, it was just Al and Buster. Al lost his job with the city and went to work in the shipping department of Bethlehem Steel, where he wrapped hot metal support rods with wire and cleaned up around the place. It was a dirty job. At the end of a shift, he often threw away his torn and dirty clothes. When this job ended, he collected scrap metal to try to make a few dollars. Buster knew how hard his father struggled to make a life for him and his brother. Al told him, "Everybody has hard times. We're scuffing right now and hardly got anything to eat, but it ain't going to be like this all the time."[40]

Though intelligent and curious, Buster began flunking classes at Washington Junior High. "He was not a kid that got into a lot of trouble," recalled the principal, Frank Fidler, "but he wasn't doing well academically."[41] His father cut his hair, his shoes had holes, and his clothes were out of fashion. For dinner they often ate horse meat—it was cheaper and didn't shrivel up as much as beef. Once or twice, when Al didn't pay the light bill, the electricity was shut off. At night they used candles and kept warm with an oil heater. Sometimes, probably because he was black, Al couldn't get work. He would see a job advertised in the paper, go to the site, and be told it had just been filled, but he'd find it still in the paper a few days later.

In September, the bank repossessed the house. Al and Buster moved to a boardinghouse on Twenty-Ninth Avenue run by Mrs. McKay, whose paraplegic son had discarded a beat-up acoustic guitar with one string that she sold to Buster for five dollars. Al wouldn't pay, so Ernestine Benson gave Buster the money to buy his first guitar. Jimmy experimented with every sound this junked instrument could produce. "He had only one string," Ernestine observed, "but he could really make that string talk."[42] He started carrying the guitar around, slung across his back as he had watched Sterling Hayden do as Johnny Guitar in *The Guitar Man*. "He loved the way that guy looked with the guitar on his back," recalled Johnny Williams. "He carried his guitar exactly like that guy in the movie."[43]

Classmates remember him taking the crippled guitar to school. He never let the guitar out of his sight. He even put it on his chest when he went to sleep at night. When he finally acquired strings, Buster, left-handed, restrung the guitar to play with his left hand. "My dad thought everything left-handed was from the devil," remembered Leon, so Buster "learned to play left and right because every time my dad came into the room he'd have to flip it and play upside down or my dad would yell at him. . . . Dad was already unhappy that he was playing guitar all the time and not working."[44]

In the fall of 1957, Buster made friends with a girl named Carmen Goudy, who also lived in a boardinghouse and was almost as poor as him. "If we had enough money between us for a popsicle, that was a big deal," remembered Carmen. They spent much time walking around in local parks. On a few occasions, they'd watch a matinee because Carmen had palmed her coins for the Sunday school collection plate. Even to Carmen, Buster seemed more than just poor. "He used to wear these little white buck loafers," she recalled. "He had a hole in the sole, so he'd cut these pieces of cardboard and put that in the bottom of his shoes."[45]

Together they shared their dreams. Carmen wanted to be a famous dancer; Buster wanted to own a real guitar and become a famous musician. When playing his air guitar, he also made sounds with his mouth. "It was a bit like scat singing," said Carmen. "He actually could sing a guitar solo, not with words, but with sounds he made in his throat."[46] He still had a childhood stutter, but it rarely came out unless he was nervous, and he would never sing, no matter how much Carmen urged him, because he thought his voice was inferior.

For a while, Leon shared a tiny room in the boardinghouse with Buster, who was in better spirits with his brother around. Buster's grades showed some improvement, even though he was truant at least once a week, walking the neighborhood with his guitar slung over his back.

The boys hadn't seen their mother in months but heard she had married a longshoreman nearly thirty years older. In fact, Lucille was on the skids. Twice in the fall of 1957, she was admitted into Harborview Hospital suffering from cirrhosis of the liver. In January, she was back in the hospital with hepatitis. Aunt Delores took Buster and Leon to visit her. Her health had deteriorated since the last time they had seen her. They were shocked when they saw their mother sitting pallid in a wheelchair. "She used to always look gorgeous and glamorous," Leon said. "She always wore jewelry and smelled nice. But this time there was none of that."[47]

No matter how bad times had been in the past, Lucille had always maintained a sunny disposition. It hurt Dolores to see her sister so downcast. Her condition did improve, and she was released from the hospital. Then, on February 1, 1958, Delores received a call that said Lucille was found unconscious in an alley next to a tavern on Yesler and taken to Harborview Hospital again. Delores and Dorothy Harding immediately went to see her and found her among the patients crowded in the hospital hallways. The women complained until Lucille was put in a room, but by the time a doctor arrived, she had died of a ruptured spleen. Spleens rarely rupture without blunt force trauma, but no exact details of her injury were ever discovered. Had she fallen or been struck outside that tavern?

Buster cried when he heard the news. His father borrowed a truck and took the boys down to the funeral home in Chinatown. When they arrived, Al decided not to let them see their mother's body and went inside alone to pay his respects to the woman with whom he had had six children. "Al was the only man Lucille ever loved," Delores said. "She may have gotten in with other men, but she never loved anyone else."[48] The funeral was scheduled for 2 P.M. the following Sunday at a Pentecostal Church. Nora Hendrix came down from Vancouver to attend; everyone was there except Al and his two sons. They held up the service for two hours, but Al and the boys never arrived. "We both wanted to go," Leon recalled, "but my dad wouldn't let us."[49] When Dorothy Harding visited the boardinghouse that night, she smacked Al on his head and then embraced the two children.

Missing their mother's funeral left a bitter memory. "He never really forgave our dad for that," said Leon of his older brother. Buster began to idolize his lost mother, writing poems and songs about her that spring. He had always been interested in science fiction but added to this pursuit a new fascination with angels. "Mama became an angel to him," remembered Leon. "He told me he was sure she was an angel, and she was following us around."[50] Buster also became more withdrawn, rarely conversing with anyone but his closest friends. "He became extremely sensitive," Ebony Harding recalled. "He was very, very sad."[51] He seemed to feel nothing no longer mattered and began living every day as if it was his last, a trait many noticed when he was an adult. Buster continued to dream but became resigned when things went wrong.

Despite his frustration and debauchery, Al was a stern disciplinarian who held his children to high moral standards. "I couldn't speak unless I was spoken to first by grown-ups," remembered Jimi Hendrix. "So I've always been very quiet. But I saw a lot of things. A fish wouldn't get into trouble if he kept his mouth shut."[52] If his father gave little of the warmth his sons wanted, at least he asked no more than he asked of himself. To keep Al's anger in check, Buster mostly went along with his demands so he could be alone with his guitar. From his mother's death and the grim home life he faced every day, music provided the perfect escape. "It was in him to do it," recalled Al years later. "He felt it. It was no job—he enjoyed it. He just picked it up all of a sudden. He had no formal lessons. He used to practice a lot. I'd come home from work and he'd be there, plunk, plunk, plunk. If I disturbed him or something, he'd go into the bedroom and he'd be there, plunk, plunk, plunking. And I'd say, 'Jimmy, sweep the floor,' or something, and he'd say, 'Okay, Dad,' and he'd do that. And after he finished doing that, he'd go back to plunk, plunk, plunking. I used to hear it constantly."[53]

Al with young Buster

Hendrix Family
(Leon, Buster,
Lucille, and Al)

School photo of Buster

Buster posing as a football player

A Musician Begins to Emerge

In the spring of 1958, Leon returned to foster care, and Al and Buster moved into a small house on Beacon Hill with the Bensons. Ernestine took Buster to Bob Summerrise's World of Music on Jackson Street and let him pick out a record from the large selection of blues and R&B artists. When he played the record at a friend's house, they played along with their guitars. On many afternoons in the neighborhood, Buster sat at the feet of Randy "Butch" Snipes. Butch could play the guitar behind his back like T-Bone Walker and could duck walk like Chuck Berry.

During that time, Buster became more truant, and his grades continued to decline. Carrying his guitar to school did not impress the music teacher, who advised another career path. "I couldn't tell if it was because of his home life or just a lack of interest in regimented academics," observed Jimmy Williams. "Jimi was always a free spirit, and school just didn't really fit him."[1]

Instead of going to school, Buster stopped at the homes of musicians. "Guys were really open, and they would show you riffs and share stuff with you," recalled Lester Exkano, who remembered that Buster's favorite guitar players at the time were B. B. King and Chuck Berry.[2] A family named Lewis inspired many nascent musicians in the neighborhood. They had a basement with a piano, and the door was always open. Dave Lewis Sr. played guitar and was always encouraging. "He had shown Ray Charles and Quincy Jones some licks," remembered Jimmy Ogilvie.[3] These families encouraged creativity. In many ways, this informal school of rhythm and blues practiced in the basements and on the back porches of central

Seattle became Buster's higher education. He became more proficient with his acoustic guitar, but what he really wanted was an electric model.

Turning sixteen in the fall of 1958, Buster was held back a grade because of his failing marks. He and his father had moved in with Grace and Frank Hatcher, who quickly tired of Al's troubles. "Al was so inconsistent: drinking, gambling, and coming home any old time," remembered Frank.[4] So in April 1959, they moved again, this time to a rodent-infested apartment on First Hill, across from a juvenile detention center where prostitutes worked the street. Despite the bleak surroundings, Buster found his greatest childhood joy. Ernestine Benson had been nagging Al to "get that boy a guitar;" Al finally relented and bought an instrument on time payments from Myer's Music.[5]

Buster's first electric guitar was a right-handed white Supro Ozark that he restrung to play leftie. "I've got a guitar," he yelled into the phone to Carmen Goudy before dashing over to her house. As they walked to a park, he was jumping for joy with his guitar in his hands.

"Remember," Carmen said, "we were kids who were so poor we didn't get stuff for Christmas. . . . You couldn't help but feel happy for him. I think it was the happiest day of his life."[6]

Buster and Carmen had begun exploring a physical romance, but in the park that day, he was more interested in his guitar. This made him more attractive to her, which Buster quickly realized and sharpened to his advantage in the years to come.

Buster often carried his guitar in a dry cleaner's paper sack, which made him look like a bum, and would play his guitar with anyone in the neighborhood and wail away when he could plug into an amplifier. He often played with Jimmy Williams. "It was a lot of Frank Sinatra and Dean Martin stuff," remembers Williams. "Jimi really worked on getting down the rhythms to those songs." He loved Duane Eddy and quickly learned "Forty Miles of Bad Road," and "Peter Gunn." He picked up songs so fast, learning a new one every day, that Jimmy Williams joked he was like "a human jukebox."[7]

In September 1959, Buster entered tenth grade at Garfield High School, a huge school in the heart of the Central District and one of the city's best, where, among the 1,700 students there were as many black and Asians as there were Caucasians. Because he was tardy and so uninvolved in class, one of his teachers described him as "a nonstudent student." Buster went there mostly to reconnect with friends in the neighborhood. They would sit at the back of the room during class and talk about music.

A lot of kids were forming bands, mostly informal neighborhood bands with revolving lineups. Buster's first gig with a band was in the basement of the Temple De Hirsch Sinai Synagogue, playing with a group of older guys. "During the first set, Jimi did his thing," recalled Carmen. "He did all this wild playing, and when they introduced the band members and the spotlight was on him, he became even wilder." After the break, the band returned to the stage without him. Carmen worried he had fallen ill, but she found him in the alley, where Buster looked so despondent, she thought he was about to cry. He told her that he had been fired. She suggested that maybe he should play with more tradition and less flash. "That's not my style," he insisted. "I don't do that."[8]

He was soon playing with a band named the Velvetones. "We were really just a bunch of kids," recalled Luther Rabb. "We had a lineup that changed a lot, but included four guitar players, two piano players, a couple of horns, and a drummer."[9] Buster was becoming a much better guitarist. His long fingers allowed him to reach around the neck to hit high notes difficult for other players. He used this advantage creatively, playing individual notes not in the original compositions. The results weren't always pleasing, but it drew the crowd's attention. The Velvetones had a regular gig on Friday nights at the Yesler Terrace Neighborhood House that didn't pay but gave the band the chance to experiment. "They were playing R&B and some blues," recalled a local musician. "Jimi was already something to watch; just the very fact that he was playing this right-handed guitar upside down was enough to keep you fascinated."[10] On a visit to Birdland, a legendary club at Madison and Twenty-Second Street, Dave Lewis let Buster solo while the band went on break. These ten-minute spotlights allowed him to rehearse in front of a crowd and try out some of his antics. Lewis later said, "He would play this wild stuff, but the people couldn't dance to it. They just stared at him."[11]

Al thought Buster spent too much time playing his guitar. "His father was pretty much against it and music in the house, even practicing," remembered a band mate.[12]

Several band members saw Al hit his son in a rage. "He was a brutal man," remembered Pernell Alexander. "Part of it was the times and the way men were then. When the wife wasn't around to beat, they would beat the kids. It was a rough scene, man. It was straight-up ugly."[13]

Anthony Atherton was afraid of Al. "Anyone who came around with an instrument was really in trouble. He'd say 'put that damn thing down; that's not going to get you a job.'"[14]

One night when Buster left his guitar backstage at Birdland, thinking it would be safer there than at home, the guitar had been stolen by the next day. "He was absolutely crushed," recalled Leon. "I think he was even more upset that he knew he had to tell our dad, and he knew he was going to get a big whipping."[15]

Buster soon met Betty Jean Morgan. "He was a sweetheart," Betty Jean recalled. "My parents liked him because he was polite."[16] They took walks to Leschi Park, and, while he still had his guitar, he sat and played on Betty Jean's porch. He had no money and dressed in old clothes, wearing black peg pants with a half-inch belt and a black-and-white striped shirt with the collar up.

Sometimes he helped his father mow lawns. "If Jimi worked really hard all day," said Leon, "he'd get a dollar. But it was hard work and Jimi hated it."[17] Buster finally told his father about his lost guitar, received the lecture of his life, and for several weeks, whenever he appeared in school, he looked depressed and defeated.

He had been playing with the Rocking Kings, a band of high school kids. "He seemed really straight," recalled drummer Lester Exkano. "He didn't smoke and he didn't drink."[18] He may have been quiet offstage, but onstage, with an amplifier and spotlight, he was transformed. The manager had a strict rule that everyone in the band had to wear suits. Buster rented a red jacket for one show that cost him more than his take for the gig. To replace his stolen guitar, several members of the band pitched in to buy him a white Danelectro Silvertone at Sears Robuck for $49.95 that came with a matching amp. He painted it red and wrote "Betty Jean" in two-inch letters on the front. The band covered hits by the Coasters, Fats Domino, Duane Eddy, and Chuck Berry, and played local favorites like "Louie, Louie."

"We played anything that would keep people dancing," recalled Exkano. "It was absolutely a black sound, but our shows were mixed and everybody came."[19]

Buster ended his sophomore year at Garfield with a B in art, a D in typing, and Fs in drama, history, and gym. "He just wouldn't study," recalled a friend. "Then he'd get these failing grades and that would further hurt his self-esteem."[20] However, Buster did bond with a white girl named Mary Willix. They spoke about UFOs, the unconscious mind, and reincarnation. It was one of the few times in youth he made friends with a white girl.

Buster and his father moved again at the end of the school year to a small house on East Yesler Way. When school started in September, he showed up for a month before completely dropping out. At the end of October 1960, he was taken off the student roster. "He was so far from graduating, it wasn't a matter of a few credits or classes," recalled the principal, Frank Hanawalt. "He had missed so much it was really impossible to make it all up. There were laws then that we couldn't keep a student on our books if they didn't attend classes regularly."[21] Though Buster had flunked out of high school, the many friendships he made there would leave a lasting impression. "The multiculturalism that Jimi experienced at Garfield would stick with him for the rest of his life," said Mary Willix. "It was truly a special place."[22]

Buster Hendrix continued playing music. There was a legendary dance hall between Seattle and Tacoma known as the Spanish Castle; built to look like a Moorish Castle, it had a capacity of two-thousand, and to play there was the dream of any local musician. Big bands played on its stage for many years, and then in the late fifties the music switched to rock and roll. Buster first visited in 1959 to see the Fabulous Wailers, the most popular band in the region, and returned whenever he could. His first time playing on the stage came in late 1960, when the Rocking Kings opened for another band. Most of the audiences at the Castle were white, but the club was integrated, and many of the white musicians in the area were influenced by African American culture and embraced jazz and rhythm and blues. "There was an originality to Northwest Music, part of which came out of the fact that Seattle was so geographically isolated," recalled jazz guitarist Larry Coryell.[23]

The music had a "dirty" sound that was partly the result of using low-fi equipment at high volume levels, but also the result of intentional experimentation. "We would actually cut the cones of the speakers, put towels on them, and stick toothpicks in the woofers, all to get crude feedback," recalled one of the musicians.[24]

At about this time Buster Hendrix accidentally dropped his amp, and, discovering that the jostling deformed the sound of his guitar, began experimenting with distortion. The original Rocking Kings dissolved, but the manager, James Thomas, re-formed the band as Thomas and the Tomcats and gave Buster the added duty of backup vocals, though Buster rarely sang. Rural audiences loved the band, particularly some of Buster's guitar solos, but the band's cars broke down when they went on the road and sometimes they missed bookings. When he got free tickets to see Hank Ballard and the Midnighters, Buster attended the show with his guitar on his lap. Afterward, he followed Ballard's guitar player around until he consented to teach him some licks. Having dropped out of school, his career options were limited. If anyone asked, he always said he played with the Tomcats.

His poverty stood out even among the other musicians he played with, none of whom knew affluence. A friend who worked at a burger joint across from Garfield High gave Buster the unsold hamburgers and French fries the restaurant threw out at closing time. Like a starving wild animal, he would scarf down the food right there in the parking lot. The staff was at first taken aback by what was essentially begging until they realized his pitiful circumstances. Earning less than $20 a month with the Tomcats, he was still dependent on his father to survive. Al wanted his son to work with him in landscaping, but during the times they worked together, Buster complained that Al was often abusive. A client once watched Al punch his son. Jimi Hendrix spoke of this incident in a 1967 interview: "He hit me in the face and I ran away."[25] Leon remembered that Al still whipped Buster with a belt.

Buster was arrested on May 2, 1961, for riding in a stolen car, then taken to the juvenile detention center across the street from the apartment where he had lived the year before. When Al came to bail him out, Buster told him he didn't know the car had been stolen. Al kindly understood. Four days later, Buster was again arrested for riding in a stolen car. This time, he spent eight days in juvenile jail.

The Seattle Police Department was known for overactive prosecution of black males. "The cops would stop you even if you were just walking down the street," recalled Terry Johnson. Common beliefs among police included, "All Negroes carry knives," and, "Any Negro driving a Cadillac is either a pimp or a dope-peddler."[26] Buster swore he hadn't stolen a car nor knew it was stolen. Still, eighteen and no longer a juvenile, he faced up to five years in prison on each of his criminal charges.

Standing before a judge a few days later, he seemed a "classic case": a mother deceased, a father who mowed lawns, a brother in a foster home, a teenager expelled from school and now an adult on the streets and out of work. He was unskilled, black, and poor. The judge didn't want to send him back to jail and suggested enlistment in the military. Buster knew he couldn't make a living as a musician in Seattle, and, since prosecutors accepted a stint in the service as a plea bargain, he seriously considered joining the armed services. He asked a recruiting office if enlisting could earn him a position with the storied 101st Airborne Division that had jumped behind enemy lines on D-Day with its Screaming Eagle patch. At a hearing in juvenile court on May 16, 1961, the prosecutor agreed to suspend a two-year sentence if Buster joined the army. The next day, James Marshall Hendrix signed up for three years in the U.S. Army to begin basic training at Fort Ord, California, late in May. Other than a few trips as an infant, Buster had never been more than two hundred miles outside of Seattle.

On the night before he left for training, Buster played a last gig with the Tomcats at an outdoor festival across the street from Birdland. Leon and Betty Jean Morgan attended. Buster asked Betty Jean if she would keep his guitar until he could send for it.

The street dance drew several hundred people, one of whom was Carmen Goudy with a new boyfriend. As one of the few people who had seen his first public concert in the basement of a synagogue at a show that got him fired, she noticed how much his playing had improved in such a short time. "He was still a wild man when it came to playing," she recalled. "But he was good. He was really good."[27] Overly flashy but confident, he played with a kind of panache that forced audiences to watch him. The next day, boarding a night train at a station he had lived within walking distance of all his life, leaving home, sitting alone, he probably felt as lonely as a person could possibly feel, and then the train began to move.

Jimi's first electric guitar

Early Seattle band (Buster on the left with guitar)

Marbles

Departing from the King Street Station on a southbound train to Monterey, California, James Marshall Hendrix left behind the scattered remains of a poverty-stricken childhood. His life would never be easy, but he was discovering his soul in music, and he had begun a relentless pursuit of his dreams. His journey would be difficult, but he was nearly always in the right places and would never waver as he constantly absorbed the beat of music with visionary knowledge. No longer known as "Buster," except to those he had grown up with in Seattle, Jimmy was 5'10" and weighed 155 pounds when he arrived at Fort Ord on May 31, 1961, to begin basic training in the United States Army. The instant shock of unrelenting discipline, the structure and formality of what you ate and wore, the strict order of every day, was a complete change to anything he had known. It may have been a welcome change for a time—he was getting three healthy meals a day, the most consistent nutrition of his life—but he felt lonely and estranged, soon finding the military harsh and mundane. He leaned on the one source of consistent love he had always known, however erratic, by writing his father frequent and lengthy letters during these months of duty.

"I just wanted to let you know that I'm still alive, although not by very much. Oh, the army's not too bad so far. It's so-so, although it does have its 'ups and downs' at times. All, I mean all my hair is cut off and I have to shave," and "although I've been here for about a week, it seems like a month. Time passes pretty slow."[1] Al wrote, too, but his letters were shorter and less regular.

Being so far from family and friends, Jimmy's feelings softened about home. Despite his father's many flaws, Al was at least understanding about his travails. Their affection came through in these letters more than in any other way. At Jimmy's request, Al picked up his guitar from Betty Jean Morgan's mother and sent it to him at Fort Ord. When the guitar arrived, Jimmy wrote his father a six-page letter: "[The guitar] was a welcome sight. It made me think of you and home," he wrote, endearingly adding, "As long as you're around, things are perfect for me, because you are my Dear Dad and I'll always love you."[2] He ended the letter with a small illustration of his Danelectro guitar.

For two long summer months, Jimmy learned how to live in a barracks full of other recruits, shoot a rifle, throw a grenade, march ten miles with a fifty-pound pack, make the blanket on his bunk so tight the sergeant could bounce a quarter on it, and clean a stinking latrine. Life was well-ordered but uninspiring. Completing basic training in early September, and making the rank of private, he bused to Seattle on a one-week leave, taking his guitar along. "He looked so handsome in that uniform," recalled his cousin Dee Hall. "He was proud to show it off to everyone."[3] Al was proud of Jimmy and thought he had matured. Leon was dazzled and amazed when his older brother gave him five dollars. Jimmy visited Aunt Delores, Dorothy Harding, and many old friends, but he spent most of his time with Betty Jean Morgan.

"He told my parents he was going to marry me as soon as I got out of school and that I'd be an army bride."[4] On his last day in Seattle, he gave Betty Jean a silk pillowcase brought from California. He told her he had slept on it every night thinking of her and signed it, "Love forever, always yours, James Hendrix, September 7, 1961."[5] He left his guitar with her again, too.

His orders came through in October. Posted to the 101st Airborne Division at Fort Campbell, Kentucky, he wrote home enthusiastically, "I wouldn't mind breaking a leg or something if I can come out wearing that Screaming Eagle patch and those Airborne wings."[6] Fort Campbell straddles the border between Tennessee and Kentucky, sixty miles northwest of Nashville, the home of country music, and two hundred miles northeast of Memphis and the start of the Mississippi River Delta, the birthplace of blues. Jimmy would have been well aware that he happened to be in the heartland of rhythm and blues.

Arriving on November 8, he soon detailed the physical challenges in letters to his father. "We jumped out of the 34-foot tower the third day," he wrote. "It was almost fun," and "There's nothing but physical training and harrasement [*sic*] here for two weeks, then when you go to jump school, that's when you get hell."[7]

When not training or writing letters, he often practiced guitar at a service club with instruments and amplifiers available to rent. One rainy night, through an open window of Service Club 1 while waiting for the downpour to ebb, Private Billy Cox heard a solo guitar playing in a wildly unique manner. He later claimed it was as if Beethoven and John Lee Hooker had merged. "It was something the human ear hadn't heard," Cox said. "I went in and introduced myself to him and said I played a little upright bass."[8] Cox, one year older than Jimmy, played the violin, piano, and various horns, but became fixated with the electrical bass sound he heard in R&B bands. Cox checked out a bass and they began jamming. Suddenly Jimmy's purpose of being dramatically shifted away from his military duties.

The army was still a part of him as he made his first jump that winter, also the first time he had ever been on an airplane. "That first jump was really outta sight," he later said in an interview. He was fascinated by the sounds of the plane ("the plane is going 'rrrrr'"), and of the jump itself ("the air is going 'sssshhhh' past your ears"[9]). In a letter to Aunt Delores, he wrote, "I'm in the best division: the 101st Airborne. That's the sharpest outfit in the world. If any trouble starts anywhere, we will be one of the first to go."[10] But he was also feeling homesick for a place he had never really liked. "You know," he wrote to his father, "I've been having dreams of coming home and seeing you and everybody. It seems kind of funny. I must really want to come home for a while."[11] In January 1962, he completed the requirements to earn his 101st Airborne Division patch and was promoted to private first class, an achievement that was fast overshadowed, for as his interest in music grew, his enthusiasm for the army melted.

Al sent the Danelectro Silverton guitar stashed at Betty Jean's. With its rosewood neck that fit comfortably between his long fingers and "Betty Jean" written on the body, the allure of the Airborne faded even more rapidly. Jimmy felt safe with his guitar in his hands. He talked to it and called it by name. He even slept with it, which made him seem odd to the others, a reaction that increased when he began walking to and from the mess hall and everywhere else on the post, picking an imaginary guitar and making strange noises. He began noticing and examining the sounds in his daily environment with the idea to re-create them on his Danelectro: the clatter of automatic weapons on the firing range, the metallic thump and bangs of airplane doors when he jumped, and the rush of wind as he whistled to earth. He experimented with his guitar, bending musical notes with the vibrato bar, trying to duplicate the sounds, and working them into popular songs. He developed calluses on his fingers from nonstop playing and annoyed his fellow soldiers with constant strumming and the eerily bent notes he made on his guitar. In the barracks, his withdrawn personality and obsession with his guitar made him a source of ridicule.

In Seattle, Betty Jean noticed a lack of interest in his letters and sensed they were drifting apart. Meanwhile, Jimmy and Billy Cox formed a small band called the Casuals with a black officer named Charles Washington, who played the saxophone. Performing a standard selection of hits by King Curtis, Booker T. and the MGs, and others, they performed at service clubs at Fort Campbell and small noisy roadhouses near the army base, and, occasionally, in Clarksville, Tennessee, at a place called The Pink Poodle Club, a dive often under the scrutiny of the local police for allowing minors to loiter where alcohol was sold. "We were gigging on the base at all functions," remembered Billy. "We practiced all day, every day. . . . We did steps and everything. We had a lot of energy."[12]

Always short of funds, Jimmy often pawned his guitar and then asked the others to help repossess it so he could play the next gig, creating a scramble to get the Danelectro out of hock. Washington noticed Jimmy was uncomfortably distant from the other musicians. "Jimmy in many cases was never really with us," Washington said in an interview. "He did a lot of concentrating on his music, and a lot of the small talk the typical group of guys would make, sometimes he would not enter into it . . . we'd look over at him occasionally and there he is, staring. . . . You didn't really get to know him that closely as far as the exact line of thinking."[13] But Cox saw past Jimmy's casual and introverted demeanor and recognized his serious commitment to music.

While at Fort Campbell, Jimmy first discovered true racial segregation. Though the army was officially integrated, soldiers socialized by race, and many places off base were off-limits to blacks. Even music was defined by race, with blacks mostly interested in blues and rhythm and blues. Cox remembered Hendrix becoming deeply interested in Albert King, Slim Harpo, Muddy Waters, and Jimmy Reed—all blues legends that had gotten their start in the South.

One night, Jimmy wandered into The Pink Poodle, whose clientele was almost exclusively black, and became entranced with a guitarist named Johnny Jones from Tennessee, playing with a local pickup band from Clarksville. Jones had experienced Chicago, where he had seen and was strongly influenced by blues greats Muddy Waters and Howlin' Wolf, and had steady gigs at a club in Nashville with his group, the Imperials. Jimmy mustered the courage to approach Jones during a break.

"He sat there all night and watched the show," remembered Jones, "and then asked to hold my guitar. I was kind of skeptical about letting anybody hold my guitar because you can easily drop one if you didn't know how to hold it right. I didn't know he played. . . . I left my amp on low and went over to the bar to take a break . . . and Jimi was up there picking away on my guitar. When he flipped it around and put it on upside down, that's when I got a cold chill."

Jones played a cherry-red Gibson ES 335. This was the first time Jimmy had held and played a fine guitar, let alone had a front-row seat in front of a player who spun off authentic blues licks learned from watching the masters.

"You know Jimi came from out there in Seattle," said Jones. "He didn't have much black on him when he got here. No, he'd talk like a white boy. His diction was real good. He was kind of shy but once you got to know him and watched him play, there was some kind of fire inside him, man."[14]

For ambitious young guitar players, there were two major black rock and roll idols: Bo Diddley and Chuck Berry. Both had successfully crossed over into white pop music in the 1950s. Diddley exemplified Jimmy's desire to manipulate tone, using the tremolo to fluctuate the volume at pulsating intervals. Chuck Berry accented his guitar work with provocative body language, often using his famous "duck walk" with the knees bent in a low side-profile with guitar in a somewhat phallic position. Their expansion of technical and showmanship boundaries, and their growing audiences, would have encouraged young Jimmy Hendrix, who began missing bed checks at the post, failed to pay overdue laundry expenses, and was demoted to private and given a fourteen-day restriction to barracks.

The one place he felt comfortable was in the band with Billy Cox, who admired the astonishing inventiveness and the sonic experimentations Jimmy Hendrix made with his guitar. Popular guitar instrumentals in the Casuals' club sets gave Jimmy a chance to step forward, and as the band built a reputation, the local girls took notice of the flashy, young guitar player with the shy smile. However, Jimmy quickly discovered that African American bands in the South could usually only play to black audiences. "He wrote and told me he had a hard time down there being in a black band," said Betty Jean. "He said he saw prejudice in Tennessee that he had never seen in Seattle."[15] The large Southern black population supported a number of clubs, however, and Jimmy, handsome and flashy on stage, met more available black women than he had ever known in Seattle.

Private Hendrix felt trapped in the army and became more delinquent on the base. After late-night gigs with the band, Jimmy napped the next day during duty. He was a terrible marksman, labeled "unqualified," having been ranked lowest on the list of recruits during basic training. With Billy and Jimmy both full-time soldiers, touring possibilities with the band hit a snag. Cox was near the end of his enlistment, but Jimmy had served only ten of his thirty-six-month enlistment. He didn't want to stay in the army alone, but if he deserted, a prison term awaited. He found the situation so untenable that he concocted a ruse to convince the base psychiatrist that he had homosexual tendencies and was fantasizing about bunkmates. The doctor first told him to get some rest, but Jimmy was persistent. He said he could not stop masturbating and claimed he couldn't sleep and woke up in terror, repeatedly wetting himself, and had lost fifteen pounds because he was lovesick over a squad mate. These were desperate, fabricated admissions. No soldier wanted to be known as gay in a homophobic army, where to be even perceived as gay could earn you a blanket party (a beating by other soldiers in the barracks at night) or a stray bullet. In May, Captain Gilbert Batchman requested a physical and psychiatric examination. His report concluded: "Individual is unable to conform to military rules and regulations. Misses bed check; sleeps while supposed to be working; unsatisfactory duty performance. Requires excessive supervision at all times. Was caught masturbating by member of the platoon."[16] Board proceedings were ordered concerning Jimmy Hendrix's status in the U.S. Army.

A week later on Saturday afternoon, Cox and Hendrix drove to Nashville for a show at the Club Del Morocco. Jimmy managed to get back to the post in time for bed check. On May 22, he received a "mental hygiene consultation" to determine if he was mentally stable for his board hearing (it was determined he was so). However, his squad leader filed a report stating, "In my opinion, Private Hendrix is unadaptable to military service and should be eliminated from the service." He continued to miss bed checks and was again caught masturbating in the latrine, this time by his platoon sergeant, James C. Spears, who filed another damning report: "He has no interest whatsoever in the Army. . . . It is my opinion that Private Hendrix will never come up to the standards required of a soldier. I feel that the military service will benefit if he is discharged as soon as possible."[17]

Finally, the army gave in. In the medical records of James Marshall Hendrix, Captain John Halbert typed: "Homosexual; masturbating; dizziness; pain and pressure in the left chest; loss of weight; frequent trouble sleeping; personal problems."[18] Halbert recommended a discharge because of "homosexual tendencies." Jimi Hendrix never admitted this subterfuge, not even to close friends. Instead, when asked why he got out of the army, he said he broke his ankle leaping out of a plane. On June 29, 1962, Jimmy was approved for an honorable discharge from the army for "unsuitability." Though he had no idea where he was destined to go, at long last, Jimmy, already free from his father, was also free from the yoke of the military. Psychologically, he couldn't cope with the military, yet he had absorbed much military doctrine. He never lost respect for those in the armed services and would remain mostly conservative in his outlook on foreign affairs.

On July 2, 1962, standing outside the gates of Fort Campbell, Kentucky, Jimmy Hendrix had about $400 in his pockets, the most money he had ever had, and could buy a bus ticket to Seattle, reunite with Betty Jean Morgan, and work in his father's landscape business while continuing his pursuit of music there. But Betty Jean was a fading memory, and his greatest enjoyment was playing live music with Billy Cox, who had another three months in the army.

Al knew the conflict inside Jimmy: the exultation of being away from Seattle tempered with exhaustion and unfamiliarity. He wrote to his son, "There's nothing going on back here in Seattle in the music world. If you come back here, you'll just be sitting around idle. There's always a home for you, but I understand your situation. You want to go out there and see what's happening. That's the way I was."[19]

So, Jimmy spent his first day of freedom in Clarksville, where his gigs at The Pink Poodle had been so energizing. "I went in this jazz joint and had a drink," he remembered. "I liked it and I stayed. People tell me I get foolish, good-natured sometimes. Anyway, I guess I felt real benevolent that day. I must have been handing out bills to anyone who asked. I came out of that place with sixteen dollars left."[20]

With almost all his money gone and knowing he couldn't call his father to wire money for a ticket to Seattle, he stayed in town and waited while Billy Cox served his final months at Fort Campbell.

In stark contrast to the racial demographics of Seattle, Clarksville, a town of about twenty-five thousand, lived in the shadow of racism stemming from the time of slavery. The antebellum separation was still present in the economic difference between the white and black neighborhoods. "Whites Only" signs were commonplace in the county, and a small section in the *Clarksville Leaf Chronicle*, titled "Happenings Among the Colored People," announced funeral services, baptisms, and barbecue chicken dinners at the Faith Temple Church of God in Christ. Strict segregation such as this was only just starting to break down throughout the South. Here, Jimmy began a relationship with a local woman, which was probably his first consummate sexual experience, a relationship that put an end to his fantasies of marrying Betty Jean. The idea of marriage had been a powerful daydream, but once it passed and he discovered the pleasures of the flesh, it would be years before he'd ever speak of settling down with one woman. Even his Danelectro Silvertone became part of the past, consigned to a pawnshop when he purchased a new Epiphone

Wilshire guitar in a Clarksdale music store. Jimmy worked a few odd jobs, made a little money playing gigs with a band ("Man, they paid us so little," he remembered[21]), and survived for the next three months, as he would do on and off for the next four years, sleeping on friends' couches or shacking with girls he'd met in clubs.

He made a few forays to Nashville to the heart of country music. Country music was totally alien to Jimmy, and to Billy, too, though he had grown up in Music City. They didn't listen to the country stars of the time nor drink in the bars along Broadway by the Ryman Auditorium. Their haunts were in the black neighborhoods south and east of downtown, where the music was predominantly blues. Even so, the glamour was intoxicating to Jimmy. This was the first big music scene he had ever experienced. He had never even seen the outside of a professional recording studio, and the studios in Nashville had an open-door policy. Jimmy walked in to take a look and was inspired to return and make a record.

When Billy Cox was discharged in September 1962, they formed another band playing mostly blues. "We'd sit around, pass the Jello . . . and pull out an Albert King or B. B. King record and get a lick or two," remembered Cox.[22] On one occasion they piled into Billy's beat-up 1955 Plymouth and drove four hours to a booking in Indianapolis, but when they arrived, the club didn't want an all-black band. Without money for gas home, they entered a "battle of the bands" contest in a bar on Indiana Avenue, the Main Stem of the city. The house band was a popular R&B band called the Presidents, founded by guitarist Alphonso Young. After the Presidents had impressed the crowd with a scorching forty-five-minute set, Jimmy and Cox approached and asked if they would back them during the competition.

"They looked kind of scruffy to me," Young admitted, "but we let them sit in anyway."[23]

When they played "Soldier Boy," a hit by the Shirelles, Jimmy instantly made it his own, bringing deep sentiment to a song that ironically reflected his own mixed feelings about being in the army. "He started off that song like I've never seen anyone play before," recalled Young, "so we backed them up."

The boys played well and came in second place. "We would have won if there wasn't another band . . . that the local girls liked better," recalled

Cox.[24] Alphonso Young quit his group and joined up with Jimmy and Bill to form the King Kasuals, with Hendrix as the centerpiece, Cox on bass, and Young on rhythm guitar. Young sometimes played with his teeth during sets, upstaging Jimmy in his own band. "Jimi's eyes lit up when he first saw me play the guitar with my teeth and behind my back. I was always a show-off. The girls loved it."[25] Jimmy closely observed his friend and quickly copied his style.

He was still shy about singing, thinking he didn't have a good voice, but his shy, sensitive demeanor brought him female fans, some of whom took care of his stage clothes when he sheared off shirt buttons during his wild stage acrobatics. When Club Del Morocco in Nashville needed a new house band, the King Kasuals auditioned for the job and were hired. For the next several months, Jimmy had a home to hone his rapidly developing skills. Jimmy's greatest period of learning—not with sound experimenting, but styles and techniques—was in Nashville, not only because of his curiosity but also because of the competition. Nashville was "one of the hardest audiences in the South," he insisted. "Everybody knows how to play the guitar. You walk down the street and people are sitting on their porch playing more guitars. . . . That's where I learned to play, really, in Nashville."[26]

In the early sixties, Nashville's music industry emerged as a considerable force. Every major label and scores of small companies set up recording studios in town and attracted big names. Four professional studios handled the majority of acts, while six successful smaller studios took up the slack, producing demos and advertising jingles. Two hundred and seventeen BMI publishers also did business in Nashville, collecting license fees on behalf of songwriters, composers, and music publishers, and distributing royalties to their members. There were over a thousand musicians and hundreds of songwriters and publishing houses. When Jimmy and his mates arrived there, half of all American recordings issued from Nashville. Nashville's black population stood at about 20%: its entertainment was segregated along Fourth Avenue and Jefferson Street.

The Del Morocco, at 2417 Jefferson Street, became the home base for Jimmy and the King Kasuals. A refurbished hotel for Pullman porters turned into a nightclub, it was packed every night with black soldiers from Fort Campbell. The club had a capacity of about two hundred people, with the bar in the back behind the tables. Upstairs was an elegant dinner club called the Blue Room. The owner, Uncle Teddy Acklen, was so impressed with the King Kasuals that he gave them a one-year contract and bought Jimmy and Cox new amps to pump up their sound. He also provided the band with a place to live above the beauty school salon he owned down the street. Teddy Acklen Jr., the owner's son, admitted, "These were single rooms. Ain't nothing in them but a bed and a chair, and there was one bathroom everybody shared. Nothing fancy like a hotel, just the bare essentials."[27] That fall, Jimmy, Alphonso, and Billy Cox shared rooms over Joyce's House of Glamour on Jefferson Street in Nashville's sprawling black ghetto.

During the week, the King Kasuals took whatever gigs were available, playing pool halls and roadside juke joints, and on the weekends, they performed at the Del. They would do their set and remain on stage, playing behind guest singers. It was a time of joyful, rambunctious exuberance. They encountered the likes of Aretha Franklin and Etta James getting their hair done downstairs at the House of Glamour for upcoming Del Morocco gigs. Acklen's wife, Muffy Walker, convinced her husband to book Vegas-style lounge acts and the occasional stripper. The diversity of the acts was remarkable. Uncle Teddy handled the Imperials as well, whose lead guitarist was Johnny Jones, who still remembered the night at The Pink Poodle in Clarksville when Private Hendrix strummed his guitar during set breaks, more to discover the secrets of Johnny's tone than to entertain the audience. The Imperials' singer, Johnny Snead, took Jimmy and Billy Cox into his group to work for more local clubs.

As poor as ever, making no more money than when he played with the Velvetones at high school sock hops, Jimmy shared a single bed with Alphonso. "Sometimes Jimi had a girl over," recalled Alphonso, "and we all three slept there, though it was just sleeping."[28]

Girls were the upside to Jimmy's life that fall. He had grown out his hair and fashioned it into a "conk," a version of the "marcel" hairstyle made famous by Little Richard. Though quite penniless, using this neediness to its full advantage, Jimmy was handsome, soft-spoken, polite, and obviously talented. Shrewd and tender—and tender was sexy in R&B clubs where sexuality was loud and overt—he met many women who would romance, mother, bed, and, usually, feed and clothe him until the rescuer discovered their tender young lover was a Romeo with another girl already lined up.

In a time and place where even flirting with a white girl could get a black man killed, his girlfriends were exclusively black. Schools and housing were still segregated. Some lunch counters had only recently been integrated after a massive civil rights sit-in. Jimmy lived an insular life, spending much of his time in three or four area clubs open to blacks. When the band did tour, he was immediately reminded of his skin color since many gas stations in the South refused blacks the use of restrooms. But Jimmy was not an activist seeking social change. His focus was on music, which he saw as being without color. In fact, when he practiced his guitar, he loved to play the surf music popular with white audiences. His bandmates laughed when he suggested they include these in their sets.

Jimmy practiced on the way to gigs, played up to five hours during an all-night show, and continued to practice on the car ride home. "He always had that guitar," Young said.[29] Jimmy practiced on his guitar before going to sleep, slept with it on his chest, and practiced again when he woke up. To find more time to practice, he sometimes bought cheap amphetamines to stay up all night. His obsession garnered him the nickname "Marbles," because people thought he had "lost his marbles" and was crazy from excessive practicing. This practicing slowly paid off. His development as a player came from his natural ability and an obsession to learn every nuance of the instrument. His bandmates joked that Jimmy could play blindfolded, upside down, and behind his back. In fact, he became capable of all three.

He hoped studio work might help support him. Before joining the service, Cox took part in Saturday afternoon jam sessions at King Studios in Nashville, where DJ Bill "Hoss" Allen, from WLAC AM, listened to the tape. If he found something worth using, he sold it to a local label. WLAC had switched to all-black programming, its signal blasting rhythm and blues and gospel music to a wide audience all over the South and parts of the Midwest. In the 1950s, Allen played hot new releases by Chuck Berry, Jimmy Reed, (Sam) Lightnin' Hopkins, and Etta James, and with this new exposure, more R&B records appeared in the 1960s pop charts than in any previous decade. Allen was a white man, and Cox convinced him to listen to his new and extraordinary guitarist friend.

Jimmy arrived at the studio, where "I got him plugged into the board," remembered Allen, "and said I just wanted him to play a New Orleans rhythm, a simple 4/4 . . . and we kicked it off. The next thing I heard in the headphones is BLLAAMM WEE WOO. I stopped and said, 'Hey, man, just give me a good straight four. We've already got a guy playing lead.' He never looked up and we started again. Same thing. BLAAMM WEE WOO. I yelled to the engineer, 'Cut that mother off. Cut him off the board.'"[30]

When the session was finished and Allen played it back, Jimmy's burst of improvisation had been left out; however, used to this lack of acceptance, he said nothing. His refusal to play "normal" guitar lines caused him trouble time and again.

From the fall of 1962, when he began scuffing for work in Nashville clubs, until late summer in 1966, after he quit his backup guitarist position for Little Richard and put his own band together in Greenwich Village, Jimmy crisscrossed the country many times, playing in at least two dozen bands and in more than a hundred towns and cities. Though there's hardly any documentation—Jimmy wrote few letters, and the musicians kept no records—everyone remembers the feel of the time, and many events and names stand out.

The King Kasuals started working a series of black music clubs a few hundred miles from Nashville. These were small joints holding only about fifty people, often had pot-bellied stoves, and served chitlins (cooked pig intestines). The band added singer-songwriters Jimmy Church and Bobby Hebb.

"I remember when we played Clarksville," said Church, "[Jimmy] came up to me and said, 'Hey, Church, listen to this sound, man.' I looked at him kind of funny and said, 'Your speaker's busted.' He said, 'Yeah, but listen to that tone, man.' He was so far away from reality compared to what we were playing, hearing stuff that nobody else could hear."[31]

On stage, Jimmy couldn't create the sounds he heard in his head. Southern audiences encouraged physical showmanship, but even in the Del Morocco, he got odd looks and catcalls when he experimented with the sounds from his guitar. He was wild at this time and lacked the distinctive individual tone a great player brings to the instrument.

He constantly practiced with his extraordinarily long fingers, which gave him a skillful ease of playing. The King Kasuals's set list included a mix of blues and popular cover songs by the Isley Brothers, Jimmy Reed, Bill Doggett, and Bobby "Blue" Bland. When Jimmy and Cox created some of their own pieces, during rehearsals Jimmy would say to Cox, "Man, if we played that they would lock us up."

In Nashville, Jimmy attended every Imperials concert hoping to learn from Johnny Jones. "My guitar was already talking," Jones said. "And when your guitar is talking, it's like you are writing a letter and all you need is the punctuation marks." Only twenty-six, Jones had learned his playing from the successors of Robert Johnson, players like Muddy Waters and T-Bone Walker. Just as important, he had grown up in rural Delta poverty and carried those troubled life experiences into his playing. "Jimi had been listening to records, but he hadn't rubbed elbows with someone who had mud on him like me," Jones said. "That's what he needed to be a blues artist—you gotta be low down and funky. Jimi couldn't get the big strings talking enough to be funky."[32] Jimmy knew about poverty and "low-down and funky," and when Jones took a closer look, he saw a natural bluesman.

A showdown between Jones and Hendrix happened one night at the Club Baron. Jones was not only technically brilliant but also physically imposing at 6'4" with a gravelly voice; Jimmy was humble, soft-spoken, about 6 feet, and skinny. "He come at me one night during intermission," remembered Jones. "Larry Lee came in the door pushing Jimi's little amp with wheels on it. . . . Jimi carried a guitar on his shoulder because he never had a case for it. Larry was doing all the talking, 'Yeah, he's coming at you tonight, Johnny Jones.' I looked up. There was Jimi, standing right behind him, head down, not saying a word."[33]

Always broke and in need of a decent guitar, Jimmy borrowed one from George Yates, a lefty who played rhythm in Jones's band. Jimmy patiently set up his gear and waited to be called to the stage.

The duel began: Jimmy used a small Fender Reverb concert amp, while Jones plugged into a dual Showman amp with two 15-inch JBL speakers easily pumping out a hundred watts. They traded licks, both furiously inventive, but Jones's guitar could be heard more clearly and he got all the applause.

Jimmy's friend, Larry Lee, grabbed him and demanded, "What happened up there?"

Jimmy, in his articulate, soft voice, mumbled, "I was trying to get that B. B. King tone down and my experiment failed."[34] Failures are essential to developing a distinct style—a long line of guitar players could imitate B. B. King, but there was only one B. B. King. When Jones saw Jimmy the next night, he assured him he wasn't bad, it was just that Jones was louder, a lesson Jimmy wouldn't forget. In the future, he did everything he could to be loud enough to be heard and appreciated.

Jimmy Hendrix and Johnny Jones became friends. Many nights after shows, they sat in the front seat of Johnny's car while Jimmy asked questions about music. Most blues players had a sense of machismo and were unwilling to ask questions and show their inexperience. This didn't bother Jimmy, and many of the established players, feeling unthreatened, gladly shared their trade secrets, convinced this skinny, unkempt boy would never develop enough to challenge them. But Jimmy quickly assimilated different styles of playing and mastered techniques far quicker than his mentors thought possible. "I adore 'folk blues,'" Jimi Hendrix later wrote. "'Blues' to me means Elmore James, Howlin' Wolf, Muddy Waters, and Robert Johnson. . . . That sort of music gets the message over and comes through so easily."[35]

Hendrix knew about stylish Delta blues guitarists of the past. In the late 1920s, people traveled distances to hear Charley Patton from Bolton, Mississippi, make his guitar "talk" at regular Saturday shows on Southern plantations. According to legend, Patton could attack the neck of his guitar like a dog shaking a stick, play it between his legs or behind his head, beat it like a drum, and ride it like a pony while still keeping the beat. Patton later taught Howlin' Wolf to play guitar and was said to be such a strict taskmaster that if you played the wrong note, he'd smack you upside the head. And in the 1930s and 1940s, there was Aaron "T-Bone" Walker from Linden, Texas, one of the first electric blues guitar players to use his amplifier's volume control to sustain pitches and combine it with a single string bending and finger vibrato. As part of his dance routine, T-Bone jumped straight up in the air with his guitar high above his head and landed in a split with the guitar behind his head, still playing a fluid line.

Jimmy's own feel for electric blues was noticed by no less than John Lee Hooker: "He was . . . always in my heart from the first time I heard him," remembered Hooker. "He came out of nowhere and wrecked the world. 'Red House' was my favorite song of his. He really had his heart and soul in what he was doing. There was no end to what he could do."[36]

Living in Nashville gave Jimmy a close view of racial hostility. On December 3, 1962, the *Nashville Tennessean* reported several organized sit-ins taking place, one outside of Herschel's Tic Toc restaurant on Church Street. "We don't serve niggers here and you ain't going to get inside," shouted an angry employee as he blocked the entrance, moments later turning a fire extinguisher on black demonstrators who were arrested on charges of disorderly conduct.[37] For the next three weeks, during a subzero cold snap, crowds of up to sixty people marched and demonstrated, trying to desegregate downtown restaurants along the crossroads of Church Street and Fifth Avenue. Most were arrested for not following orders to disperse, some serving up to fifty-five days in jail. The more the Negro community spoke up and poured out its communal anger, the more police turned out *en masse* and turned up the heat.

Disgusted with the situation, Jimmy and Billy purposely ignored a "whites only" sign in a Nashville diner and were taken to jail for sitting in a section designated for whites. Uncle Teddy Acklen, who was light-skinned and often passed for white, bailed them out and got the charges against them dropped, but the fines were deducted from their paychecks. Shortly afterward, expressing insecurity, Jimmy wrote to his father about his incarceration: "Dad, I did just what I figured you'd do. I hope I didn't do anything wrong."

Al Hendrix, a tough, occasionally neglectful father who had denied his sons the opportunity to attend their mother's funeral and only reluctantly encouraged Buster's musical talent, showed an uncharacteristic warmth and support of Jimmy taking a stand against bigotry. Assuring his son he had done no wrong, Al replied in a letter, "If that had been me, I'd be doing the same thing. As a matter of fact, I participate in a lot of activities in Seattle, even though it isn't as bad as the South. You stand up for your rights."[38]

Life became hard for Jimmy in Nashville. There was no studio work, and except for a handful of musicians and club owners and a few fans, he knew no one. He was learning a lot about music and his talent was growing, but the King Kasuals were going nowhere and he was feeling discouraged. He could not move out of his room above Joyce's House of Glamour. The additional cleanup work he did there was viewed by Acklen as compensation for meals and for the sound equipment the club had loaned him.

The band did not earn enough to break the musical servitude that kept them at Del Morocco. Bookings weren't improving, so Jimmy decided to recharge his soul and borrowed money for a bus ticket to Vancouver, British Columbia, where, through the winter of '62–'63, he stayed with his grandmother Nora. Though Seattle is only 130 miles south, he didn't visit during his stay. While he expressed his love for his father in letters, he didn't particularly want to be near him. He wanted the consistent love of his grandmother Nora, with whom he had spent happy times as a child, and to immerse himself in the peace and beauty of a city he knew and loved to keep his vision alive.

There was an after-hours club in Vancouver in the basement of the Embassy Ballroom on Davie Street called the Elegant Parlour, partly owned by Tommy Chong, who was half-Irish and half-Asian and would later achieve fame as half of the comedy duo "Cheech and Chong." Jimmy found his way to it and played rhythm guitar on stage with singer Bobby Taylor and Tommy Chong on lead guitar. "They played Motown stuff," recalled a friend. "They also had a bit of a surf, garage kind of rock to their sound."[39]

On the weekends at a club on the corner of Alma and West Broadway, the group played Taylor's original arrangements of popular hits of the day. But Jimmy grew bored playing "twist songs." Their music was too tame, not what Hendrix envisioned, and he was also dismayed that their audiences were almost exclusively white. He loved his grandmother, but living with her cramped his style. When he didn't come home for several nights, she worried. And when he did come home, he often arrived just as she was getting up.

Feeling rejuvenated enough, Jimmy Hendrix left Vancouver in February and took a southbound train heading back toward the Mississippi Delta where the music was intensely original and fired his imagination.

The Del Morocco Club

Johnny Jones

Private Hendrix

King Kasuals – Jimmy on the left

Chitlin' Circuit

In the South, where soul and blues infused with jazz, and where he could grow as a musician, Jimmy spent another four years working a circuit of small black nightclubs, perfecting a style no one could emulate. Whenever he stayed in Vancouver with his grandmother Nora, who was a cook at Vie's Chicken and Steakhouse in Hogan's Alley, he filled himself with traditional Southern Soul Food—turnip greens, grits, ham hocks, catfish, cornbread, hush puppies, and sweet potatoes—served at the restaurant. Nora ran a yearly church fundraiser that featured such "delicacies" where among the entrees served were pig intestines called chitterlings, a longer word for "chitlins." In homage to this black Southern delicacy, the name "Chitlin' Circuit" was used to describe the circuit of African American clubs in the Deep South, a route that grew from mob-backed installations of coin-operated phonographs in every colored café on the Main Stem "strolls" of any southern town in the 1930s, to booking big band orchestras molded from music students at high schools and small black universities. They were booked from the largest ballrooms in New Orleans and Dallas to the most ramshackle barns in the Carolinas. The harsh post-World War II economic conditions forced black promoters to turn from big, expensive swing bands to small, cheap, rhythm and blues combos that revolutionized black music. The dark town's lively atmosphere inspired violent, sexual, hedonistic lyrics. The word "rock," originally used to mean coitus, went from sexual to musical connotations as rhythm and blues transformed into black rock and roll and went mainstream in the 1950s with acts like B. B. King and Little Richard.

The route began in New York's Apollo Theater, ran through Washington, D.C.'s Howard Theater, and then farther south and west to small, shabby venues in rural areas. "The Chitlin' Circuit was basically any place where you were playing to black audiences," observed blues legend Bobby Rush. "It could be a roadhouse, barbecue joint, pool hall, or a bar."[1]

From 1963 through 1965, this circuit was the home turf of Jimmy Hendrix. Playing with the King Kasuals, or more often as a backup musician in other bands, he felt he had seen the inside of every juke joint throughout the South. Even with a gig every night, it was hard to make a living, but it offered Jimmy invaluable lessons on showmanship, interaction with the audience, and survival as a touring musician, which included being an entertainer. With each passing gig, his own playing matured as he learned more of the Delta tradition.

When Jimmy returned to Nashville in the winter of 1963, the King Kasuals added a horn section. "We wanted to have the 'show,'" said Alphonso Young.[2] The "show" was the term for large revue-style bands then in vogue. Many audiences in these clubs expected more than just music—they wanted a full night of entertainment that included comedy, live theater, and pantomime. The Kasuals added an emcee who opened their shows with an impersonation of comedian Moms Mabley.

Hendrix was already a flashy player, but he perfected his first real "act" in the Chitlin' Circuit where he began playing with the guitar behind his back like T-Bone Walker and mimicking Alphonso Young's trick of playing with his teeth. Cox bought him a fifty-foot guitar cable that allowed him to move out onto the dance floor and sometimes outside on the street. He dueled onstage with Young, which made their sets more exciting. Young also suggested that rather than practice during set breaks, he mingle with the audience. "He was shy. I told him to stay and mingle, get to know the crowd, and talk with them. That was the way to build fans who would come to see you night after night."[3] Jimmy quickly discovered it was also a good way to meet girls.

The Kasuals played throughout Tennessee, Kentucky, Arkansas, and Indiana. They were basically a dance band playing R&B hits to exclusively black audiences. Most band members had part-time jobs outside of music, but Jimmy favored spending more time with his guitar than working a part-time job, and that meant he had to live off the generosity of others. Sometimes he squatted in a house under construction, rising before the workers arrived in the morning. He took many musical side jobs during these years and toured as backup to Carla Thomas, Tommy Tucker, Slim Harpo, Jerry Butler, Marion James, Chuck Jackson, and Solomon Burke.

The Continentals, a popular band playing a four-week engagement at Del Morocco, asked Uncle Teddy to help recruit a temporary guitar player. The band was integrated with three whites and three blacks and had difficulty playing in Nashville's white clubs, where racists in the audience often called the police to shut down the show. Larry Perigo, a white sax player, recalled Acklen saying he had a guy staying in his apartments who did some cleaning up and played guitar. "I don't know if he'll work out, but you can use him until you find someone else." So Jimmy joined the Continentals while they headlined at Del Morocco, and served in the backup band when the big stars came through on Friday and Saturday. Always a quick study, he learned the songs easily during rehearsals, despite not being able to read music. "He was a little strange," claimed Perigo, "and we called him 'Marbles.' He didn't seem to mind. Any type of conversation he had with you he'd cover his mouth and whisper, even if it was, 'I'm going to go have some lunch,' like it was some big secret. He didn't sing with us. We didn't even know he sang."[4]

Repressing his impulse to cut loose with wild guitar lines, Jimmy tried to play a subservient role as rhythm guitarist. Once, when he pawned his guitar, he offered Larry Lee as a replacement. Perigo complained about Larry's skills. "After the first show, I told Jimi, 'You got to do something. This guy isn't that good.' Jimi took Larry's guitar, flipped it around so he could play it, but the strings were now upside down. He played it that way the rest of the night and he was great. Jimi later told me he learned how to play the guitar that way."

But left- or right-handed, Jimmy was still wild and too much of a problem for the band and they took a vote and let him go. "The last time I saw him," said Perigo, "he was walking down Jefferson Street with his guitar in his hands, not in a case, and an amp cord was still plugged in. The other end was bouncing on the sidewalk."[5]

Jimmy posed numerous problems for existing bands in Nashville because of his use of stage tricks; while exciting some audiences, it annoyed the players onstage. Jimmy Church remembered, "He played the guitar with his teeth. . . . He'd play behind his back. . . . He was left-handed and had a little effeminate thing about him: soft-spoken, smiled a lot. And when he was on stage and flicked his tongue out, the girls really went for that. They didn't always like the macho guys."[6]

Already noted for his unorthodox personal behavior, Jimmy was also forgetful and late for gigs, an attitude likely fueled by his frustration with his surroundings. The low pay and lack of creative freedom were confining to the King Kasuals, and they focused their resentment on Teddy Acklen. "They didn't give us any raise," explained Billy. "We decided we weren't going to take it anymore."[7] Uncle Teddy caught wind of their plans and told them to start packing. Guitarist Johnny Jones visited them prior to their eviction from their rooms above Joyce's House of Glamour. Jimmy was lying on a mattress on the floor. All he owned were a few scattered clothes.

In March 1963, an R&B tour package passed through Nashville with a variety of talented artists that included a young Aretha Franklin and Hank Ballard and the Midnighters. The show's flamboyant emcee/singer, "Gorgeous" George Odell, needing a guitar player for his backup band, hired Jimmy Hendrix. Gorgeous George introduced top R&B acts on various touring venues for Henry Wynn's Supersonic Attractions. A self-promoter with a sharpened awareness of stagecraft, he wore a silver wig and his motto was "Don't look back; if you do, it holds you back." He came from a tradition of traveling musical revues, where the person who introduced the acts was seen as a "cleanup man" responsible for telling jokes or dancing during the transitions between performers. "I would change after each performance," George remembered, "and I usually had twelve acts to introduce. My outfits would kill because I dressed in European-cut pinstripe suits." George liked Jimmy's eagerness to tour.

The pay wasn't much, but Jimmy said, "You don't have to pay me, just feed me, and let me play behind you when you go onstage."[8]

Touring on the road required stamina and tolerating the mood swings of bandleaders and other players. The players were affected by cramped quarters, boredom, and repetition. The food was not the best and there was little time for decent sleep. Touring with Gorgeous George, even with limited musical participation, clearly had an impact. Larry Lee observed that the most important lesson Jimmy gleaned on that first tour with Gorgeous George was the importance of a complete performance from beginning to end, offering the audience a consistent level of entertainment. Lee said of George, "He needed no rehearsal. The cat could put on a four-hour show in itself, and he knew about people and how to make them happy."[9] Jimmy acquired a general sense of showmanship by watching Gorgeous George's energy, commitment, and flair.

To assuage Jimmy's frustration about not performing more during the tour, George told him Hank Ballard might be able to use him as a guitarist. Jimmy was a fan of Ballard's risqué hits, which were often pulled off radio station playlists because of their sexual content. In 1954, Ballard's "Work With Me, Annie" caused an uproar with music critics and broadcasters with its suggestive lyrics ("Annie, please don't cheat/ Give me all my meat"), but sold a quarter of a million copies and became a number one R&B hit. He also wrote and recorded "The Twist," which Chubby Checker recorded and made into the biggest dance-fad record ever. Like Gorgeous George, Ballard was every inch the showman. Jimmy had seen Ballard perform in Seattle with the Midnighters in 1959 and became enthralled with guitarist Billy Davis's style of playing, watching him swing the guitar behind his head and play it fiercely, and stepping up close to the amp and using the feedback to sustain a note.

Davis remembered Jimmy, who was allowed backstage at that concert: "I opened the dressing room door," said the guitarist, "and there was this kid with a big smile on his face. After we talked a while, he invited me back to his house so I could show him some of the things I did on the guitar, and for some reason I went twice. Hank was in town for a week. Jimi introduced me to his dad and showed me this little cheap guitar he was playing, and I showed him some licks on my Stratocaster." Davis told Jimmy about legendary guitarists T-Bone Walker and Eddie Kirkland and how they charted new territory for black guitarists. When they again crossed paths on Jimmy's first tour with Gorgeous George, Jimmy asked for some help. So "I pulled a few strings and got him in the Midnighters," recalled Davis.[10]

The Midnighters had a Billboard Top 100 hit and Jimmy was thrilled. It was his first road tour experience with a major R&B act. But he could not break a growing pattern of landing a gig, learning the music, trying to branch out, getting fired, and then being picked up by another band. Hank Ballard and the Midnighters were even less tolerant than smaller acts in Nashville, and Jimmy was fired from the group in the middle of the tour.

"He couldn't play the music right," explained Davis, although it would probably be more accurate to say that Jimmy refused to play the way he was expected. "So they left him stranded with no money in Knoxville, Tennessee."[11]

Jimmy also toured with Solomon Burke, a legendary soul singer and preacher who had a big voice, weighed 250 pounds, and was a bona fide star with two Top 40 hits. "I had a record out called 'Just Out of Reach (Of My Two Open Arms),' and Jimi could play that so well it would make you cry," Solomon recalled.

Included on this tour were Otis Redding, Joe Tex, Sugar Pie DeSanto, and comedian Pigmeat Markham. Even among this stellar lineup, Jimmy stood out as one of the best guitarists, though his flashiness put him at odds with Burke. The sets would go along fine until, "he'd go into this wild stuff that wasn't part of the song," said Burke. "I couldn't handle it anymore." One night on the bus he traded Hendrix to Otis Redding for two horn players. Jimmy lasted with Redding for less than a week before being fired for the same reasons. "We ended up leaving him by the side of the road," remembered Solomon.[12]

Similar incidents followed. When a short gig with Bobby Womack fell apart, Jimmy's guitar was thrown out the bus window. But he could always turn to Billy Cox, who, like a brother, always rescued him from a lonely train station or roadhouse. Returning to Nashville, Jimmy patched things up with Acklen, again lived upstairs at Joyce's House of Glamour, played gigs with the King Kasuals at the Del Morocco, and backed up other groups coming through town. The grinding poverty of Seattle and the regimentation of the Screaming Eagles might not have taught him discipline, but it gave him an amazing surplus of resilience and confidence. His correspondence to his family was short and limited to postcards, but he stayed in touch as he moved from town to town. He wrote his father, "Dad, Here's a picture of our band named the King Kasuals. We're one of the two best Rhythm and Blues bands in Nashville."[13]

Renaming the band the Sandpipers, Billy Cox lined up a gig in August at The Jolly Roger. "[We] added a horn player and a rhythm guitar player, and then as an opening act billed as 'Jimmy Hendrix and His Magic Guitar,' we backed Jimi doing all of his stage tricks."

Jimmy was getting a reputation among musicians as not just a wild man on stage but also a phenomenal talent. Later, tutoring a young guitarist named Velvet Turner, Jimmy taught the importance of learning chords when starting out. "Forget about playing lead in the beginning," Turner remembered him saying. "The main thing I want you to learn are chords. Everyone puts so much emphasis on lead guitar, but chords are more important. Because with those you can always paint colors and then put your lead on top. They're the most important part. I've been playing chords half of my life in all those rhythm and blues bands."[14] Besides his innate creativity, passion, and obsession with music, pure genetics aided Jimmy's talent: His long fingers and thumb stretching over the fretboard allowed him to simultaneously play lead runs and low parts.

Jimmy Hendrix grew and learned from every artist he met, saw, or played with in Nashville. In the summer of 1963, he gigged at the Club Baron with R&B singer Roscoe Shelton. Shelton was born in 1931 in Lynchburg, Tennessee, and had sung with gospel groups and became friends with Sam Cooke when Cooke was lead singer with the gospel vocal group the Soul Stirrers. Jimmy gained a further appreciation of gospel when he and Cox backed up singer Marion James's band and did short road trips to surrounding cities. Marion's husband, Jimmy Stewart, was an accomplished trumpeter who had played with B. B. King. The couple's apartment served as a way station for struggling, hungry musicians coming and going. Lattimore Brown, a singer on the Chitlin' Circuit, spent a good deal of time at their home and recalled: "At any given time there'd be six to eight of us up there. . . . It was a two-bedroom apartment. I'd be in there cooking neck bones and pinto beans, corn bread. If a musician only had one piece of bread, he'd break it in half for his friend. . . . It was a bonding, like family. We had Billy Cox up there, Larry Lee, and this kid that didn't have no name. He was just another guitar player . . . Jimi motherfucking Hendrix, man!"[15]

During this time Jimmy met Albert King, who was also left-handed and obsessed with the guitar from an early age. As a child, King made "one strand on the wall," a wire fastened to a wall at the top and to a brick at the bottom. He'd play the crude instrument with one hand and use a glass bottle as a slide. It wasn't until 1961 that he had a major hit with "Don't Throw Your Love on Me So Strong." He was twenty-two years older than Jimmy and stood 6'4". He liked Jimmy and showed him some of his techniques. Because his hands were so big, King had trouble holding and using a pick. To compensate he developed a technique that used the meaty part of his thumb and bent two strings at the same time, achieving several tones from a single note. King also showed Jimmy how he tuned to an E minor chord, with a low C on the bottom, and mainly concentrated on the top three higher strings. "Hendrix used to take pictures of my fingers to try and see what I was doing," recalled King.[16]

Years later in an interview in *Rolling Stone*, Jimmy told the reporter, "I like Albert King. He plays completely and strictly in one way, just straight funk blues,"[17] and King would later say about Jimi, "He's had it tough, but Jimi is a born blues man."[18]

Jimmy's young friend Larry Lee had developed into a much better guitar player, becoming the featured guitarist with a band called the Bonnevilles with a hit record called "Cherokee Twist." Lee and Billy Cox, who occasionally played bass for the group, suggested to the band's leader, Robert Fisher, that he meet their friend Jimmy, who still lived in a room above Joyce's House of Glamour. Fisher recalled, "[Jimi was] plucking the guitar upside-down and left-handed. . . . I guessed this Hendrix fellow had not been eating too regularly. So, that weekend I let him play with the Bonnevilles." Fisher bought him two guitar strings and got his suit out of the cleaners. When they played a gig in Huntsville, Alabama, Jimmy stepped forward with his solos and bowled over the entire black audience. Fisher was impressed by Jimmy's performance skills. "Whether it was playing the guitar behind his back or picking it with his teeth, his antics really fired the crowd up. . . . Jimi's stage presence added confidence to the band. He took a group of musicians and made an even better band out of them."[19]

Jimmy later looked back with affection on some of his Southern gigs outside Nashville. "It's fun to play little funky clubs because that's like a workhouse. . . . Everything is sweating. It seemed like the more it got sweaty, the funkier it got and the groovier. Everybody was melted together . . . and the sound was kicking them all in the chest. I dig that."[20] Fisher was soon distributing concert posters that featured Jimmy as the main performer.

In August an opportunity arose for the Bonnevilles to back the Impressions, a vocal trio featuring Sam Gooden and Curtis Mayfield, for an upcoming tour of the South with twenty-eight shows in thirty days. Hendrix later remembered, "The best gig was working with Curtis Mayfield and the Impressions. Curtis was a really good guitarist, but he was the star and thought I was flighty. I learned quite a lot in that short time. He probably influenced me more than anyone I'd ever played with up to that time, that sweet sound of his, you know."[21]

One reason Mayfield may have thought Jimmy flighty was because the Bonnevilles used the amps supplied by the Impressions, and, according to Larry Lee, Jimmy hit a note at the end of the Bonneville's set that blew out the amplifier. Mayfield demanded to know what had happened to the amp, but Jimmy feigned ignorance.

Despite their lack of camaraderie, Mayfield's smooth style of playing and his political consciousness clearly moved Jimmy. Mayfield's song "Keep on Pushing" delivered a message of hope, strength, and unity in the wake of the June 1963 murder of Medgar Evers and the Ku Klux Klan's bombing of the Sixteenth Street Baptist Church in Birmingham that killed four young black girls.

Near the end of their run with the Bonnevilles, Larry claimed the promoter owed him money. A heated argument ensued with Robert Fisher, who "warned Larry that he had better watch himself and reminded him that Nashville had more than its share of unemployed guitar pickers."

Jimmy intervened, reminding Fisher that Larry was still in college, trying to work his way through school. Jimmy then told Fisher he would be leaving the group. He wanted to record some songs he had composed using his own vocals.

"I could see he had visions of his own," remembered Fisher, who skeptically observed, "I thought to myself, yeah, sure, Jimi Hendrix on vocals. Give me a break."[22]

In a vain effort to keep Jimmy, Fisher took the band to Fidelity Recording, a small studio on Broadway Street by the Ryman Auditorium, where they recorded a demo of four songs. He took the tape to Boss Allen, who was impressed with the sound but not interested in producing the Bonnevilles.

But by the fall of 1963, Jimmy Hendrix had played with some of the best bands in the nation. Playing for groups he had grown up admiring gave him a greater sense of destiny than playing for a cover band in Nashville. When there appeared a dapper, sophisticated concert promoter from New York named Carl Fisher, who saw Jimmy perform at the Club Baron and offered to bring him to New York and make him the star he deserved to be, Jimmy, with stardust in his eyes, made the decision to leave. He tried to convince the Kasuals to accompany him, but none wanted to leave Nashville. Alphonso Young, listening to Jimmy's promises of fame and riches, was more concerned over his friend's increasing use of amphetamines. "He was taking these Red Devils and other pills they called speed."[23]

Jimmy, just turning twenty-one, headed for New York City in December, once again carrying his guitar on his back in the style he had seen in *Johnny Guitar*. It was cold and there was snow on the ground in Nashville. At the Greyhound bus station, Larry Lee took off his overcoat and gave it to Jimmy to buffer the New York winter. "Jimi had no responsibility," remembered Larry. "He was just foot-loose and fancy-free. I knew it couldn't be that easy in New York. It scared me."[24]

Everything Jimmy owned was in the small duffel bag he carried onto the bus. He moved to the back and started playing his guitar. Any seasoned blues lover within earshot would have been warmed, for beyond the fast playing and skillful technique was the first hint of tone smoothed out by two years of struggle in the South. The bluesman in the back of the bus had begun to sound like no one else.

Albert King

Jimmy playing guitar with his hair styled

Hank Ballard

Solomon Burke

Manhattan Rhapsody

In January 1964, Jimmy got off the bus with Carl Fisher in New York City. They took a room at the Hotel Theresa in Harlem, on the corner of Seventh Avenue and 125th Street. The Hotel Theresa had been a transit place for many famous black entertainers over the years: Cab Calloway, Billie Holiday, Louis Armstrong, and many others. When Jimmy arrived, Malcolm X had an office there.

After growing up in Seattle, Jimmy must have marveled at the size and vibrancy of the black population of Harlem. But just a few days after arriving, when Fisher walked in on Jimmy and a woman copulating, the offer of work disappeared. Carl Fisher, Jimmy learned, was a female impersonator and exotic dancer who occasionally performed at Apollo's Jewel Box Revue (now he understood why Fisher scrutinized him whenever he got out of the shower). He threw Jimmy out, ending their brief professional relationship.

Almost immediately he became friends with two other struggling musicians, R&B singers Dean Courtney and Johnny Star. Courtney was living in a suite in the Theresa, paid for by Little Richard. Jimmy moved in as he adapted to life in Manhattan with its great, seething variety. His soft-spoken, kind demeanor made him appealing to many people, including the gay hotel beautician. But when a large woman named Big Sandy picked up his guitar in the hotel room one night, he revealed a sharp, dark, angry side: "If you drop my guitar," said Jimmy, shattering his polite demeanor, "I will choke your neck."[1] When she knocked it over, he dragged her into the bathroom and choked her with her head in the toilet. Star and Courtney, hearing gurgling sounds, rushed in and pried loose his fingers.

Jimmy started hanging around 125th Street, Harlem's main thoroughfare, frequenting Small's Paradise and the Palm Café, looking for gigs with little success. His stage tricks—louder amplification, short bursts of feedback, and playing behind his head or with his teeth—didn't impress the denizens of 1960s Harlem.

During the 1920s and '30s, the years of the Harlem Renaissance, an influx of creativity in literature, drama, music, visual art, and dance changed Black America. But by the mid-sixties, Harlem's music audience had retrenched: Floor shows and dancing waiters no longer presided. Broadway musicals and Fifty-Second Street jazz clubs reduced the amount of jazz found in Harlem, as sophisticated rhythm and blues had become its most popular music.

Guitarist Horace "Ace" Hall, who soon worked with Jimmy, saw that Jimmy's style of playing, onstage behavior, and appearance did not fit with the clubs in Harlem. "Jimi turned his amplifier up and wanted to be heard at those clubs. But when he wanted to sit in again, those cats would tell him, 'Well we're just going to intermission' or 'You can catch us on the next set,' . . . they'd always give him some excuse. . . . Most of the guys then had their conked and Marcels [hairstyles] and not in a do-rag [a close-fitting cloth tied around the top of the head] like Jimi would wear. He was just different."[2]

In New York for less than a month, Jimmy had no money, no job, no leads, and the coldest part of winter was coming. Not only was the New York music scene hard to break into, he also found it exceptionally narrow. R&B, jazz, and blues were the accepted genres, and there was little diversion from how they had been done before. "Black people didn't want to hear any rock n' roll in Harlem," recalled TaharQa Aleem, and "there was a dress code—if you didn't look or sound a certain way you were shunned."[3]

Jimmy had to rely on women again. Hanging out at clubs, he soon found his way into the heart of a flamboyant, promiscuous woman who did not want to fall in love with him. Courtney introduced Jimmy to Lithofayne Pridgon, a street-smart, beautiful African American, who, at nineteen, was already a Harlem fixture, and she guided and protected Jimmy in the hard indifference of New York City.

Known as "Apollo Fay" because she frequented the famous Harlem theater of that name, Lithofayne, or Faye, was born in Georgia and came to New York at sixteen. Her sexual daring, according to her friend Etta James, resulted in many lovers who performed at the Apollo. Etta said she called them "my repertoire;" allegedly, among whom were Jackie Wilson, Otis Redding, Brook Benton, Wilson Pickett, and Sam Cooke.

"She was pretty and perky," according to Etta, and "thin-framed and big-breasted and wore spike heels and scandalously short skirts where you could see the cheeks of her ass."[4]

When Jimmy told Faye that he was desperate to find work, she introduced him to Jerry Cuffee, Sam Cooke's valet. Faye and Jimmy followed Cuffee up a flight of backstage stairs at the Apollo Theater to Cooke's dressing room. Jimmy had his guitar in hand, ready to play from a large number of R&B songs in his head. But Cooke already had a guitar player, and Jimmy stomped down the stairs, grumbling about not getting the job, a job that wasn't really offered, and burst through the backstage door onto 126th Street with Faye behind him. They walked downtown past prostitutes, hustlers, and desperate junkies of whom Jimmy barely took notice.

Through Faye, he met the Aleem twins, TaharQa and Tunde Ra, who were born and raised in Harlem. On their first night together, Jimmy regaled Faye and the Aleems with stories of touring in the South and playing the guitar. The Aleems had temporarily abandoned music for drug dealing. Harlem was an epicenter for heroin distribution: Most of the city's addicts lived there. The Aleems worked for "Fat" Jack Taylor, who was a powerful, ruthless drug boss. He ruled Harlem's 116th Street and was, according to Dean Courtney, "just under six feet, soft-spoken, with a dazzling, winning smile." Taylor was a homosexual with an uncanny ability to charm and manipulate people. "It was hard to get him out of Harlem," remembered Courtney, "because he took care of a lot of the people in the area. During Thanksgiving, Christmas, and all of the holidays, he'd pull up in a big truck and make sure all the kids got toys, or at Thanksgiving everyone got turkeys."[5]

A lover of music, Taylor had once started a record label, Rojac Records, trying to capture the musical pulse of Harlem as Berry Gordy had done with Motown in Detroit, though not nearly as successful. Etta James knew him and went to him for help when a pimp she dated had beat her and sent her to the hospital. Taylor loaned her his feared brother, Willy Jack, as a bodyguard.

The Aleems thought dealing was a way out of poverty. No one was more impoverished than Jimmy, and Fat Jack offered him a job hustling drugs. Steadfast in his belief that music was his only calling, Jimmy declined. "People would say, 'If you don't get a job, you'll just starve to death.' But I didn't want to take a job outside of music."[6] Jimmy's devotion to music was only possible through the patronage of friends like the Aleems, who, he knew, helped pay rent and bought food with drug money.

Faye Pridgon studied Jimmy Hendrix. "Jimi was kind of naive to what was going on around him. . . . He had processed hair and shiny black pants that showed where the knees bent. But he had something about him, a warmth that none of the other fast-rapping dudes had. He thanked me for getting him backstage to see Sam Cooke. He referred to Sam as 'what's-his-face.'"[7]

When they left Sam Cooke, they had walked to West Ninety-Eighth Street and dropped in on Faye's mother, Mrs. Pridgon, who liked to cook. Jimmy was nearly starving. Mrs. Pridgon also had a collection of blues records—Muddy Waters, Lightnin' Hopkins, Judy King, Junior Parker—that Jimmy loved. They ate and talked and ate some more. Faye found him surprisingly old-fashioned, often talking about his old high school girlfriend, Betty Jean. Jimmy endeared himself by playing along to the blues records. When they left, they went to the Hotel Cecil "where I was staying with a girlfriend," remembered Faye. "I made the decision just to take care of him."[8]

They moved in together. "All our activity took place in bed," she wrote. "He was creative in bed too. There would be encore after encore." According to Faye, his sexual appetite was insatiable. "There were times when he almost busted me in two." His only equal passion was music; she thought of her competition "not as a woman, but as a guitar."

They had frequent disagreements. One argument ensued when he refused to take her out one night. "You know how I hate to go out when my hair doesn't look right," he said.[9] He was obsessed with his hair, spending hours making sure the curls were right. His clothes were ratty, his shoes ill-fitting, and his borrowed coat barely kept him warm, but before he ventured out his hair had to be perfect.

When thrown out of their hotel room for nonpayment, they stayed at Mrs. Pridgon's on the sly. "We'd sneak into her place after she left for work," recalled Faye. "We'd come in and go to sleep. We'd get up before she got back and straighten up or be gone or sit around like we just walked in." At Mrs. Pridgon's, Jimmy discovered a Robert Johnson single, "Walking Blues." He listened to certain riffs repeatedly. "Jimi used to play a stomp-down, funky blues," Faye recalled. "Elmore James was his favorite. He used to take one of those little hotel glasses and put it on the strings and get that sound Elmore got. He tried to make his voice sound like his too."[10]

Mrs. Pridgon, initially fond of Jimmy, began to resent his regular presence in her home and his lack of employment. She doubted Faye had much of a future with him and warned Jimmy to start looking for another girlfriend.

Since 1934, the Apollo had offered its stage to aspiring performers: Sam Cooke, Little Richard, and the Isley Brothers had all launched their careers there. The theater conducted a weekly Wednesday night amateur competition. First prize was $25 and the opportunity to return the following week and play with the house band. It was a hard audience. They booed and jeered when they did not approve, or threw bottles and chairs from the balcony. Jimmy showed up on a Wednesday in January along with several other anxious contestants. Billy Mitchell, later tour director at the Apollo, remembered the night: "He came out and played a popular R&B hit with the Apollo Theater house band, led by Reuben Phillips. The audience loved him, and he really got into his groove."[11] Jimmy won the competition, but $25 didn't last long in New York.

Barred from Mrs. Pridgon's place, for a while they slept on the floor of Etta James's hotel dressing room. Faye noticed Jimmy's stress causing weight loss and chest pains. He was generally nervous, chain-smoked, and had trouble sleeping, but there was an even more troubling condition. "Jimi would like to play the guitar on the bed," observed Faye, "and he'd often fall asleep on his back with his guitar lying on his chest . . . and he'd make these choking sounds, followed with muscle spasms in the middle of the night that woke me up. Many times I'd have to roll him over on his side to make him stop."[12] (Faye wasn't surprised when she learned years later that Jimi died from choking-related circumstances.)

"About this time, I met Jimi Hendrix," Etta James later wrote. "It was Faye who said the boy was talented, but to me he looked like a roadie working the R&B circuit. Someone said he could play the blues—the John Lee Hooker blues—but back then, we were looking at country blues like sharecropper's music."[13]

Faye remembered, "We used to have to get up and get out early before Etta returned. . . . Etta didn't like Jimi and she didn't want him staying in the dressing room. He was brokenhearted because the image he held of these entertainers was much different [than the] reality. Most of them didn't want him around unless they had ulterior motives."[14]

What Jimmy wanted and probably needed most was a touring gig with a big-time band, and it was just at this time that the Isley Brothers needed a guitarist.

The Isley Brothers had started off singing gospel music but had turned to rhythm and blues and rock and roll with a series of high-energy hits in the early sixties. The brothers wrote and recorded "Shout," a hit record that sold over a million copies. Their next hit, "Twist and Shout," shot to number two in rhythm & blues, and stayed on the charts for nineteen weeks (a new rock group from England named the Beatles would do even better when they covered the song in their first album, *Please Please Me*). With their hits selling millions of copies, the Isleys became one of the biggest R&B bands of the era. Early in February 1964, with a spring tour and recording dates booked, their guitarist quit. Dean Courtney mentioned Jimmy as a possible replacement to a friend of the Isleys named Tony Rice, who knew about Jimmy as "the guy who plays the guitar upside down." Ronnie Isley remembered, "Tony said this kid . . . was the best and that he played right-handed guitar with his left hand. I said to Tony, 'Aw, come on, man, he can't be that good . . .' and then I started naming all the guitar players we knew we'd like to have in our band, and Tony said, 'He's better than any of them.'"[15]

Jimmy looked like an itinerant musician with all his worldly possessions inside his guitar case when Ronnie took him to the house the Isleys rented in Englewood, New Jersey, where the band assembled in the basement. Jimmy leaped into "Twist and Shout," "Respectable," and "Shout." He knew and fluidly played them all.

"He knew how to pull off a dazzling cover version," remembered Ronnie. "Man, I never heard anything like it. We hired him after about thirty seconds."[16]

As a member of the backup group, the I. B. Specials, Jimmy received a spare room in the house. The younger Isley brothers nicknamed him "creeper" because he moved about so softly. "He was quiet, well behaved, and minded his own business," remembered Ernie Isley, who was eleven at the time and watched Jimmy quietly sit and play his guitar while looking out the front window. "Jimi would practice phrases over and over again, turn them inside out, break them in half, break them in quarters, play them slow, play them fast."[17]

On Sunday night, February 9, the Beatles were on *The Ed Sullivan Show*. The Isley Brothers and band watched the historical appearance, not knowing that this one event would transform America and make rock and roll the dominant musical genre on the charts. The Beatles had sex appeal, harmonies, and amplified rock music that buoyed Jimmy's hopes.

Earning thirty dollars per night on tour with the Isley Brothers, Jimmy's individuality was beginning to show. The Brothers prided themselves on a clean-cut, well-tailored look, but Jimmy would wear brightly colored scarves, earrings, shiny bracelets, and, at one concert, used a gold chain for a belt. They eventually enforced a strict dress code. The tour began in early March with a concert at the Grand National in Montreal, Quebec.

At a local club after the first show, Jimmy met a seventeen-year-old drummer named Buddy Miles, who remembered: "This one guy came through that was a little bit different from everybody else. He had the same garb on, but he had chains and stuff, and his hair was, like, down to his shoulders. . . . We were doing one of Wilson Pickett's songs and I was singing too. After we got done, he came backstage and says, 'Hey, man, I must say, you about the funkiest drummer I ever heard, man.'"[18]

The tour then bounced from Canada to a crowded baseball stadium in Bermuda, where the I. B. Specials also backed the local opening acts. While the Brothers were in their dressing rooms, they heard a loud roar from the audience. When they looked, they saw the commotion was for Jimmy, who was on his knees biting the guitar strings.

Jimmy felt more comfortable on stage with the Isleys. They developed a call-and-response routine: The brothers sang a phrase and Jimmy mimicked their voices on his guitar. Ronnie Isley recalled that when Jimmy's guitar was stolen at one stop, they didn't see him until a week later in New York. The Isleys traveled on to Atlanta to perform at a street dance near Georgia Tech without Jimmy's proven stage persona. And yet, missing that concert provided a stroke of luck for Jimmy, because in New York, he heard from a friend that soul singer Don Covay needed a guitarist for his latest single.

Jimmy arrived at A–1 Studio on Broadway and was told to play a simple R&B riff and not overstep his boundaries at the song's dramatic pause. The song, "Mercy, Mercy," later hit number thirty-three on *Billboard*'s pop chart and eventually covered by England's newest hit makers, the Rolling Stones.

When the Brothers returned to New York, Kelly Isley took Jimmy down to Manny's Music Shop in Manhattan and purchased a white Fender Duo-Sonic. Jimmy customized it with an Epiphone "Temtone" vibrato unit that changed pitch and volume on demand—a quantum leap for Jimmy.

The Isleys made a deal with Atlantic Records to distribute their independent label, T-Neck, and went into a studio and recorded "Testify," which ran just over six minutes. The engineer made it radio-friendly by editing it into two parts and splitting them on sides A and B of the single. Jimmy's brilliant guitar is clearly heard on both sides. It is an upbeat song with each Isley brother individually "testifying" about R&B acts such as James Brown, Jackie Wilson, and Little Stevie Wonder, paying tribute to their unique singing style and stage performance. After the session, Jimmy remarked, "Oh, is this how you make records?"[19]

On June 19, the Isley Brothers played a gig at the Rockland Palace in the Bronx billed as a farewell dance and show for the Magnificent Montague, a trailblazing DJ leaving to work in Chicago, who had championed integrated radio playlists and had popularized the phrase "Burn, baby burn" for records he loved. In a six-hour lineup, the Brothers joined thirty other performers that included Solomon Burke, King Curtis, Don Covay, and Wilson Pickett.

After Rockland Palace, the Brothers headlined for a week at the Apollo Theater on a bill with Dionne Warwick. Jimmy, winning the amateur contest and then returning to the Apollo to play with a major group in just a few months, had come full circle in Harlem. But his brilliance as an artist was offset by a unique mixture of talent, single-mindedness, self-confidence, naïve relentlessness, and fatalistic inflexibility that both served him and proved his undoing time after time.

Jimmy was terribly nearsighted, vanity prevented wearing glasses, and once, on a short-distance gig, he took over driving duties, and doing about eighty-five miles per hour, hit an eight-point buck. The hood peeled back upon impact, and the two-hundred-pound animal went through the windshield. The car was demolished, but everyone was all right, even laughing at this brush with mortality.

Jimmy began realizing that few black guitar players were noted for their hot licks and wild stage antics. On their summer tour, the Isleys played with Carla Thomas, Joe Tex, Esther Phillips, and the Drifters in an R&B revue, giving them each thirty minutes of stage time in which Jimmy was lucky if his solo lasted thirty seconds.

Occasionally, if the tour intersected with a British invasion band, the Isleys would put their guitar player in the spotlight. "'Come on out here, Jimi, and show them how it's done,'" Ernie Isley recalled his brother Kelly saying, "and he'd do something like play the guitar behind his back."[20]

Jimmy became unhappy with the Isley Brothers. Though they treated him respectfully and were the closest notion of a family structure he had experienced since his days in Vancouver, once again, without an alternative, he was about to reject comfort and the strict stylistic parameters he was held to in both music and fashion.

"I had to conform," he said in a 1967 interview. "We had white mohair suits, patent leather shoes, and patent leather hairdos. We weren't allowed to go onstage looking casual. If our shoelaces were different types, we'd get fined five dollars. Oh, man, did I get tired of that."

On the revue-style shows, Jimmy was mostly seen if not unheard, placed in the back row on the crowded bandstand. Shortly after the August gig in Macon, Georgia, he was again fired from a group. In an interview with filmmaker Tony Palmer, he said, in essence, that he could not help himself, despite trying to fit in with other groups: "I was a backing musician [but] it was really getting to be a hang up because I might have an idea for song—because I got tired of playing the same song over and over—and they would say, 'No, man, you have to do it exactly right. You have to do the steps. . . .' You can get very bored."[21]

The Apollo

Etta James

Jimmy (left) with the Isley Brothers

Lithofayne Pridgon

On the Road Again

"If I'm free," Jimmy often said, "it's because I'm always running."[1] After being fired by the Isleys, he went to Atlanta, where Gorgeous George again helped the struggling guitarist find work. Putting him on a Midwest tour that featured Solomon Burke, Jerry Butler, the Drifters, and Patti LaBelle & the Blue Belles, the girls screamed for Jimmy, who had not toned down his stage persona.

Bobby Womack remembered, "Jimi would take the guitar and be playing it with his teeth while George be singing a ballad," and the emcee would turn around, and in rather threatening words, tell him to stop it.[2] Womack thought Jimmy played so loud it dominated the other instruments.

The complexity of Jimmy's musical mind and the exponential growth of his abilities meant he could sound like two guitarists at once as he played solos and rhythm seemingly simultaneously with a technique that far outstripped his fellow musicians. In addition, according to Womack, Jimmy's unkempt image alienated him from the other artists on the tour. "If you didn't have a process, a trim haircut, and suit and a tie, you wasn't in it. . . . He wore raggedy old clothes and looked like a beatnik."[3]

Jimmy remained on the Chitlin' Circuit, where life on the road was a series of tiny motel rooms or fitful nights aboard a crowded, noisy bus, irregular meals, and performances night after night. There was never enough money—sometimes Jimmy wasn't paid on time, was given partial payment, or wasn't paid at all—and no home to return to at the end of a tour. He couldn't afford to have his hair styled, so he kept his conk in place with a comb and hot Sterno. Yet Jimmy never complained in the few postcards sent home.

"Dear Dad," he wrote, "I hope everything is fine. Well, here I am again, traveling to different places. I'm on a tour which lasts about thirty-five days. We're half through it now. I've been up to about all the cities in the Midwest, the east, and south. I'll write soon. Jimmy."[4]

When they arrived in Missouri, Jimmy went missing. "I got stranded in Kansas City because I missed the bus," he remembered.[5] He took a bus back to Atlanta, where he found a place near Gorgeous George, who hired him for an upcoming tour with Jackie Wilson and Sam Cooke that also included the Upsetters and Hank Ballard and the Midnighters. The Cooke/Wilson tour left Atlanta on the next day, October 16, 1964.

"Every night was a packed house," recalled Upsetters's band leader, Gene Burks. "Sam Cooke and Jackie Wilson would switch it up, but the crowd loved us too."[6] Cooke was moved by Bob Dylan's "Blowin' in the Wind," interpreting it as a plea for social tolerance, and would soon write the first draft of "A Change Is Gonna Come."

Tours were often threatened by racial hostilities. "You always kept a good watch and a good ring. You never knew when you'd have to hock it to get out of town," remembered Womack. At earlier Cooke shows, "the whites would come in and be seated. Then the blacks would come in and be seated, and you had a stage in the middle. The K9 dogs would be going up and down the aisles."[7]

While Cooke and Wilson often traveled in limousines, the rest of the artists rode the bus. Fellow left-handed guitarist Womack often sat behind Jimmy. Womack was both fond of and annoyed by Jimmy, who habitually practiced and only put his guitar down when he went to the bathroom. "Ting, ting, chink, ting. That's all I heard, all night, every night," remembered Bobby.[8]

The Rolling Stones were currently having their first number one hit with Womack's song, "It's All Over Now." British groups were opening a new market for American R&B music. In December 1966, *Ebony* would publish an article by Eric Burdon, contending that if it weren't for British rock's interest, many of America's black performers would have disappeared into obscurity. Womack would probably have agreed. The best he and his brothers could do with "It's All Over Now" was two weeks at number ninety-four.

Guitarist B. B. King briefly joined the tour for a few shows. Although they didn't meet then, Jimmy watched King every night from backstage. "I knew I didn't have Sam's good looks or Jackie's dance moves," remembered B. B. in his autobiography, "but I was going to give them a taste of the in-your-face blues and give it to them good."[9]

Jimmy took note of King's signature riffs and approach. Through King, he eventually saw a way to break out of the R&B mold and be recognized as an accomplished electric guitar player, but whereas King's repertoire was strictly blues, Jimmy felt there had to be a way to add a hard-driving rock element to the sound as well. Years later, he updated King's "Rock Me, Baby" into a fast-tempo song he called "Lover Man."

After a show in Nashville, the tour stopped in Memphis, where Jimmy entered Stax Records on McLemore Avenue looking for Steve Cropper. "It was pretty obvious when I first met Jimi that he was a special person," remembers Cropper. "I really don't remember when he left for England, but he did become famous over there and I didn't see him again til after that, but he did remember meeting me and our brief studio encounter."

Along with Booker T. Jones, Al Jackson, and Donald "Duck" Dunn, Steve Cropper formed Booker T. & the MGs, a half-white, half-black instrumental band. Steve had co-written "Green Onions," which was a number one hit, selling over a million copies. By 1964 the group served as Stax's house rhythm section, and Cropper had been promoted to session producer and songwriter. Stax was housed in an old movie theater, and the company had taken out the concession stand and replaced it with a small record store. Steve was tied up in production when Jimmy arrived, so, after milling about looking at the records, he left word he was going across the street for a bite to eat.

"I came out of my mixing session to get something to eat," says Steve, "and thought I was the only person still there at Stax because it was after five, but Deanie Parker [Stax receptionist] was still there and she said the guy that drove down from Nashville to meet you was across the street eating. . . . I went over, set down, and introduced myself." Steve Cropper played the blues with dignity and authenticity. Hendrix was surprised that he was white. Like many listeners, he had imagined Cropper's funky guitar could only be played by a black man. Jimmy knew Cropper's entire discography; Steve found him remarkably polite.

Hendrix mentioned having played the introductory guitar riff on Don Covay's "Mercy, Mercy." "That about knocked me to my knees," admitted Cropper, "because that was one of my favorite records at the time. After we ate, I asked him to come back to the studio and show me the lick he played on the Don Covay record. When I handed him my guitar, he turned it upside down and I quickly said I can't learn it that way. At that time he still had the little strings on top like Albert King. He always played a Fender Stratocaster upside down. I don't remember when he restrung it with the big strings on top."[10]

When the tour ended in November, Jimmy returned to Atlanta. He was staying at the Bellevue Hotel, courtesy of Gorgeous George, when the Tams, playing at the Soul City nightclub, offered him a temporary gig. Guitarist Herman Hitson recalled, "Jimmy was staying in room seventeen. [We would] visit him and he'd always be sitting in there playing his guitar. . . . I noticed Jimi started wearing some of Gorgeous George's fancy clothes. We'd all go up to the Royal Peacock and sit in."[11]

Sam Cooke had a five-day engagement at the Royal Peacock from November 26–30. Less than two weeks later, in the Los Angeles suburb of Watts, Cooke was shot and killed by a motel manager after a drunken liaison with a woman went wrong. Jimmy had been moved by the singer's style and smoothness during their brief time on the road together and was devastated by the news.

Gorgeous George knew Jimmy was barely surviving. While playing with the Tams, Jimmy pawned his guitar and amp and again relied on the largesse of women. Little Richard was in Atlanta at this time and wanted to meet Gorgeous George, who, like him, dressed and performed flamboyantly. George met with Little Richard, and to help Jimmy, who he described as his cousin "Maurice James," persuaded Little Richard to take the talented and handsome young man.

"He didn't really want to tour with Little Richard at first," remembered George, "because the Sam Cooke tour was getting ready to go back on the road in a few weeks, but I took him down to meet Little Richard, and he hired him."[12]

Little Richard recalled that Jimmy was playing "B. B. King blues" at this time and attempted to take sole credit for Jimmy's interest in mixing rock and blues. Richard had also claimed himself as the inspiration for Jimmy's stage moves, style of dress, and even his moustache. Even if this was braggadocio, Little Richard was a matchless, groundbreaking performer to whom many musicians that came of age in this era owed something.

Born Richard Penniman, Little Richard had first been a popular, groundbreaking act in the fifties. A black singer and pianist whose up-tempo hits, flamboyant wardrobe and makeup, and vocal delivery punctuated with wild falsetto shrieks, theatrical moans, soaring whooos, and breathless panting, revolutionized the sound and style of rock as he outraged conservative America, wailing "Tutti Frutti" and "Good Golly, Miss Molly" while sporting a turquoise suit and mascara, singing about a girl who "sure likes to ball." Little Richard brought something new to music and was one of the first black rock performers to attract a large white audience. He was one of the half dozen most popular performers of his time, until he made a sudden shift in profession by somehow persuading himself that the launching of Sputnik, the Russian satellite, was a sign he should forsake rock and roll for the ministry.

When Little Richard reconverted back to music several years later as the self-proclaimed "King of Rock and Roll," he had become a tough act to sell to a new audience of rebellious youth. In the early sixties, his only major bookings were in Britain and on the European continent, where he was regarded as sort of a demigod. Some of the acts that opened for him were the Rolling Stones and the Beatles. "The Beatles were with me, opening my show," Richard recalled. "I didn't know that they would get to be famous. If I'd have known that, I'd have had a contract as long as from here to my toenails."[13] In the United States he was almost disregarded, playing in small clubs in black neighborhoods. Still, hoping to capitalize on the British Invasion, Richard hired a six-piece band called the Crown Jewels.

When Little Richard first saw Jimmy Hendrix, he said he knew the guitarist was a star. More likely, he recognized a superb musician willing to go anywhere for little pay. After all, Richard was the only star of his show—the others were musically competent individuals who had to be on time, faceless, and willing to put up with Richard's flaming ego. Jimmy's future with Little Richard should have been bright, but it turned out more contentious and troubling than his time with any other group.

For more than a year, off and on, Jimmy traveled with rock and roll's Muhammed Ali, playing an amalgam of gospel and early rock, keeping the pant creases in his black suit sharp, his hair greased into the still popular conk, and his developing public personality in check. Little Richard may have been a has-been in the early sixties, but he hadn't forgotten how to entertain, and Jimmy was watching closely, never interfering, never competing, but learning what made an audience twitch.

Jimmy loaded his guitar, wrapped in a potato sack with only five strings, onto the tour bus. "The road was so much a part of my soul that I can't imagine life without riding the highway," remembered Hendrix, "the rhythm of the road rocking me to sleep, making me feel like I'm moving on and going where I need to go. . . . It's monotonous but steady. In a strange way, it's secure. Moving on means I'm never where I am; I'm always leaving the past behind and heading into the future."[14]

The tour played two gigs in Atlanta: one at the local branch of the Whisky a Go Go and the other at the Royal Peacock. Fans who saw Jimmy perform in Atlanta claimed that when he suddenly launched into one of his wild solos, Richard beat on his piano, yelling, "Stop the music! Stop the music!" The band started the song over. The audience, used to Little Richard's outlandish theatrics, did not fully realize this was not part of Little Richard's act.

At a performance in Mobile, Alabama, Jimmy worked up the courage to speak to B. B. King backstage during an intermission. They sat on stools. Jimmy told King how long he had loved his music.

"I noticed he was left-handed," remembered King, and, seeing his guitar was strung right-handed, asked, "Why didn't you change the strings?"

Jimmy replied, "That's just the way I learned."

B. B. later noted that, at that time, even in the Deep South, rock was making an incursion on audiences who listened primarily to the blues. "They didn't care much about blues because Little Richard was so electrifying that when he got through everyone was ready to leave."[15]

Although Richard's show was full of high energy R&B, the next few stops were in decidedly blues territory: Louisiana and Texas, which, along with Mississippi, were the spawning ground of most of America's blues singers from 1943 to 1966.

Backing Little Richard was Jimmy's highest profile job, but it was not creatively satisfying: Little Richard was strict and controlling, dictating how his band members should dress, where they stood on stage, and how they should play. The crowds went wild when Richard played "Tutti Frutti" and "Good Golly, Miss Molly," but Jimmy had little challenge repeating the same guitar chords night after night. When the tour hit Nashville, Johnny Jones, Jimmy's friend and former mentor, observed, "Jimi was getting better and was more flashy, but I knew he wasn't going to be with Richard very long. Jimi was pretty, and Little Richard wasn't going to let anyone be prettier than he was."[16] Jimmy was paid $200 a month as a touring musician, a fair wage, but after deducting his fines, his actual salary was usually less.

In Los Angeles on New Year's Eve, on a rare night off, Jimmy watched the *Ike and Tina Turner Revue* at the California Club. There he met a young singer named Rosa Lee Brooks. He told her that she looked like his mother. They left the club together and spent the night in Jimmy's hotel room. "We celebrated New Year's all night long, until the early, early dawn," recalled Rosa.

During part of the evening, Jimmy complained about the demeaning way Little Richard treated him, his sexual advances, and the formulaic music he had to play night after night. "I prefer Curtis Mayfield myself," he told Rosa.[17]

He accompanied Rosa to a few of her gigs that week; at one, he met Glen Campbell, then an unknown backup musician, surprising Rosa, and probably Campbell, too, by knowing all of Campbell's studio sessions, especially his work with the Beach Boys.

In a lull between gigs with Little Richard, Jimmy performed with the *Ike and Tina Turner Revue* at a newly opened rock club called Ciro's Le Disc on Sunset Boulevard. Ike Turner was even more of a temperamental taskmaster than Little Richard, and, not about to tolerate any of Jimmy's tendencies toward showmanship, quickly and methodically fired Jimmy Hendrix. "He was a real good guitar player," Ike later stated, "but his problem was that he liked gimmicks. He would fuck up the whole solo to the song trying to stop the feedback or bring up the volume. . . . I'd give him a guitar solo and he didn't have balanced lines. I told him about it three times. It was a case of three strikes and out."[18] Now going by the name Maurice James, Jimmy rejoined Little Richard.

Eager to start a joint career, Rosa introduced Jimmy to a young musician friend named Arthur Lee from Memphis. Lee later joined the band Love, but at this time was an oddball walking around Hollywood in one shoe and wearing sunglasses he couldn't see through.

"Jimmy Hendrix was one of the first long-haired black cats I'd ever seen," Arthur said. "He had a suit like a priest, a hoodlum priest, with his hair directly in place and runned-over shoes. We became friends. He liked the way I wrote, I liked the way he played guitar, so we started jamming over near Fifty-Fourth and Western. . . . Jimmy was backing up Little Richard and other bands in L.A. at the time and I needed a guitar player who could play like Curtis Mayfield. You know, like on 'Gypsy Woman.' I wrote a song called 'My Diary' and Jimmy played on it. Rosa Lee Brooks was the singer."[19]

The song was a heartfelt ballad about Lee's first love and the misfortunate discovery of a tell-all diary, which they auditioned for Billy Revis, a local R&B producer, who asked them to pull a band together for a recording session. They recruited a bassist and drummer from Major Lance's band, then performing at Ciro's. The session was in Revis's garage, which he had converted into a recording studio. Jimmy was encouraged to be daring with his solo, and the group nailed "My Diary" in two takes. They wrapped up the session in two hours, and the tapes were taken to Hollywood's Gold Star Studios for mastering. The song received airplay on Los Angeles radio, and though some listeners mistook Jimmy's guitar solo for Curtis Mayfield, it was not a hit.

Rosa saw Jimmy was pleased with the new recording and that he was also extremely uncomfortable with Little Richard's controlling behavior and sexual advances. "He was ready to get away from that," she recalled.

Rosa witnessed Jimmy's challenge to Richard's dress codes during an April concert in Huntington Beach: "I did Jimi's hair before the show. I gave Jimi a white, puffy, Errol Flynn-type of blouse to wear with the big sleeves and pointed collar. I also gave him a bolero. . . . Jimi said to me, 'I'm going to show you something special tonight. . . .' He played the guitar behind his head, between his legs and with his cuff links. After the gig . . . Little Richard called for a meeting with his two guitar players."

Mimicking his shrill voice, Jimmy later imitated Richard's lambasting: "I am Little Richard, and I am the King of Rock and Rhythm, and I am the one who's going to look pretty on stage."

Little Richard demanded, "Take that shirt off."[20] Jimmy was fired and then rehired the next day after selling the shirt.

Hendrix had his moments of full musical expression and sonic revenge on Richard using his Fender Jazzmaster guitar. The Jazzmaster was popular with rock players because it had a long tremolo arm to facilitate controlled note bending and it tended to produce feedback, especially if the body cavity was left without magnetic shielding. There were times when Jimmy whipped Richard's head around with frenzied bursts of sound. "I found it difficult to constrain myself," reflected Jimi on his time with Richard. "It was okay at first, but then you get to a point when you can't stand anymore."[21]

He was not the only one who resented Little Richard's artistic totalitarianism. The singer would fine players $50 if they didn't call him "King," remembered Buddy Travis. He once fined a player for smiling during a performance when they were supposed to just stand without any expression.

Jimmy's last L.A. gigs took place on April 9 and 10 at Ciro's nightclub on Sunset Boulevard. The Byrds, who had debuted there in March 1965, when they were joined on stage by Bob Dylan, were the house band and were present when Little Richard and Maurice James performed. "It was early days for us then. We were unknowns and [Jimi] was an unknown," said Roger McGuinn. "I noted him as a flamboyant guitar player in a conservative setting. He was obviously a good musician and a great band player at that time."

The Byrds's bassist, Chris Hillman, also remembered Hendrix. "The 'Palace guards' escorted Richard onto the stage, and he wore a huge red cape. One couldn't help but notice Hendrix on the other end of the stage as a 'sideman,' but playing so well. Not moving much, just playing guitar, but what a guitar player even back then in a diminished role."[22]

When he left Los Angeles, Rosa Lee Brooks recalled, "I remember the day he left. . . . It was raining, and I remember Jimi telling me, 'I wish I didn't have to go.'"[23]

In New York City, the "Little Richard Revue" was part of the week-long *Soupy Sales Easter Show* at the 3,660-seat Paramount Theater in Times Square. Putting on a raving, energetic show, taking off bits of his clothes and throwing them to the screaming audience, Little Richard became upset when promoter Morris Levy shortened his act. They got into a heated argument, with Levy jumping up from his desk. Later onstage, as described by theater manager Bob Levine, "Little Richard did about ten minutes or so, but then turned to the audience and said, 'Management doesn't want me to play any more music. How do you feel about that?' The crowd went wild and he continued performing. We immediately closed the curtains and had the house band play over him. Richard stormed off the stage in a fit of rage."[24] Still raging in an elevator, the young black kid trying to hold him went by the stage name Maurice James.

Little Richard was bleeding cash. By May 1965, his accountant calculated it was costing twelve thousand dollars per week to maintain the extravagant production. As a result, many venues couldn't afford his show, and bookings declined. When the tour played for a week at the Apollo, Little Richard demanded royal treatment for his shows regardless of the expense. However, Apollo emcee Ralph Cooper said, "We could seat fewer than fifteen hundred people, which meant we couldn't pay an act $40,000 or $30,000 or even $25,000, which by the late sixties was cheap for a big-name group."[25] Little Richard's shows weren't profitable, and bandmates eventually found themselves locked out of their rooms in Harlem's Hotel Theresa. With Little Richard sliding, it was unlikely Jimmy could hold back his resentment.

"Little Richard's style of playing was much different than Jimi's," admitted Dewey Terry, who played with the revue in May. "Jimi would let the guitar feed back some nights and that would piss Richard off because . . . it covered up Richard's vocal."[26]

Jimmy was fired after playing the Apollo Theater. According to Robert Penniman, Richard's brother and tour manager, "He was a damn good guitar player, but the guy was never on time. He was always late and flirting with girls. . . . I finally got Richard to cut him loose. . . . We had some words."[27]

Jimmy's version was different. He claimed he quit in July because he hadn't been paid for over five weeks. Fellow band member Glen Willings said, "We did have a problem getting paid sometimes, and I think Jimi just quit before they fired him. . . . Richard felt upset after he found out Jimi had gone from the band."[28]

For all the disagreements, sexual tension, and false firings, Little Richard eventually paid Jimmy an unreserved compliment: "He was the greatest guitar player I ever had," he said. "Not one of my men has ever come close to him. He would wander off stage playing his guitar. He was into his guitar, really wrapped up in it, and that's the way it should be. He put his heart into it. He never sounded like just one man."[29]

Despite their tumultuous time together, Jimmy once told a reporter, paying his mentor a supreme compliment, that he wanted to make his guitar sound as wild as Little Richard's voice.

Gorgeous George

Little Richard

Sam Cooke

Steve Cropper

City Streets

In the summer of 1965, Jimmy rejoined the Isley Brothers for a month at a resort in New Jersey. But the life of a backup musician had grown so stale he reconsidered his career. "I'm starting all over again," he wrote to his father. "When you're playing behind other people, you're still not making as big a name for yourself as you would if you were working for yourself. But I went on the road with other people to get exposed to the public and see how business is taken care of, just to see what's what. After I put a record out, there'll be a few people who know me already and who can help with the sale of the record." He boasted that he might be heard on the radio, "Just in case about three or four months from now you might hear a record by me that sounds terrible, don't feel ashamed, just wait until the money rolls in."[1]

Jimmy later claimed New York became so hard that he ate orange peels and tomato paste to survive. "I didn't know where my next meal was coming from," he recalled. "I didn't want to take a job outside of music. I tried a few jobs, including car delivery, but I always quit after a week or so."[2]

With few places to turn, Jimmy called upon one of his first and most loyal friends in Manhattan—Dean Courtney—who let him share his room at the American Hotel, where Jimmy spent most of his time playing his guitar. He listened to the sounds of his environment, using his guitar to imitate the rushing clatter of New York's subway trains, the high-pitched release of the air brakes on a bus, the energetic honk of a saxophone. Slowly his style continued to emerge, but it wasn't easy.

Living in boardinghouses and cheap hotels in seedy sections of Times Square, he made friends with local musicians, jammed with them, tried to pick up work, and talked about how he would make it if only he got the right break.

His fortunes improved when he encountered Mr. Wiggles, a singer who toured with R&B revues and had a knack for merchandising. Mr. Wiggles was a friend of Little Richard and understood Jimmy's frustration with Richard's tight control of his band's image. He encouraged Jimmy to explore a more flamboyant style of dress. "[Jimi] always wanted to be a star. . . . I used to take him down to Stone the Crow and help him shop for clothes. All those crushed velvet shirts and those funny-looking hats—I started him wearing that."[3]

Mr. Wiggles used Jimmy on some recording sessions in mid-July. Jimmy played rhythm and lead on Mr. Wiggles's "Fat Back" and "Wash My Back," but more notably on a session with sax player Grady Gaines and the World Famous Upsetters. Their session yielded the single "K.P." and "Cabbage Greens." Both tracks were upbeat instrumentals that featured Jimmy's solos, complete with enough distortion to rival any rock record for 1965. "He was just a hurricane on the guitar," Wiggles recalled.[4]

Soon parting ways with Mr. Wiggles, on July 27, Jimmy signed his first exclusive recording contract with Henry "Juggy" Murray, head of Sue Records and Copa Management in New York. Murray had seen Jimmy perform with the Isley Brothers in 1964 and was so impressed with his talent he could scarcely believe it when Jimmy walked through the doors of Juggy Sound studios looking for work with a demo in hand. Ike and Tina Turner had given Murray five Top Ten R&B singles a few years earlier, but with Stax, Atlantic, and especially Motown churning out hits on a regular basis and leaving Sue Records behind, his label was suffering financially. His solution was to make R&B crossover hits that could be played on white as well as black pop stations. Jimmy returned several times to Murray's studio on West Fifty-Fourth Street to rehearse with other session players and witnessed the speed with which Murray produced sessions, often completing two albums worth of music in three hours. Murray went over the contract line by line so Jimmy could understand it, but Jimmy never kept a copy for fear he would surely lose it.

In October, Jimmy was living with Faye Pridgon in another cheap midtown hotel. With no work, he had to pawn his guitar to pay the rent.

At this desperate moment—one Jimmy Hendrix knew well—he met a fellow musician in the hotel lobby named Curtis Knight, who sang in a rhythm and blues group called the Squires and was looking for a new guitarist. Jimmy's Chitlin' Circuit stories and list of famous entertainers he had played with impressed Knight. When Jimmy returned to their hotel room, Faye wasn't interested in hearing about his promising encounter with Knight. "I was always hearing this stuff, that he was going to get a guitar and get this and that," she remembered. "'Yeah, well is this . . . going to pay the rent, because tomorrow we're out of here.'"[5]

Dean Courtney happened to know Knight. "Curtis was a full-time pimp when he didn't have a music gig," said Dean, who took Jimmy to the Lighthouse on Broadway, where Knight was playing.[6]

Knight brought Jimmy on stage for a solo "and Jimi rocked the whole place. . . . He did things with that guitar that I had never imagined possible."[7] Knight lent him a guitar and hired him. The Squires were vastly inferior to the other bands Jimmy had played with, but Knight put him front and center and gave him creative freedom.

Knight introduced Jimmy to a curly-haired record promoter named Ed Chalpin, known for packaging old tapes and selling them at discount prices. Knight had penned a civil rights-themed song, "How Would You Feel," and Jimmy arranged a melody influenced by Bob Dylan's "Like a Rolling Stone." Chalpin saw its commercial potential and set up a recording session.

Ed Chalpin was an independent New York record producer who had formed PPX Enterprises in 1961. He found a niche making cover versions of British and American hit songs in the language of other countries and distributed through major labels with an international market. Chalpin recorded at Studio 76 on the seventh floor at 1650 Broadway in the heart of New York's music district. There was no upfront money for "How Would You Feel," (when it was released radio station managers considered it too controversial for airplay) so Jimmy left town for a quick $30 with the Isley Brothers for a weekend show at DePauw University in Greencastle, Indiana.

Jimmy's inability to read music did not impress Chalpin. But after hearing Jimmy play, Chalpin realized he had talent, and on October 15, eight days after Jimmy's recording session with Knight, Chalpin signed him to an exclusive, long-term recording deal, a single-page agreement contracting Jimmy to produce and play exclusively for PPX for three years with a minimum of three sessions. Jimmy's contract stated he would receive only a minimum scale for any arrangement he offered, would have no control over the release of the recordings, would not be compensated for equipment costs, and would receive a 1% royalty on the retail price of all records sold after PPX had recouped its studio expenses. He was paid a one-dollar advance. Jimmy later testified that he hadn't read or completely understood the PPX contract before signing it, but at the time he didn't care. "He would sign a contract with anybody that came along that had a dollar and a pencil," said Faye Pridgon. "Jimmy just wanted to record, to make records."[8]

The contract was signed in a coffee shop. "The man was happy to sign it," Chalpin recalled. "He knew that no backup musician ever gets a royalty. I was giving him a good royalty with no deductions. And he knew he was going to be an artist. If it was a hit, and his name was on the label, he would get a royalty."

Chalpin had used the word "artist" to lure Jimmy. The suggestion that he was an artist and not just a backup musician put Jimmy into a trance. "He was so happy to be an artist on his own right," Chalpin observed, "he would have signed anything."[9] Jimmy's carelessness eventually led to legal proceedings that haunted him for the rest of his life. Over the next eight months with Curtis Knight and the Squires, Jimmy played two dozen studio sessions for Chalpin. The best that can be said is Jimmy learned the basics of how to record and overdub in Chalpin's studio. Most of the tracks were notable only for Jimmy's guitar solos.

Curtis Knight and the Squires played regularly in New York clubs but never drew much of a following. Jimmy made very little money. Late in October, Joey Dee & the Starliters, the house band at the Peppermint Lounge, needed a new guitarist. They'd had a number-one hit with "Peppermint Twist," and unlike other white band leaders, Joey Dee purposely integrated his group: three whites, three blacks. To keep the racial balance in the group, he wanted a black guitarist. The drummer, Jimmi Mayes, got a lead from Johnny Star that the former guitarist with the Isley Brothers was staying in a Midtown hotel. Mayes found Hendrix in his hotel room, heard him play, and called Joey to say he'd found the right man. "We then went over to Joey's house in Lodi, New Jersey, and plugged him in," remembered Mayes.[10]

Halfway through Jimmy's second audition number, Dee told him to stop. He had heard enough and offered the job. "Hendrix told me how frustrated he was with Little Richard," recalled Dee. "He was such a taskmaster, and you could never steal any of his thunder. It was just the opposite in my group. . . . I'd share the spotlight. I gave him a few solos and even had him sing the 'bop-a-shu-bop' parts in 'Peppermint Twist.' That's when I found out he couldn't sing too well, but he more than made up for it on the guitar."[11]

The Starliters were more rock and roll than his earlier bands, and they played army bases, a few black clubs in the South, and sometimes in auditoriums with crowds as large as ten thousand, the most people Jimmy had ever played before. Even in 1965, during the height of the civil rights movement, an integrated band experienced hostility. When they toured in the South, they slept in black-owned hotels, sometimes as far as fifty miles from the venue. In many venues, the black musicians weren't allowed to leave the backstage area during set breaks. But his tenure with the Starliters showed Jimmy Hendrix that many white musicians were willing to stand up for human rights.

"There were many times I was offered more money to tour without the black players, but I refused," recalled Joey Dee.[12] "There were many instances where we'd all walk into a restaurant or a bar and get stared down, and we decided it was just easier to leave."

They gave Jimmy a solo every night, and he played his guitar behind his head. "He was really shy at first," recalled band member David Brigati, "but he opened up and told some wild stories about being on the road with the Isleys and Little Richard."

Playing before white crowds, Jimmy was amazed that the white girls liked him. "Jimi had a lot of acne," Tunde Ra Aleem recalled. "That added to his withdrawn nature."

These young white fans helped boost his self-confidence, and he began to brag to his bandmates about his girls. "He was a magnet for them," Brigati remembered. "There was something he had that just seemed to draw girls in."[13] In Buffalo, three East Indian women, who weren't even fans of the band, slept with Jimmy, declaring he had the face of a Hindu god.

Jimmi Mayes and Hendrix shared a room and became friends. "He was going by Jimmy James," recalled Mayes.[14] In addition to his band, Dee's entourage included attractive female go-go dancers, and on some nights, Hendrix and Mayes would have a couple in their room.

Jimmy celebrated his twenty-third birthday while on tour with the Starliters. Bitter about the paltry "'Peppermint Twist' salary" and the lack of originality in the group, who played their hits note for note, he felt no closer to his dreams. "I had all these ideas and sounds in my brain," he later said, "and playing this 'other people's music' all the time was hurting me."

His tenure lasted about two months and was concluded by mid-December. Jimmi Mayes said, "Jimi was like a jewel. We didn't realize we had this genius in our midst. Many entertainers he'd work with didn't respect him or his talent. When he left us, he pawned one of his guitars with Joey but never came back to get it."[15]

Jimmy confessed to friends that he dreamed the coming year would change his life. "I used to dream in Technicolor that 1966 was the year that something would happen to me," he told a reporter. "It sounds a bit silly, but it's the honest-to-God truth."[16]

On New Year's Day 1966, Jimmy was back in New York, broke, trying to pick up the occasional studio gig, and wondering how he was going to eat. Moving into a cheap hotel, he soon faced eviction for overdue rent. Often, he didn't eat. On the back of a postcard of the Empire State Building, he wrote his father, "Everything's happening bad here." Poverty, segregation on tour in the South, and loneliness had made 1965 a difficult year.

Thinking of himself as more than just a backup guitarist, Jimmy reconsidered singing. "Nowadays people don't want you to sing good," he wrote his father. "They want you to sing sloppy and have a good beat to your songs. That's what angle I'm going to shoot for."[17] However, at the beginning of 1966, Jimmy didn't have the confidence or artistic direction to create his own band. He didn't have enough songs to create an album, and his hesitancy about his own singing voice held him back from achieving the success he so much wanted. Consciously living the blues, he was still playing other people's music.

Casual observers saw Jimmy offstage as quiet, contemplative, polite, absent-minded, and ethereal, yet his temper was often out of control.

"Jimi fought a lot," remembered Faye. "Once at a club, he had me pinned down under a booth with his knee on my chest. Billy Hamburg, an albino dancer, tried to talk to him. [Jimmy] turned around and lunged at him and Big Johnny, the bouncer." She also remembered, "One time someone told me to get over to the Hotel Theresa. Jimi had gone mad, all crazy. He tore up the room and pulled the phone out of the wall, but when I got there, things had got back to normal." Faye had likely experienced the repressed anger Jimmy harbored from an upbringing in an alcoholic household full of infidelity and domestic violence. "He used to always talk about some devil or something that was in him that he didn't have any control over," Faye sadly recalled. "He didn't know what made him act the way he acted, and what made him say the things he said. . . . When he'd really done me in . . . he would say: 'I don't know what came over me. I really can't understand.' He would grab his hair or cry. . . . It was sad when he would cry."[18]

Jimmy Hendrix was conflicted in several ways. He could not suppress the Seattle childhood that haunted and had shaped him, and despite his youthful energy and love of the road, the constant travel and lack of a permanent address wore him out. Unable to alleviate the need to impress his father and assure him that he had indeed followed the right path in life, Jimmy sent his father postcards.

Always he was a musical gypsy with an innate love of all kinds of music and the ability to play any style the gig required, but Jimmy felt divided about which musical genre was truly his. His relentless pursuit of an experimental rock sound consistently led to him being fired by rhythm and blues bands, and rock and roll was a genre in a state of change itself. And yet the desperately poor little boy who had politely accepted the generosity of neighbors and friends in Seattle had become a stunningly gifted young man with a persistent belief in his own eventual success, who devoted his waking life to playing his guitar and trying to find opportunities for work.

On January 6, Faye and Jimmy went to the Apollo to catch the last night of a big blues show that included Sonny Terry, T-Bone Walker, John Lee Hooker, Muddy Waters, and headliner Bo Didley. Jimmy reveled in the performances even though he was already edging away from rhythm and blues as a career choice.

In mid-January, when a vacancy opened in King Curtis's band, the Kingpins, Jimmy joined them. King Curtis, a tenor saxophonist, had been featured on hit records such as Ben E. King's "Spanish Harlem," Bobby Darin's "Splish Splash," and the Coasters's "Yakety Yak." In 1965 he opened for the Beatles on their American tour. The band included Bernard "Pretty" Purdie on drums and Cornell Dupree on guitar, both to become legends. Playing with Dupree, Jimmy learned interplay and how to play "more greased," as Dupree put it, adding more feeling and more soul. Jimmy quickly learned the band's material. "In all my years, I've never seen another guitar player pick up the material like that,"[19] Purdie recalled. He lay back as part of the rhythm section, but when he gave his first solo, he nailed it.

During a recording session, singer Ray Sharpe remembered, "It was phenomenal to watch Jimi work. I could tell he came from a blues background, but that wasn't the only way he played. He could interject just about any style he wanted in whatever he was playing."[20]

When King Curtis played at a party at New York's Prelude Club for Percy Sledge, who had delivered the number-one hit "When a Man Loves a Woman," after the show Sledge told King Curtis, "I'd really like to steal your guitar player." Curtis had hoped to hang on to Jimmy for at least another year or so, but "Jimi left us shortly after that show," remembered bassist Chuck Rainey. "Like me, he must have got tired of playing the same songs over and over again."

Shortly after parting with Curtis, Jimmy played briefly for the legendary duo Sam & Dave. At his first gig at a Midtown New York hotel, Sam Moore remembered, "We start doing 'Hold On, I'm Comin',' and he starts doing this *nawaaaaaahhh*. You know how Jimi played. I cut my eyes over at him. Next time, I go over to him and said, 'There is no solo in that, Jimi, stop.'"[21] When Jimmy did it again, Moore fired him on the spot.

Jimmy rejoined Curtis Knight for an afternoon audition at the Club Allegro in Garfield, New Jersey, where his playing was more than good, and though he was not aware of it, he came close to being discovered there by legendary guitar player and pioneer of multi-track recording, Les Paul. Paul had transitioned into management, and among his acts were Simon & Garfunkel, Willie Nelson, and guitarist José Feliciano. He and his son Gene were taking tapes from their home in Mahwah, New Jersey, to Columbia Records in New York City when they dropped by the Allegro. "I believe if you want to stay at the top of anything you've got to remain curious," said Paul. "That's why I dropped by places like the Allegro."

Les parked the car and Gene went inside. Gene returned and said, "Father, you better look for yourself. There's a guy playing all over the guitar." Les stood in the doorway and was impressed by what he heard. "That dude was really working his guitar over. He was bending strings, playing funky as hell. I'd never seen anyone so radical." They had to push to New York for business but afterward tried to "hurry back to the club and nail that guy."[22] When they returned a couple of hours later, a bartender told them a black dude was auditioning earlier but his playing was too wild and too loud, so the group wasn't hired.

Les Paul searched for Jimmy in local musician unions and clubs in north and central New Jersey and in Harlem. No one could match a name to the description. He asked his manager to hunt him down and was told that the left-handed guitar player had died in a fire started by a cigarette. In 1967, when London Records asked Paul to come out of retirement and produce one more album, he agreed but wanted to hear what the current crop of guitar players sounded like. "Walt McGuire with London [Records] brought over ten albums . . . and said, 'Here are some of the best guitarists. . . . One of them, the picture, as soon as I saw it, I said, 'There's my guitar player!' He didn't die in a fire.'"[23] He was looking over the cover of *Are You Experienced?*. In addition to all his other accomplishments, Les Paul missed, by about two hours, his chance to be forever known as the man who discovered Jimi Hendrix.

That winter, Jimmy, hungry and broke, was sitting alone late at night in a coffee shop on Fifty-Second and Broadway when he smiled at a young, attractive, light-skinned black girl. She was a sixteen-year-old runaway named Diana Carpenter, who, to survive, had become a prostitute using the street name Regina Jackson.

"I saw this real skinny guy," Carpenter remembered. "He had a hole in the bottom of his shoes . . . but he had the biggest, prettiest eyes I have ever seen."[24] He told her she looked like his mother, a favorite line that usually had some truth. Her pimp told Jimmy to shut his mouth and yanked her out of the restaurant. They met again a few weeks later, without her pimp, and began a torrid relationship.

At first her profession was an asset. She was making more money than he, and even after a day's work, she was still equal to his sex drive: "two or three times a night," she recalled.[25] When Carpenter revealed to Jimmy the nightmare of being molested by an uncle when she was five, he broke down in tears, and according to her, he, too, revealed he had once been molested. "I don't recall if it was a police officer or a youth counselor, but it was somebody Jimi had confidence in that sexually molested him as a teenager. He said he was afraid to tell anybody and lived with this secret until now."[26] It was a story he never shared with anyone else.

They stayed in cheap hotels, and some thought Jimmy was Carpenter's pimp, but, though living off her as an "easy rider," he didn't pimp for her. At night they walked along Fifth Avenue together, dreaming about being rich and famous. When he asked her to pick out what jewelry she wanted, she pointed to a fabulous gem in a window. "Oh, I'll buy you that," he boasted, despite feeling increasingly desperate.

"If I don't get rich and famous in a year, I'll go crazy," Jimmy once told her.[27] He spent hours a day practicing, dragging a borrowed amp four blocks from a nearby club to their hotel room because he couldn't afford a taxi.

Jimmy once returned to their room to find a "John" choking Carpenter. He grabbed the man and threw him out of the room. The incident soured him on her job. That same week she was arrested and put on a bus to the Midwest. When she escaped and returned to Jimmy, he was in tears, saying he feared a trick had killed her.

To avoid further arrests, she only worked during the day and was free at night to attend his shows. "He was always complaining that Curtis Knight owed him money," she recalled. "But even if Curtis paid him, Jimi wasn't making enough to cover rent."[28] At times they resorted to shoplifting food. Once, a shop owner caught and chased them down the street. Carpenter laughed as Jimmy dropped some fruit while they ran, but Jimmy was furious and disgusted with the way they were living: "I gotta change this bullshit," he raged.[29]

"We didn't always know if we were going to have a place to stay," said Carpenter. "I told Jimi, 'You have a daddy. Why don't you call him and let him know what's going on?' Jimi said no and didn't want to let his father know what was really going on in New York. He wanted his father to be proud of him."[30]

Carpenter discovered she was pregnant that spring. Jimmy pleaded with her to give up prostitution, but, secretly, Carpenter continued to work the streets. When Jimmy found out, he hit her with a belt. "When I tell you to do something, you do it," he bellowed. "It was the only time he was like that," she recalled, shocked by the meanness unleashed.[31]

Diana was soon arrested by an undercover cop and given the choice of three years in jail or a bus ticket home to her parents. She took the bus ticket home. In February 1967, she gave birth to a daughter, Tamika, who weighed five pounds. Carpenter was convinced the child was Jimmy's, but she had no idea where to write him and gave up on ever finding him until after Jimmy had become a major act in Europe. Through the years, through letters from her attorney, she kept reminding him that he was the father of her little girl. When Jimmy died in September 1970, he hadn't given the court a requested blood test to determine if he was Tamika's biological father.

Jimmy rejoined Curtis Knight in May when his band got a well-paying gig at a stylish new club in Midtown Manhattan. The Cheetah was an elaborate three-floor discotheque on Broadway and Fifty-Third Street that opened in April with an 8,000-square-foot dance floor and capacity of 1,800. The opening was described by *Time* magazine: "Men in flowered shirts and wide ties squired girls wearing everything from Pucci prints and Paco Rabanne disks to weirdies from London's Carnaby Street and vinyl suits from Manhattan's Third Avenue boutiques."[32]

Curtis Knight and the Squires did a two-week run at Cheetah. To stand out, the band wore attire that fit the name of the club. "Jimi and I thought we'd better get some of those way-out clothes ourselves," said Knight. "We went down to the Village and found some material that was almost the same [as the] décor at the club, and we designed ourselves shirts and jackets out of it. We added white bell bottoms and we looked like we were coming out of the walls," which were decorated with spotted fur wallpaper.

Squires drummer Marion Booker remembered, "Bands would come from all over with their mouths and eyes wide open just watching us.

Jimi played the guitar with his elbow, tongue, teeth, and everything else he could use to get a new sound. I'd do all these tricks with my drumsticks, where I'd throw them up and catch them behind my back . . . bouncing them off the drums. They would look at us like, 'What planet are you guys from?'"[33]

One of those at the Cheetah who watched with delight was Salvador Dali, the surrealistic painter, who told his table guests that he thought the music emanating from Jimmy's guitar was psychedelic.

Richie Havens was at the Cheetah on May 26, when Jimmy was a guest player with Philadelphia-based Carl Holmes and the Commanders. Havens walked up to the stage during the show, knelt, and looked up to see if Jimmy was using some special equipment to get his sounds. When a fan walked up and asked Jimmy how he created the sounds with his guitar, Havens heard Jimmy, in his low-key, dryly humorous manner, reply, "I don't play guitar, I play amplifier."[34]

One night Jimmy met a blond call girl named Carol Shiroky with whom he had another brief, tumultuous relationship. "Jimi used to come home really pissed off, four nights out of six," said Shiroky, "for whatever reason: angry at Curtis, fighting with the band, fighting with the material." Shiroky urged Jimmy to go out on his own. "Jimi always used to say he was not from this planet. He was from somewhere out in space. That was his great line when he got in a crazy-ass mood. 'I'm not from this planet.'" Jimmy admitted with shame that he stayed with the Squires because he used a guitar owned by Knight. "Two days later," Shiroky said, "we went down to Manny's [Music Store] and I bought him his first Strat [Fender Stratocaster]. It was all white with a rosewood neck. I watched him for a week—a week—before he played it. He was filing the frets so he could change the strings. For a week, that was like his baby. He gave birth."[35]

While taking a shower one day that summer, when he heard "Wild Thing" playing on the radio, he jumped out of the shower, hair in rollers, picked up his guitar, and gave Shiroky a performance, naked and dripping wet. Fortunately, his new Stratocaster was not plugged in.

Shiroky introduced him to Mike Quashie, the extravagant singer and dancer from Trinidad, who did fire-eating and fire-walking in his nightclub act and introduced the limbo to America. He was 6'2" and could shimmy under an 8" bar. When they met in Shiroky's hotel room, Mike assumed Jimmy was her pimp because he wore pink and had yellow curlers in his hair, but Mike soon found Jimmy quiet and withdrawn. "He was very down," Quashie said. "He would talk about his depression, frustration, and anxiety. It was not easy for him."[36] Some of the act Jimmy later shocked the world with—wearing scarves, playing on his knees, and the use of pyrotechnics—he copied from Mike Quashie.

Because of Jimmy's spontaneity and lack of regularity, Shiroky realized they could never have a long-term relationship. "There were nights when he didn't come home," she remembered, "and I knew he was in someone else's bed and I would never question him because if I did, he'd be gone."[37] He had few friends and was often despondent, writing poetry about his dissatisfaction. But life was about to change for Jimmy. A confluence of varying influences would tap into his inner resources and open a world of possibilities, changing what seemed, until then, his sideman fate. This next phase of his life would be powerful and lasting.

The Cheetah Club

Curtis Knight and the Squires

Les Paul

Mike Quashie

Backing Wilson Pickett

Discovery and the Village

In the cold early months of 1966, Jimmy lived in the tawdry Times Square area, a neighborhood of big movie theaters, grimy bars, and no-questions-asked hotels. Bobbing and weaving from place to place, he moved along the noisy, dirty streets. He had fallen under the influence of the outrageous black performer Mike Quashie, who gave Jimmy ideas about voodoo and fire, as well as introducing him to the idea of tying colorful "calypso scarves" around his biceps, thigh, and head. Jimmy had a good rapport with this jive-talking black man and would laugh at his good-natured kidding.

"I was working in the African Room," Mike remembered, "right across the street from the Lennox Hotel where Jimmy was stayin'. He was goin' by the name of Jimmy James . . . and the owners of the place would freak. He'd have these three hookers with him. At least they looked like hookers, and the owners thought Jimmy was a pimp, with his wild clothes and his processed hair and his do-rag. They didn't want him in the place, didn't want that crowd at all."[1]

A miracle transformation happened when he met twenty-year-old Linda Keith, a strikingly beautiful British model. Jewish, well-off, and well educated, she had lived a life very different from James Marshall Hendrix. Most impressively, her boyfriend was Keith Richards of the Rolling Stones. In with swinging London's in-crowd, Linda had been dating Richards since 1963 and had witnessed the rise of the Stones, who were soon to arrive in the U.S. for their 1966 American tour. Linda came over early to get a taste of New York's club scene. In late May, smart, savvy, and traveling with a case of her favorite blues 45s, she walked into the Cheetah where Jimmy was playing another woeful gig with Curtis Knight and the Squires. The Cheetah, which had once housed a grand, turn-of-the-century ballroom, had a bar lining one side of the room and a fifty-foot-wide stage for the performers but had not yet caught on as a sophisticated spot. On this night, the club was almost vacant.

Linda recalled that there were fewer than forty people in a room that could hold two thousand. She paid little attention to the band until she noticed the guitar player. "The way his hands moved up and down on the neck of the guitar was something to watch," she remembered. "He had these amazing hands. I found myself simply mesmerized by watching him play." She recognized an extraordinary ability, but seeing him play to a tiny and unappreciative crowd aroused her sense of justice. "He was just a brilliant player and a brilliant blues guitar player," she recalled.[2]

When the set ended, Linda and her friends invited him to their table and lavished him with compliments. "We chatted," recalled Linda. "I wanted to know everything: who he was and where he was from and what he was doing." Attention from beautiful models was rare for Jimmy.

When the show ended, Linda invited Jimmy to her friends' apartment on Sixty-Third Street. "I played him loads of my favorite tracks," said Linda. "We bonded."[3]

When asked if he wanted to take some acid, he answered, "No, I don't want any of that, but I'd love to try some of that LSD stuff," an answer that showed his naivete and inexperience with psychedelics.[4] Partially due to poverty, Jimmy's drug experimentation had been limited to marijuana, hashish, cheap speed, and, on rare occasions, cocaine.

"In Manhattan, the drugs of choice were cocaine and marijuana," TaharQa observed. "Nobody in Harlem was doing acid then."

Later that summer, Jimmy tried to talk an uptown friend, Lonnie Youngblood, into tripping with him. "Jimi was saying all that crap you have in your mind, the spider webs, this clears and focuses it." Lonnie gave Jimmy a lecture about the dangers of LSD, how it could make you think like a white person. "That was white kids' drugs," Youngblood said. "I didn't want hallucinations."[5]

Lysergic acid diethylamide was discovered in 1938 by Dr. Albert Hoffman by accidentally dosing himself while researching the ergot fungus. He later wrote about the hallucinogenic effect in a memoir: "In a dreamlike state with eyes closed (I found the daylight to be unpleasantly glaring), I perceived an uninterrupted stream of fantastic pictures, extraordinary shapes with intense, kaleidoscopic play of colors."[6] By the forties, Sandoz Pharmaceuticals was commercially marketing lysergic acid diethylamide as a cure for everything from alcoholism to schizophrenia. Official distribution of LSD would cease in 1965 after it became controversial, but the drug was still legal when Jimmy first took it in 1966, though it would become illegal the following year. Dr. Timothy Leary, one of the first scientists to do extensive testing of LSD, much of it on himself, proclaimed that the "set" and "setting" of LSD experiences were as important as the dosage. The "set" being the mindset of the user; the "setting" being the environment. Jimmy's first time was ideal: being gently befriended by a brainy British model who knew the music and legend of Robert Johnson, in a rather lavish apartment listening to an excellent collection of blues singles.

Linda played Bob Dylan's new album, *Blonde on Blonde.* Jimmy was probably tripping when he first heard "Stuck inside of Mobile with the Memphis Blues again" and "Most Likely You Go Your Way (And I'll Go Mine)"—songs that would have made a strong impression anyway. Linda later described this evening as "a night of magic," but nothing sexual happened between them. "I was going out with Keith," she said, "and I was a middle-class girl with middle-class values."[7]

But the evening was intimate for Jimmy in a new and different way. Their passionate discussions about music and the guitar were not the kind Jimmy usually had with a woman. Linda's friends eventually became exhausted with the talk about whether Delta or Chicago blues were preferable, but Jimmy and Linda stayed up all night talking in the living room.

He was different and enthralled her in the open and naive way he talked about his career. He was not afraid to talk about the disappointment he felt, and when he pulled pink plastic curlers from his guitar case and inserted them in his hair, she was shocked he would do it in front of sophisticated people. Sharing a strong love of the blues, Linda produced several obscure 45s from her traveling case, many from Keith Richards's personal collection. When she had played all the singles, they returned to

Blonde on Blonde, which they both agreed was a work of genius. Jimmy played along with his guitar. "It was the most special concert you could imagine," Linda recalled. "I would play him a record, and he would either play along or play me back his own version. It was like a private recital."[8] By then she was certain he was special.

She was interested in his personal life and asked if he had a girlfriend. "Many," he replied, naming only "Auntie Faye," who he said he ate with once a week uptown. Sometime during the night, he told her his real name was Jimmy Hendrix, not Jimmy James. She asked why he didn't sing. "Well, you know, I'm not that great a singer." Jimmy had felt his singing voice was weak since junior high, when he compared himself unfavorably to friends who could sing (and, also, quite likely to his aunt Pearl and her sister Eleanor Collins), but, listening to Dylan, he began to reevaluate his voice. "Sure, you're a good singer," Linda Keith replied that night after hearing him sing for the better part of several hours.[9] There, too, from the blurred cover of *Blonde on Blonde*, was a skinny fellow with wild curly hair and a scarf wrapped around his neck. Except for the color of his skin, he was very much like Jimmy, with a voice he couldn't forget.

Jimmy Hendrix's first LSD experience had a profound effect on him. (The red velvet walls and décor of the apartment influenced his classic electric blues number "Red House.") The drug profoundly affected his perception of life and his music, and he tripped quite a lot thereafter. He did not create all his work stoned, but, once he entered the realm of acid, what he played and wrote was suffused with psychedelic thinking. He insisted that he played colors, not notes, and that he saw the music in his head as he played it, a creative process similar to what Dr. Hoffman wrote in his notes: "Every acoustic perception . . . became transformed into optical perceptions."[10] LSD took such a strong hold on Jimi Hendrix that he tripped even when he played concerts.

As Jimmy began using LSD more frequently, he saw its growing influence on popular culture. In an interview in *Life*, Paul McCartney said, "After I took it, it opened my eyes. We only use one tenth of our brain. Just think what all we could accomplish if we could tap that hidden part. It would mean a whole new world." He then added the naive presumption, "If politicians would do LSD, there wouldn't be any more war or poverty or famine."[11] The Beatles's seventh album, *Revolver*, released in

1966, was a forerunner of the psychedelia that would soon permeate rock music. *Revolver* offered up the mind-altering, ethereal "Tomorrow Never Knows," with its highly compressed drums, reverse cymbals, reverse guitar, processed vocals, looped tape effects, and two East Indian instruments new to pop music: the sitar and the tamboura drone. John Lennon was inspired to write the song on LSD after reading Dr. Timothy Leary's *The Psychedelic Experience*. That year, Jimmy, who had been fascinated by science fiction as a boy in Seattle, read *Night of Light* by Philip José Farmer, which later influenced his writing of "Purple Haze."

Though *Blonde on Blonde* accelerated Jimmy's ambition and belief that he could sing, his interest in Dylan had started long before the night with Linda Keith. It was an almost obsessive admiration at odds with his friends in Harlem. Faye Pridgon, to her chagrin, remembered him spending his last few dollars to buy *Highway 61 Revisited*. Earlier, when he had an unknowing DJ play "Blowing in the Wind" at a Harlem club, he was run out of the club by a mob yelling, "Get out and take your hillbilly music with you."[12] After hearing *Blonde on Blonde,* he bought a Bob Dylan songbook. He kept the songbook with him always; frequently it was the only item in his travel bag. Using curlers, he styled his hair to look like Dylan, who had miraculously fused folk music and rock and roll, and was about to become one of the most influential performers of his generation.

Robert Allen Zimmerman, the oldest child of Jewish parents, was born in Duluth, Minnesota, in the spring of 1941. He was a beautiful child with a head full of golden hair. When his father lost his job at Standard Oil, he moved the family seventy-five miles west to the rich iron ore fields of the Eastern Masabi Range. Once there, Abe Zimmerman joined his brothers in selling furniture and electrical appliances at their store in the small town of Hibbing, where the summers were warm and the winters frigid. Rich from the giant ore pit, there were no poor, no wrong side of the tracks. Except for occasional circus visits, the town held a boring sameness for the sensitive nature of Bobby Zimmerman, for whom music and words resonated deeply. He started writing poetry while still a boy, and then, as a budding adolescent, picked up an acoustic guitar and began playing in bands and roaming the streets with his guitar slung over his shoulder on a leather strap. As he grew, he grew inward, experiencing a volatile flow of emotions, sometimes moving faster than he knew how to express.

Enrolled at the University of Minnesota in Minneapolis in the fall of 1959, Bobby took the last name Dylan and attended no classes, preferring an enclave of poets and musicians, where, with astonishing progress, he absorbed and played all kinds of music, especially the folk ballads of Woody Guthrie, who for a time took over his soul. When Dylan heard that Guthrie was suffering from a neurodegenerative disease in a New Jersey hospital, Bob hitchhiked east with a suitcase and guitar and found his idol inside what he would describe as an insane asylum. More compassionate than discouraged, Bob played songs while Woody lay on his bed. From there, Dylan crossed the river to New York, where he found his way to Greenwich Village and began playing in the clubs along MacDougal Street, where a breadbasket was passed between sets for the performers to split the coins. Dylan could imitate any accent or style, and though he never learned to read music, once he heard a song, he had it forever.

"There were so many places to play," remembered Dylan. "You would have to make an impression on somebody. There were many, many singers who were good, but they couldn't focus their attention on anybody. They couldn't really get inside someone's head. You gotta be able to pin somebody down."[13]

Dylan was rather short and scrawny and wore plain clothes that were slightly tattered and dirty, and he was introverted, extroverted, brash, and shy. Most people liked him, although some thought he was performing even when not on stage. But from the stage with a harmonica and guitar, Bob Dylan could burn words into the audience with the songs he wrote. His good friend Dave Van Ronk, a tall, garrulous folk singer, tried to interest him in the French symbolist poets. Van Ronk thought the poets would be a good influence on Dylan's lyrics until he found translations of Villon, Rimbaud, and Apollinaire on a shelf in Bob's hovel that looked like they had been thumbed through for years.

Dylan started working more and more, opening for John Lee Hooker at Gerde's Folk City and performing at the Folklore Center, which charged two dollars a ticket. When John Hammond Sr. read an article about twenty-year-old Dylan in the *New York Times*, he set up a recording session for Columbia Records. Dylan's first album was mostly old folk and blues songs that he sang with conviction but not with a fine and beautiful voice: His voice seemed to be fighting its way out of his throat, leaving the husk and bark on the notes. At first this may have inhibited him, but not for long, because his words came from deep within and the songs coming forth had lives of their own, deeply affecting people. Poet Allen Ginsberg cried upon hearing "A Hard Rain's a-Gonna Fall" because he knew the torch of the countercultural movement had been passed to another generation. When folk group Peter, Paul and Mary released "Blowing in the Wind," over a million copies were quickly sold. Soon recorded by many others, the song became a timeless anthem of the civil rights movement.

Albert Grossman, who had formed Peter, Paul and Mary, became Dylan's manager and made millions publishing his songs. Grossman, a brilliant, manipulative man, never quite figured out or fully manipulated Bob Dylan, who was too clever an opportunist to be much manipulated by anyone. Grossman did, however, put him on stage at the Newport Folk Festival in the summer of 1963, where, pairing his foghorn with the beautiful mezzo soprano of Joan Baez singing "God on our Side," he shined over everyone else there, which included Pete Seeger, Johnny Cash, the Staples Singers, and Peter, Paul and Mary. Crowned by a mass of cherubic (or perhaps devilish), unruly hair, Bob Dylan became the voice of his generation and continued writing and singing songs that kept burning into the consciousness of the nation and the world.

In a bloom of inspiration in 1965, Dylan wrote and recorded "Like a Rolling Stone." Gathering Mike Bloomfield and Al Kooper and plugging into amplifiers, the music was "electric" and loud. There was strong resistance from folk purists, but Dylan had never catered to the crowd—it was always the audience who found him. Among those who found him was Jimmy Hendrix, who, listening to "Memphis Blues Again," intuitively understood the lyrics.

Jimmy Hendrix had been a loner all his life, and the alienation and anger that Dylan expressed deeply touched him, as it touched many others. That Dylan did not have a pretty singing voice gave Jimmy as much courage as the poet's angry lyrics. "When I first heard him, I thought, 'You must admire the guy for having that much nerve to sing so out of key,'" remembered Hendrix. "But then I started listening to the words. He is giving me inspiration. Not that I wanted to sound like him. I just wanted to sound like Jimi Hendrix."[14] If Dylan could get away with singing in a weak, raspy, untrained voice and get a record contract, Jimmy reasoned he also had a chance.

On their first night together, Linda Keith and Jimmy Hendrix had listened to and exhausted the subject of Bob Dylan. When playing at the Cheetah two weeks later, Richie Havens, listening to Jimmy's guitar work, asked him where he had learned it, and their conversation turned to Bob Dylan. Richie told him he'd done a cover of "Just Like a Woman." Jimmy wanted to hear it and asked where he played. Richie, in describing the coffeehouse scene, told him about the clubs in Greenwich Village. Though Jimmy had been living in NYC on and off for two years, Havens had the impression he had just arrived. "You've got to go down to the Village," Havens said. "That's where it's happening."[15] He wrote down the names of several village clubs.

Dimly lit, tiny-tabled coffeehouses, holdovers from the folk music era, still dotted MacDougal Street. The tradition of folk singing in Washington Square Park that began in 1945 had fully blossomed by 1960, when hundreds of singers, players, and appreciative listeners congregated there on weekends. But a new crop of young people had replaced the poetry-reading coffeehouse Beats and anti-A-bomb activists from the Eisenhower era. By the mid–1960s, Greenwich Village was New York's equivalent of Haight-Ashbury in San Francisco, another perfect incubator for a bohemian cultural revolution. Village venues overflowed with people looking for fresh talent. James Taylor, Bob Dylan, and Richie Havens had all played at the small clubs where more than half the coffeehouses that featured folk music in 1964 had made the switch to rock and roll or folk rock.

That spring, frustrated by years of being a sideman, rejected by the black community in Harlem for his appearance and new musical approach, and buoyed by his experience with LSD and the rapidly evolving counterculture in America, Jimmy explored this other world thirty blocks south in lower Manhattan, walking among the clubs in his search for work. Some of the clubs on the Lower East Side were known for jazz. Others, notably those along Bleecker and MacDougal Streets in the Village, were established folk music showcases. In Greenwich Village, every variety and mix of music was available. Besides folk music and jazz, there was a fusion of rock, country, and jug-band instrumentation, most notably by the Lovin' Spoonful. As music lines were blurred or erased, other lines were drawn. With the young generation questioning the lifestyle of the older generation, seeing much of their hypocrisy, a revolution had begun that was freely expressed on the streets of Greenwich Village.

Paul Caruso, an early Village friend of Hendrix, recalled the first time he saw Jimmy walking down MacDougal Street: "He looked ridiculous. He had on striped pants, a calypso shirt with huge puffy sleeves, and those Little Richard sausage curls."[16] It was like a black pirate had been placed among the beatniks, bohemians, and radicals of the Village, where long hair and beads on men were popular, drug experimentation increased, and societal norms about sex and marriage were challenged. Jimmy hadn't fit in in Harlem, but he was embraced in Greenwich Village. "He was starting to come out of his cocoon and becoming the butterfly," observed Caruso. "He was actually very reserved in many ways until he got on stage. It took a great deal of courage for him to come out of himself. He was pathologically shy. He would stare at the ground and almost shuffle his feet when he met someone, but he had the courage to break through all that."[17]

He started performing on street corners, playing an acoustic guitar for spare change. "Jimi continued to panhandle, which he had been doing prior to meeting me," said Linda Keith. "And he would play the guitar on the street in Greenwich Village. Paul Caruso would play harmonica, and I think I sang, which is a horrible thought. But I think that was a little trio and I was the vocalist."[18]

Jimmy was not abandoning his musical roots as much as evolving into another kind of musician, and the treatment he received in the black community made his evolution even more rapid.

The Chambers Brothers experienced the same difficulties when they shifted away from their musical origins. "Even though we came from Mississippi and began by singing gospel, once we played the 1965 Newport Folk Festival and started hanging out with Bob Dylan, things changed for us. . . . Like Jimi, we were never accepted by our own people in Harlem because they said we played white music," insisted Lester Chambers.[19]

To many blacks, Dylan's voice and music sounded too "country," which often obscured the power and craft of his lyrics. When Jimmy practiced a Dylan song at Jimmi Mayes's apartment, Mayes told him, "I don't want to hear no more of this Bob Dylan music." But in the Village, where the color of your skin, the style of your hair, or the mode of your dress did not matter as much as the newness of your sound and the passion and thought behind your lyrics, Dylan's music was regularly heard in clubs and cafes.

Jimmy's exceptional musicianship made him comfortable in both the strict, regimented tradition of uptown Harlem R&B, and the loose amalgamation of folk and rock developing in the Village, yet he knew not to bring the Village to Harlem. "If he would have taken that to Harlem, he would have been laughed at," observed TaharQa Aleem, who, with his twin brother, Tunde Ra, were some of Jimi's only black friends who would go to the Village to see him play.[20]

"This revelation took place then," Tunde Ra said. "It was the epiphany for him artistically."[21] Jimmy, at long last ready to forge a new identity with his own band in the Greenwich Village music scene of 1966, did not set out to mix blues, rock and roll, and R&B, but, exposed to this cross pollination of music, his musical imagination was so wide it was natural he would combine genres. The sound he forged that summer in the basement of Greenwich Village clubs was visionary and brilliant.

The streets of the Village were filled with a varying and often bizarre parade of people dressed in a pronounced array of color, ambling among the high, old, narrow brick buildings, at odds with the outside world but not within themselves. Along with the newfound social mores of the time and place came economic desperation for the youthful counterculture as well as a once-in-a-lifetime freedom of expression. Impoverished hippies and creative artists huddled in doorways, smoking pot and begging for spare change, a surrealistic freedom that proved fertile ground for Jimmy and his music.

Linda Keith, who had helped unlock his resistance to singing his own material, said in an interview, "He wasn't going to blow any minds with his singing. But it was perfectly good and adequate. And I convinced him [of that] by playing Bob Dylan songs and made him focus in on the actual vocal tones and to see that Bob Dylan couldn't sing, but that it came across wonderfully."[22] Devoted to Jimmy, she caught as many of his appearances in the Village as she could and quickly became the unexpected force that transformed his life and career.

Performing in Greenwich Village, Jimmy was now free to dress how he liked, wearing ruffled sleeves, brightly colored shirts, bellbottoms, jewelry, capes, and wide-brimmed hats. The music that for so long only he had heard in his mind was now finding a following as he explored new lyrical territories. The more time he spent in the Village, the more he avoided the disharmony he experienced from his own race. "In the Village," he once explained, "people were more friendly than in Harlem, where it's all cold and mean. Your own people hurt you more. I always wanted a more open and integrated sound."[23]

In the Village, he enjoyed flaunting mixed-race behavior, knowing he was among open-minded friends. His dialogue was freer, too, ranging from talk about racial riots to space travel, and his drug experimentation was accelerating. By the middle of 1966, he was eating small pieces of blotter soaked with LSD two or three times a week and smoking grass almost daily. Sometimes he was seen in clubs sucking from a small plastic baby bottle filled with methedrine and water. He even once pretended to be a homosexual in front of a sailor who said he couldn't stand "Village fags." Having found the right environment to experiment and flourish, he needed a home base where people could see him perform regularly, and he found it in one of the first places Dylan had performed when he hit New York in January 1961.

The Café Wha?, located at the corner of MacDougal and Minetta Streets in the heart of the Village, was a dark basement alcove with earthen walls. Mary Travers had worked there as a waitress before her Peter, Paul and Mary days, and comedians Woody Allen, Richard Pryor, and Lenny Bruce first captured audiences there. With its burlap-covered ceilings, weird wall fixtures, and cheap coffee, Café Wha? became a popular place. Visitors were herded down a steep staircase to a dark room filled with cast-off chairs and a narrow stage. Candles in blue glass flickered at every table. At full capacity, the Wha? held 325 people. It had no liquor license and therefore attracted a crowd of almost exclusively white teenagers drinking carbonated water spiked with lime. Musical acts were paid six dollars to play five sets. In this cave, Jimmy began his effort to transform his music.

Janice Hargrove was in the audience on the day he auditioned and remembered, "Anybody could get up and try out. Most people were so-so. Jimi played and everybody in the club was totally blown away, all fifteen people." He performed several covers, with his guitar solos the centerpiece of the act. The manager offered him work, and in the excitement, he left his Stratocaster at the club and another guitar was stolen. When he returned the next night, he flew into a rage. "Someone gave him a right-handed guitar," Janice Hargrove remembered, "and without hesitation he turned it upside-down and started playing. That fact alone blew us away. He did it without so much as a pause; he just flipped it and started playing. He was as good playing someone else's guitar upside down as he was playing his own lefty guitar."[24]

When Jimmy walked into a Manny's Music store the next day to try out a new Stratocaster, he met a fifteen-year-old runaway from California named Randy Wolfe, who played guitar at the Night Owl Café. "I asked him if I could show him some things I learned on the guitar," remembered Wolfe. "He then gave me the Strat and I played him slide guitar. He really liked it and invited me down that night."[25]

Jeff "Skunk" Baxter, who later played with the Doobie Brothers, also worked at Manny's and was invited to play bass. Though the band that formed was called "Jimmy James and the Blue Flames," Jimmy soon decided to change the spelling of his first name to "Jimi" because he thought it looked more exotic. Because there was another "Randy" in the band (Randy Palmer, whom Hendrix dubbed "Randy Texas"), Jimi christened Wolfe "Randy California." The following year, Randy California formed the band Spirit and created hits like "I've Got a Line on You." Randy said, "I didn't even know his last name was Hendrix. I always thought it was Jimmy James."[26]

Many blues guitarists could bend the strings for an added tone. Playing covers such as Howlin' Wolf's "Killin' Floor" or Dylan's "Like a Rolling Stone," Jimi bent the tone of this music to make it his own and always did extended versions to stretch out their sets. The group had a version of "Summertime" that went on for twenty minutes and reworked

"Wild Thing," a number one hit for the Troggs that had been a precise two minutes and forty-two seconds, stretching it to twelve minutes with Jimi playing it differently every time. Finally holding the reins of his own musical vision, he thrived in the club's upbeat atmosphere. On his way in, while the doorman barked, "Hey folks, come on down and check out the talent at the fabulous Café Wha?," Jimi would casually bum a cigarette from someone in the gathering crowd while heading down the stairs.[27]

Drummer Danny Taylor and Jimi became roommates at the Albert Hotel on Tenth Street and University Place. It was an old building with both squared and curved balconies designed by Henry Hardenbergh, who had also worked on the renowned Dakota at Seventy-Second and Central Park West. They lived in an apartment on the twelfth floor that was wall to wall with people in the music scene.

"It was so crowded," Taylor warmly recalled, "Jimi often climbed out on the fire escape with a pillow to sleep. Some mornings he'd wake up with his hair in rollers, grab a coke bottle, pretend it was a microphone, and act like a DJ. It was hysterical."

From there, they moved into a basement apartment on 211 East Fifth Street across from ABC Studios. "It was a filthy, rat-infested place with lots of cockroaches running around," remembered a friend.[28] Jimi also lived briefly on the third floor above the United Egg Company on the corner of Greenwich and Reade streets. Village regulars used the loft for music rehearsals and informal jams lasting for hours, often attended by guitarist Roger McGuinn and David Crosby from the Byrds.

With more musical experience than his bandmates, Jimi often gave quick lessons on song structure in the boiler room, which served as their dressing room. Jimi did a cover of "Hey Joe (You Shot Your Woman Down)" by Tim Rose that had the usual blues theme of a jilted lover taking revenge, but he replaced the original country picking with a slow rock beat and alternated between interrogation and confession in an unruffled conversational manner that heightened the brutality of the tale. When the words seemed darkest, he raised a white Stratocaster to his face and produced a rippling solo with his teeth. The group also did covers of the Beatles and songs from John Hammond Jr.'s *So Many Roads*.

On most evenings, they closed their sets with disorienting amounts of feedback and tremolo, coupled with Jimi's seizure-like, onstage gyrations.

Ever since losing his guitar duel to Johnny Jones in Nashville due to lack of amplification, Jimi had been committed to always playing as loud as possible. The volume of Jimi James and the Blue Flames was startling not only to some of the crowd but also to Randy California.

One night, Randy California thought Jimi was playing too loud and reached around Jimi's back and turned the amp down. "Jimi stopped, turned around, and started cussing him out," said Taylor. "Boy was he mad. Jimi unplugged his guitar, threw it across the room, walked off stage and out of the club. We had to play the rest of the night without him."[29] He fired California the next day and the group became a trio.

In the Village that summer, Jimi began experimenting with a crude version of a fuzz box: Placed between the guitar and amplifier, it distorted a note and thickened the sound, making a light string sound heavy and a heavy string sound like a sledgehammer. He so quickly mastered these new effects and made them musical that he attracted a crowd of guitar players who marveled at his use of new technology. "The squealing he could do with that guitar was a piece of art," recalled Danny Taylor.[30] A Blue Flames show was something to watch with Jimi displaying joy and humor.

"He was really into the *Batman* TV show . . . and watched it religiously," remembered Taylor. "We'd be backstage getting ready, and right before he went on stage, he'd turn to me and say, 'Robin, are you ready?' . . . He even wore a cape."[31]

Jimi took every move he had ever watched Little Richard, Solomon Burke, Jackie Wilson, or Johnny Jones do and brought a black stage show to a white audience. He dressed exotically with scarves and jewelry, as he had seen in Mike Quashie's "Spider King" act, and once the show began, he performed every trick he knew. He played the guitar with his teeth, behind his back, under his legs, and humped it with his leg in a manner that was clearly sexual, all while keeping the musical tempo going. It was an over-the-top act that could have been laughed off the stage in other places, but the kids from Long Island who hung around the Wha? were spellbound. The "Jimi Hendrix" the world would soon come to know was created that summer in the dim basement of a Village club. By July, his pay was raised to ten dollars a night as word went out about this new guitar in town. But he needed more pay and a better venue, and the person who stepped in to help him was part of a remarkable American music family.

John Hammond Jr. was a young, white blues guitarist playing The Gaslight. His father was John Hammond Sr., the talent scout, critic, and producer (the first to acknowledge Robert Johnson) who signed Bob Dylan to Columbia Records and produced his first album. Junior told *Guitar Player* magazine, "One night between shows . . . my friend who was working at the Players Theatre on MacDougal right next to the Café Wha? came over and said, 'John, there's this band playing downstairs that you've got to hear. This guy is doing songs off our old album and he sounds better than you. . . .' I went down there and he was playing all these tunes off this album I'd done called *So Many Roads* and he was playing the guitar parts better than Robbie Robertson had." Hammond and Jimi struck up a friendship.

"He was a really handsome black kid playing with these guys who could barely keep the beat," remembered Junior. "He knew me and had my albums, and he was just knocked out that I was there. See, I had all these Muddy Waters and Howlin' Wolf tunes on the *So Many Roads* album, and he had gotten them from my records. At least, this is what he told me."

Jimi, having been exposed to blues all over the country for years with some of the all-time blues greats, may have been flattering the young guitarist because of his father's association with Dylan. If so, it worked because Hammond hired Jimmy to join him at the Café Au Go Go, another basement club around the corner on Bleecker Street that offered an audience of the socially hip, including many pop stars. Jimi went for it and pulled out all the stops. He could have been a sideman once more to John's harp and voice, but as Hammond said years later, "No way was he going to be my guitar player. He was his own star."[32]

With a staircase that circled down into a long, deep room seating only two hundred, Café Au Go Go wasn't just another small venue but a showcase club of the Village where many musicians were discovered. The food was good, the waitresses were sexy and friendly, and the lighting was as good as or better than most off-Broadway theaters. When the cafe transitioned from folk to electric rock, owner Howard Solomon upgraded the sound equipment using Fender products and tube amps, making it superior to other newly opened rock clubs. Finally, Jimi had a club where the sound system could do justice to his revolutionary guitar work with a major musician accompanying him.

In mid-August, John Sebastian and the Lovin' Spoonful dropped by the Go Go to hear Hammond. Like the rest of the crowd, they were amazed by Jimi Hendrix. He played an entire solo with one hand and was doing hammer-ons and creating transcendent but carefully crafted feedback. He was also playing louder music than anyone had ever heard it played in Greenwich Village.

Musician Kieran Kane was among the small audience at his first show there. "What he could do with that Strat was mind-bending," Kane recalled. "There was a lot of flash, but there was also substance, and it was twisted in this way that drew you in."[33]

Jimi's mastery of many music styles led to his unquenchable desire to play with a variety of musicians. Ellen McIlwaine, the headlining act at the club that first week, befriended Jimi during the run. He politely asked if he could sit in with her band during her set, and she said yes. Even as a backup player he managed to make the entire evening "the Jimi Show" and won more fans. "He just blew everybody away," observed a club worker. "He played behind his back, all that stuff he had stolen from T-Bone Walker. We thought he invented it. No one there realized there was a black tradition that went back to the twenties."[34] The crowds grew along with his reputation. Hearing that Dylan occasionally dropped by, Jimi scanned the audience every night, hoping to see his idol's face.

The blues enjoyed a spiritual revival in 1966 thanks in large part to the success of British groups such as the Animals and the Rolling Stones. Leading the pack in America was Mike Bloomfield, who performed with the Paul Butterfield Blues Band from Chicago, then playing in another Village club. "I thought I was the hotshot guitarist on the block," Mike said. "I'd never heard of Hendrix. Then someone said, 'You['ve] got to see the guitar player with John Hammond.' I went right across the street and saw him. Hendrix knew who I was and that day, in front of my eyes, he burned me to death. . . . He was getting every sound I was ever to hear him get right there in that room. . . . I was awed. I'd never heard anything like it. . . . He wasn't a singer, he wasn't even particularly a player. . . . But I found, after hearing him two or three times that he was into pure melodic playing and lyricism as much as he was into sounds. In fact, he melded them into a perfect blend."

Introducing himself, Bloomfield asked Jimi where he'd played. "I been playing the Chitlin' Circuit and I got bored shitless," Jimi said. "I didn't hear any guitar players doing anything new and I was bored out of my mind."

"As many times as I watched him play," said Bloomfield, "I couldn't figure out what he was doing. I stared and stared and stared and I couldn't understand his hand positions. His thumb was so big, his hands were so outsized, nothing looked orthodox. Even when he played songs like 'Rolling Stone,' where I really knew the chords, I could never connect what he was doing with his hands with what I was hearing. . . . And there was no great electric guitarist in rock and roll that Jimi didn't know of," Mike added. "For example, Jimi knew all about a very early Righteous Brothers record on which there's a guitarist who plays very advanced rock and roll guitar for that time. There's another record by Robert Parker . . . that has a real hot guitar player with a style more like Hendrix than most session players. Jimi said it wasn't him, but that he knew the guy—somebody named Big Tom Collins."[35]

For the first time in his life, Jimi had other great players in awe of him and he reveled in the attention.

He sometimes used the rings on his fingers as a bottleneck player uses a metal cylinder, or grabbed the microphone stand and ran it up and down the fretboard for bold, searing side effects. He would sometimes play the back of his guitar's neck nearly as much as the front, tapping it with his knuckles to bring out harmonics, and other times grabbed the neck and shook it to get a wild vibrato that couldn't be produced otherwise. In some of these sessions, his guitar work was shimmering, and on one of the songs, an original of Jimi's called "Red House," even his voice sounded practiced and confident. Jimi had spent years on the road, bouncing between groups and hotels, pawning and borrowing and losing guitars, with a single-minded insistence on playing his own way that repeatedly got him fired. But now there was a sea change in American music, and he had a venue where he could regularly be heard and a girl who would not give up on bringing important people to witness his performance.

Bob Dylan

Café Wha?

John Hammond Jr.

Linda Keith

Mike Bloomfield

Richie Havens

Ticket to London

Linda Keith worked tirelessly to bring attention to Jimi. Trying to find a producer who would be impressed, Linda took Andrew Loog Oldham, the Rolling Stones's manager, to a show at the Wha?. Oldham listened and watched carefully, with hesitation. "It was obvious that she knew him, and clear that she knew him well," remembered Oldham, "and she was the girlfriend of my lead guitarist, so that's what I was worried about; the part of me that did like the music could see that he was trouble, and I had enough trouble already with the Stones."[1]

Once Oldham passed, Linda contracted Seymour Stein of Sire Records. Stein was impressed by what he saw, particularly the fact that Jimi had a few original songs, but Stein didn't like it when Jimi began smashing his guitar in frustration. When Seymour returned a second time, only to see an argument between Jimi and Linda, he became cold and indifferent.

Linda and Keith Richards were breaking apart, and one of the reasons was Richards's jealousy of Jimi. And though Linda had feelings for Jimi, a love affair with him didn't develop. Refusing to settle down, Jimi juggled girlfriends by individually conning them into thinking she was his only flame. "He had this depth with women," Linda observed. "All the women who say they were the great love of his life, they probably were in that moment. Or at least that's what he told them." Linda felt hurt that he wouldn't be monogamous. Jimi argued that his wandering ways were part of his "nature."[2] He pined for Linda, but could not forgo the other women, and, feeling hurt and snubbed that she had higher romantic standards, he wandered away when their relationship became uncomfortable or disagreeable.

Still, Linda Keith remained determined to have Jimi Hendrix "discovered," and the opportunity came with Bryan "Chas" Chandler, the bass player for the Animals who happened to be touring in America. The Animals, all from Newcastle, a rough, sooty mill town in northern England, were hugely popular with more than a dozen hits. Chandler planned to leave the band at the end of the tour and was looking for producing possibilities. Though only twenty-eight, Chandler had a decade of experience in one of the most successful rock groups in the world and knew a "hit" when he heard one. That summer he heard a version of Tim Rose's "Hey Joe" and was convinced that if he found the right artist to cover this version in England, he would have a smash. On the night of August 2, 1966, Linda encountered Chandler at a club in Manhattan and told him there was a guitar player in the Village he should check out. They arranged to attend the following day.

On Wednesday afternoon, August 3, Linda and Chandler showed up at the Wha?. There were about two dozen teenagers inside, sipping Green Tigers (carbonated water with lime). Chandler, a large man in a suit, stood out. "He was better dressed than anyone in there, so you could tell he was a manager type,"[3] remembered Danny Taylor, who was playing with Hendrix. Jimi had been tipped off and put on his best performance. Jimi had also discovered "Hey Joe," and when he played it, Chandler became so excited, he spilled a milkshake on himself. "I thought immediately he was the best guitarist I'd ever seen," he recalled.

After the set Jimi, Chandler, and Linda talked at a table. Hearing about Jimi's life on the road, backing up Little Richard and the Isley Brothers, and impressed by his interpretation of "Hey Joe," Chandler was convinced Jimi could be a star. "I sat there and thought to myself, 'There's got to be a catch here somewhere, somebody must have signed him up years ago,'" remembered Chandler. "I just couldn't believe that this guy was standing around and nobody was doing anything for him."[4] The rest of Jimi's set reinforced Chandler's astonishment. "I remember thinking, 'This cat's wild enough to upset more people than [Mick] Jagger.'"

Chandler asked Jimi if he was under any contracts. Jimi told him about Juggy Murray and Sue Records, but he didn't mention, or forgot about, the contract he had signed with Ed Chalpin and PPX. Chas then asked Jimi if he would consider returning with him to England, where he was certain Jimi could be a success. Jimi was impressed by Chandler's attention but was not immediately convinced. Knowing little about Britain, Jimi asked if his guitar would work with their electricity. "He was worried about the equipment we had," remembered Chandler, "and what the musicians were like. One of the first things he asked me was if I knew Eric Clapton. I said I knew Eric very well and that I saw a lot of him socially at that time. He said, 'Well, if you take me to England, will you take me to meet Eric?' I told him that when Eric heard him play, he would be falling over to meet Jimi, and that decided it."[5]

When the meeting ended, they agreed and shook hands. Chandler still had a month of touring with the Animals but said he would return to straighten out the details. Meanwhile, Jimi continued to play in the Village, where musicians continued to be impressed.

Linda soon disappeared from the scene. When she broke up with Keith Richards, Richards, in anger, told her parents she was involved with a black junkie and gave her father instructions on where to find her. She was attending Jimi's shows when Mr. Keith flew to New York City and went to the Café Au Go Go on an evening when Jimi was playing. Warned that her father was about to storm into the dressing room, Jimi turned to the mirror and patted down his hair and asked Linda, "Do I look all right?"

She later recalled, "[It was] as if this wild man, by patting his wild hair down, would have made himself in any sense look acceptable to my father, this elderly Jewish British gentleman."[6] Her father took Linda, who was not yet twenty-one and thereby a minor, back to England, where she continued to write to Jimi Hendrix, care of the Wha?.

Chas Chandler returned to New York in the first week of September. Jimi had no club dates that week, so finding him was difficult. Chandler spent four days scouring fleabag Midtown hotels. When he found Jimi, they held a series of meetings, planning their strategy to launch Jimi Hendrix upon the world. Chandler worked in partnership with a man named Michael Jeffery, who managed the Animals and happened to be in New York, and Chandler brought him to the Village to see Jimi perform. Jeffery agreed to come in as a co-manager. Jimi now had managers who cared about his career.

They decided Chandler would focus on the band's music, and Jeffery would handle money and contractual matters. Chandler, a large, tall man, was outgoing and gregarious, while Jeffery, always wearing dark-tinted glasses, was private and hard to know. Though almost a foot shorter than Chandler, Jeffery suggested a sinister power; his background was dark and shady, with vague hints that he had worked for British intelligence services in a clandestine role that involved having people killed. Jeffery did little to diffuse these rumors; like many powerful talent managers, from Elvis Presley's Colonel Parker to Dylan's Albert Grossman, he used fear and intimidation to his advantage.

Chandler was ready to bring his new discovery into a heady brew of musical influences that would serve him perfectly. The British appreciation for blues, epitomized by Eric Clapton, John Mayall, and the Rolling Stones, laid the groundwork for Jimi Hendrix. "The blues boom in London was dying," Clapton later said about the time before Jimi arrived, "and it needed someone to bring it all back to life and cement it together."[7]

Jimi assumed Chandler wanted the entire Blue Flames band to go along with him. "Jimmy asked if I wanted to go along," said drummer Danny Taylor, "but I didn't want to get stranded there."[8] He also asked Billy Cox, who politely declined and wished him luck.

But Chandler did not want the Blue Flames; he wanted to build a new band around Jimi. Ellen McIlwaine remembered, "Jimi felt guilty [about leaving his newly formed band], but he was going through with it. 'I don't feel too good about it,' he said, 'but I think I'll do it.'"[9]

There was so little to keep him in America, where there was hardly any pay at the Café Wha? and no offers anywhere else. Linda Keith had given him money and a place to stay, even purloining one of Keith Richards's guitars from his hotel room in NYC and giving it to Jimi on loan, but now she was gone. And so, he reasoned, just as he had starved in America, he could also starve in Great Britain.

During one last meeting with Chandler, Jimi asked, "What's the point in me coming to England as a guitar player? You've got Eric Clapton and Jeff Beck over there. You don't need one more guitar player." Then he plaintively added, "If you can guarantee that you'll introduce me to Clapton, I'll come to London."[10] Chandler again confidently promised Jimi that he would meet Eric Clapton.

Jimi was still insecure about his voice, but Chandler told him, "Your voice is okay and you've got enough going on the guitar, so don't worry about your voice." There were problems, too, with contracts. Michael Goldstein said, "Chas kept [Hendrix] in a hotel room for three days trying to remember everybody that he had ever signed a piece of paper with. They were running around and they bought a lot of contracts back. I mean Jimmy signed anything in those early days. I think Chas told me once that they bought up about ten contracts that were on him for different things."[11]

Immigration laws in Britain were strict. Jimi needed a passport, which required a birth certificate—weeks passed before it arrived from Seattle, and he had to be up to date on his vaccinations. And, since he was a touring musician with no verified past, some documents had to be fabricated. Correspondence was forged to make it look like Jimi was being asked into Britain by a promoter.

All these matters were handled by Jeffery, who put up the few hundred dollars it cost Chandler to buy Jimi's contracts. By making a few phone calls, he bypassed immigration regulations. Finally, Chandler thought he had freed Jimi and bought two first-class tickets to London on Pan American Airways.

Jimi made the rounds to say goodbye, visiting Faye Pridgon, Carol Shiroky, the Aleems, and Lonnie Youngblood. "To someone who had grown up in Harlem, or even Seattle," Tunde Ra Aleem noted, "England was like another planet."[12] Jimi didn't phone or write to tell his father, because going to play music in a foreign country was not something Al would likely support.

On the evening of September 23, 1966, Jimi boarded a plane at John F. Kennedy International Airport. The only money he had was $40 borrowed from drummer Charles Otis at the Café Au Go Go. In his guitar case were all his possessions: a Fender Stratocaster, a change of clothes, and a jar of Valderma skin cream for his acne.

James Marshall Hendrix, an obscure rhythm and blues man with an electric guitar, whose genius had been all but dismissed in America, had spent the first twenty-three years of his life struggling to find a place in a world where he felt like an outcast. Yet after twenty-four hours in London, his life would transform so completely that even a dreamer like him had to marvel at the change. After all the struggles he had been through, his poverty and a seemingly shiftless career, his acceptance in England and other parts of Europe would be astonishingly swift. All that had once been so hard—scratching out a living to achieve recognition for the music he believed in—suddenly became so easy.

They stepped off the plane and entered London's Heathrow Airport at 9 A.M. on September 24, 1966. Jimi could not have arrived in London at a better time, coming during an explosion of fashion, photography, film, art, theater, and music.

Swingin' London

In a *Time* magazine cover story in April 1966, the article "Swinging London" had broadcast to the world that London was a cultural trendsetter. Music was king in the pop world of London. There was rock and roll around the clock and girls in short skirts and men with long hair. It was the time of the Beatles and the Rolling Stones, the Yardbirds and Cream. To be both a musician and British was an especially high realm of reality. Though the British Invasion had subsided in America, the Beatles remained the most popular group on both sides of the Atlantic, and British bands continued to dominate sales charts worldwide.

"Before the Beatles," observed Vic Briggs, "no one thought rock and roll had any future. You imagined that you'd play rock music for two years and then find a real job. But the Beatles changed everything, and people began to have actual careers in music."[1] London was filled with nightclubs, concert venues, and pubs. Simply watching the movement of the Beatles, whom Mick Jagger called "the four-headed monster," became a nightly sport.

The city was again a great cultural rose that had bloomed quite suddenly, it seemed, from staid but fertile ground. Just ten years before, with World War II fresh in memory and Winston Churchill still in Parliament, the air had been thick with the proper manners of an antique age. In New York and Paris, there was a change toward modern culture, but London was an old man's town with private drinking clubs and a formal nightlife of violin concertos.

"There was nothing for young people," remembered fashion designer Mary Quant, "and no place to go and no sort of excitement."[2] But at a few pubs and coffee bars along King's Road in Chelsea, various restless and creative young people began to gather, some from prominent old families with good educations and trust funds. They consorted with rough types and dressed outrageously in exaggerated versions of gentlemen's clothes from previous generations of English fashion, or in colorful, form-fitting pants and flowing shirts, some even wearing blue jeans, which were then generally worn by laborers.

"Our lives were built around going to parties and getting drunk and meeting gangsters," recalled Simon Hodgson, who ran with what was known as the Chelsea Set. "Everyone had to be rich, funny, or famous, or at least notorious."[3]

Chelsea offered opportunities. "You could skate by on not very much," Quant said of the feel of the time. "It grew out of something in the air which developed into a serious effort to break away from the establishment. It was the first real indication of a complete change of outlook."[4]

Chelsea became removed from the rest of London by its ideas and developing new culture, but it was a daytime culture without many night spots. For night entertainment, the Chelsea Set began to gravitate toward the bohemian enclave of Soho, where you could feel a further upsurge of change contrary to traditional England. While King's Road still had aged soldiers and genteel shopkeepers, Soho was a hardcore bohemia, where artists, writers, drunks, and loons were encountered, vice was given room to operate, and homosexuals felt relatively safe among the gangsters, pimps, hookers, strippers, pornographers, and slumming actors from the West End theaters. Italian, Jewish, and Chinese families did substantial business as restaurateurs, and the best jazz clubs, often in small dingy basements, were also found in Soho.

Quant married Alexander Plunket Greene, an old-line, wealthy Briton, who, in his mother's disused pajamas, wandered Chelsea and Soho jazz bars with a purported film script under his arm. Quant had been designing her own clothes ever since childhood in pursuit of a Peter Pan-ish idea of what ought to constitute women's fashion. "I grew up not wanting to grow up," she explained. "Growing up . . . meant candy-floss hair, stiletto heels, girdles, and great boobs. To me it was awful; children were free and sane, and grown-ups were hideous." She and her husband agreed to open a boutique for young Chelsea women, offering the sort of gear not found anywhere else. Together they leased a King's Road building with shop space on the street level, with a place below for Greene to open the jazz club of his dreams. In November 1955, Quant opened Bazaar. "I just went at it like any other design thing," she said, "which was clothes for the way I lived or the way one lived in Chelsea."[5]

Quant's shop and novel designs were an immediate, transformative success. "People were sort of three-deep outside the windows," she recalled. Bazaar became an essential destination, with young Chelsea girls popping in several times daily. The designs were simple and bold: bright colors, stripes or polka dots, dresses and short skirts with hemlines that would continue to rise. The styles could only be seen in London, and the Chelsea girls ate it up. Though ignored by the mainstream fashion trade, Quant hit a nerve with her work. Her clothes gave the sense of color, freedom, and youthfulness (and sex) that became increasingly fashionable as a youth-quake swept away old standards. Even their music was profoundly different from their elders'; not Bach or Mozart but derived from the rhythm and blues played and sung by blacks in the Deep South of America and brought to the fore by an unusually gifted man.

Brian Epstein was born into privilege as the eldest son of respected Jewish merchants living in a leafy suburb of Liverpool, England. Conscripted into His Majesty's armed forces at eighteen, he was assigned as a clerk on the staff of the Royal Army Service Corps stationed in Regent's Park in London, where he dove into the city's pleasures and rather lost his equilibrium. Given a medical discharge, he caught the train back to Liverpool and began working in his family's furniture store and partaking of the secret gay life of the city. The idea of acting popped into his head, and, with the help of a few friends attached to the theater, he enrolled in the Royal Academy of Dramatic Art in London. Again, he enjoyed London but soon lost interest in acting. "The narcissism appalled me," he recalled.[6] Returning home a bust again to work in the family furniture business, this time the winds brought good fortune.

At the end of the 1950s, with the British economy awakening from postwar lethargy, the Epstein family business expanded into music, placing outlets of the North End Music Stores into the heart of the shopping district in central Liverpool. These new stores required a certain panache, and Epstein, the creative, theatrical son with a nice way about him, made a neat fit with the new image. When the store at Whitechapel Street augmented its booming business in phonographic equipment with a record department, under Brian's genius it stocked everything—jazz, classical, pop, and imports—and had listening booths where shoppers could sample various discs. Everybody went to NEMS, and everybody knew the enigmatic, elegant proprietor called Mr. Brian, who had an encyclopedic knowledge of the records sold and an uncanny ability to forecast smash hits when everybody else only heard nice little tunes.

Epstein began sensing something musically important was going on right there in central Liverpool when bunches of excited kids, mainly girls, asked for a record cut by a local band named the Beatles. The store placed orders for the record, and when the order arrived it sold out quickly. Epstein found that the Beatles played in a basement club a few blocks from his shop, and on November 9, 1961, wearing his natty business attire, he descended into the sticky, humid air of the Cavern on his lunch break and stood among the teenagers skipping school to watch as the Beatles, four handsome young toughs in black leather, pounded through their repertoire. Epstein was electrified, and, turning to his assistant, Alistair Taylor, asked, "What do you think about me managing them?"

He returned several times over the coming weeks to see if his initial excitement would abate: It did not. Finally, on November 30, after another lunchtime session, Epstein asked the band to come by NEMS Whitechapel, where he bluntly proposed, "Quite simply, you need a manager. Would you like me to do it?"

The lads asked around town about him. Paul McCartney's dad, who had bought a piano from Epstein's dad, said, "Jewish people were very good with money,"[7] and so Epstein and the Beatles agreed to an arrangement.

Epstein's eye for rough young men, his sense of music success, and the clothes and style with which to do it, along with his ability to spot what people liked before they realized they liked it, all came together with the Beatles. The Beatles were very young, pill-popping rockers who still lived with their parents, and in Brian Epstein they found an older man with class and money who taught them about food, clothes, social niceties, and the larger world. Epstein smartened them up, gave them a more professional aspect, and assailed the London record and concert industry with news of his brilliant act. Gone were the leather jackets and blue jeans and such stage antics as swearing and chatting up the girls and drinking and smoking and eating between numbers; gone, too, were the cheap cigarettes and curly ends of guitar strings sticking out of the pegboards. Henceforth, the Beatles performed in smart suits and boots, sticking to the most professional sort of stage manner, including a full bow from the waist after each number. Some in Liverpool saw these new bits of polish as a sellout that had nothing to do with music and everything to do with image, but, said John Lennon, "It was a choice of making it or still eating chicken onstage. . . . I'm not in love with leather that much."[8]

For several months, Epstein's trips to London were fruitless. A little knot of Beatles always waited for his return at a coffee shop at Lime Street Station, and he always descended from the train dejected with the sorry news. "He'd be terrified to tell us that we hadn't made it again," remembered John. But he never lost his belief in them and his vision of their potential. "He was convinced that eventually everybody was going to agree with him. That gave him the power to make people listen," remembered Andrew Loog Oldham.[9]

Finally, in May 1962, on another bleak trip to London, an engineer at the HMV record store on Oxford Street listened to an acetate disc, liked what he heard, and made a call to EMI to an "artist and repertoire" man named George Martin, who, listening to tapes the Beatles had earlier recorded at Decca (who turned them down), decided to sign them. He flew them to London in September to cut their first record, "Love Me Do."

The Beatles became the greatest music success of the century. Within eighteen months they released five singles, three of which—"From Me to You," "She Loves You," and "I Wanna Hold Your Hand"—reached number one on the charts. Two albums—*Please Please Me* and *With the Beatles*—both reached number one. With their love of American rock and roll and the developing songwriting skills of Lennon and McCartney, they created timeless music never heard before. Their personalities, the freshness of their looks and sound, and the exuberance they radiated on stage, generated heat and hysteria and a pan-cultural recognition not seen since the explosion of Elvis Presley less than ten years before. They performed for the Queen and her sister, Princess Margaret, and before one hundred thousand people in Finsbury Park, London. They were the strongest stroke thus far of the broom of youth sweeping away the old cobwebs. Their triumph in America in early 1964 furthered the seismic cultural shift.

The Beatles were steeped in Americana. Their own music had grown from the music of Chuck Berry, Little Richard, Buddy Holly, and all forms of rhythm and blues. They so little realized the low esteem the vast American mainstream then held for the roots of rock and roll (so dismissive that its brilliant return by the waves of British bands was hardly recognized as such) that when they arrived in New York on February 7, 1964, the tumultuous reception they received surprised them because, in part, they reckoned they were doing little more than imitating their American idols. They were light and bright and brought joy and overwhelmed the public. Newspapers could barely keep up with the demand for news about the band and the phenomenon known as Beatlemania. Fans, mostly young girls, surrounded hotels and theaters, choking airports and lining streets to see their heroes come and go. Everything any of the Beatles did became news.

What hadn't been news was an encounter John Lennon and Paul McCartney had with Andrew Loog Oldham, who managed a group called the Rolling Stones. On an afternoon in early September 1963, as his band rehearsed in a Soho jazz club, nothing about them felt very good, and, feeling discouraged, Oldham decided to take a walk. On Charing Cross Road, John Lennon and Paul McCartney tipsily emerged from a taxi, having just been feted at a Variety Club luncheon at the Savoy Hotel, and caught sight of Oldham, whom they knew when he was a press agent for Epstein. They asked about his worried expression. He told them that his band needed a hit and asked if they had a song they could spare. They did, but it needed a little polishing, which wouldn't take a minute. Oldham returned to the dingy confines of Studio 51 with

John and Paul, handshakes all around, and then John and Paul taught the band the parts of the song they'd already finished. A month later, the Rolling Stones recorded "I Wanna Be Your Man."

The Rolling Stones had been building a crowd on Sunday nights at Crawdaddy, a makeshift venue at the back of a hotel in the western London suburb of Richmond, where Oldham first beheld them. The amazing trio of front men—Brian Jones and Keith Richards twining their guitars into one sound, and Mick Jagger preening and mocking and inciting with his singing voice—drew a surging crowd of hipsters who liked to make the scene. Oldham introduced himself to the band after a show and expressed his desire to manage them. "Andrew is very young," remembered Richards. "He's got nobody on his books, but he's an incredible bullshitter, fantastic hustler, and he's also worked on the early Beatles publicity."[10] He also understood the band. Some felt Jagger sounded too black to be acceptable to mainstream showbiz bookers, but Oldham thought just the opposite, and though Brian Jones stepped forward as leader, Oldham fashioned his vision of the band around Mick Jagger. The Stones were purists of rhythm and blues; Oldham knew that mattered little in the commercial world, but that the frenzy into which Jagger worked a crowd could mean quite a lot. In his mind, the Stones, dark-hearted, sexual, and predatory—actually, they were middle-class university students—were to be the antithesis of the neat and sunny Beatles, who actually were working-class leathers.

The British wave of rock and roll was a wave of small bands. Except for "soul reviews" like those Jimi Hendrix had played, rock and roll had been focused on singular artists. But small bands became the new thing, and the Beatles were so red hot that this new thing got more attention than it might have actually deserved. The flood of groups and the media's attention became an industry unto itself. The Beatles, the Dave Clark Five, Gerry and the Pacemakers, the Searchers, the Hollies, and the Animals were all spending time on the charts. It was an explosion of non-threatening, young manhood, squeaky clean, tuneful, and smiley, that swept through Great Britain and then America, where the group concept was novel outside the arena of black soul and blues. And as its music and art and clothing swept through the world, London became the hub of a great, swinging culture.

The unlikely center of this world youth movement was a lane Charles Dickens had described in *Nicholas Nickleby* as "a bygone, faded, tumble-down street" that hadn't had much to fade from.

With a name plucked out of nowhere and a history noteworthy for nothing, Carnaby Street was two hundred and fifty yards from one end to the other. It had been a nondescript street of trade shops, workrooms, and an electric station and still had scars from Luftwaffe bombing. At the dawn of the sixties, most Londoners didn't know about it, though on the border of Mayfair, Piccadilly, and Soho, between the London Palladium, Golden Square, and the shopping hubs of Regent Street and Oxford Street, it lay in the midst of everything. There was a decent pub, the Shakespeare, and a good tobacconist, Inderwick & Co, but nothing else to really recommend it, except, perhaps, that it lay a few blocks east of Saville Row, the traditional stronghold of menswear. And, yet, never thought to be a stronghold, Carnaby hijacked much of this distinction and became the locus of a boom in young men's fashion in the sixties.

When John Stephen, a grocer's son from Glasgow, came to London in the mid-fifties with dreams of entering the haberdasher's trade, he soon worked at Vince Man's Shop on Newburg Street, parallel to Carnaby Street one block east. Vince was one of the first places in London where a man could buy clothes with color and made of material other than the dullest tweed, wool, or gabardine. It catered mostly to gay men who frequented a nearby bathhouse, but by the late fifties, Vince began attracting a more varied clientele of actors, pop stars, and adventuresome sorts from Chelsea who'd shaken off the hangover of war and felt like dandying up a bit. Expanding on the patterns of colors and fabrics, Stephen soon opened his own workshop on the ground floor on Carnaby Street with a window where customers could see his clothes. He turned out new styles and colors at a remarkable pace and opened more Carnaby Street locations. The homosexual atmosphere of the shops became disregarded as rising pop stars and professional boxers began wearing the tight jeans and blazing pink sailor shirts.

At about the same time as Epstein put the Beatles into smart, collarless suits, young men in London began feeling comfortable wearing bold, bright, varying colors. "Before that," recalled Ian McLagan, keyboardist of Small Faces, "all you had was the same clothes that your dad wore. Life suddenly became colorful."[11]

Unlike beatniks, who adopted a generally shaggy, earnest appearance, these new *mods* (derived from *modernists*) were extremely particular about their clothing. They wore tight pants, colored shoes with pointed toes, jackets made of silk and shantung, carefully maintained haircuts, sharp sunglasses, and colored shirts and ties. This new breed of smart-styled young men hung around Soho favoring amphetamines, motor scooters, and clothes from Carnaby Street, where dozens more men's specialty retailers opened with names like Stephen Had His Clothes, Male West One, Adonis, Domino Male, and Gear. Their musical taste was catching on, too.

When the Rolling Stones cracked the Top 20 with "I Wanna Be Your Man," the gift from Lennon and McCartney, they became the most visible standard-bearers of the rapidly evolving Soho music scene of rhythm and blues, a style Jimi Hendrix knew intimately. It was a curious blend of beat and boom echoing the American blues masters like Howlin' Wolf, Muddy Waters, and John Lee Hooker, and was infused with the youthful energy of Chuck Berry, Little Richard, and Fats Domino. It was a movement formed in London clubs and suburban halls that had recently converted from traditional jazz into R&B and blues, places where white boys could be heard wailing and moaning and banging out stirring imitations of American originals that only a handful of Brits had ever before noticed.

The most prominent nightclub in Soho was the Marquee, a cavernous hall beneath an Oxford Street cinema. A band could leap from the Marquee to a record deal, television appearances, and even America. The Rolling Stones got their first important gig there in January 1963. Within two years, the Yardbirds and The Who would get their big break there, too. The Who came to be associated with mod, though they weren't a natural fit, not as close to American soul and R&B as were the Stones, the Yardbirds, or even the Beatles (who did covers of soul and R&B but were a nascent, Pop Art band). The Who's guitarist, Peter Townshend, was a bright art student who got a rush out of the sheer, energetic drive of the modern world of sleek cars, French New Wave films, steel-and-glass skyscrapers, and paintings by Richard Hamilton and Peter Blake. They were cast as top mods by a publicist named Peter Meaden, who heard something modern and sexy in their crisp line of attack and encouraged them to play to the hyped-up mod audience, who, he knew, that for all the specificity of their tastes didn't have a domestic pop group of their own. "Because of my art school exposure to mod," recalled Townshend, "I supported him."[12]

The Who began dressing in Carnaby Street gear and was soon managed by Kit Lambert and Chris Stamp. Peter wrote their first hit, "I Can't Explain," with its thundering opening riff and lyrics that distilled the essence of teen angst, and they soon scored a spot on *Ready, Steady, Go!*, TV's stairway to the stars which had debuted in August 1963, and became an immediate hit, spreading London's mood, look, and beat through the country with lightning speed. Kids from around the world began to partake of London's youth-quake miracle, truly in the midst of something, window shopping outside boutiques with rents that had risen thirty-fold in the half-dozen years since John Stephen opened his shop. Very soon, drawn by the Beatles and the Rolling Stones, the clothes, the rumors of sexual liberty, and the opportunities for people doing new and exciting things, Americans began making their way to London.

In January 1966, the Robert Fraser Gallery in Mayfair hung a show of young painters and photographers from California called "Los Angeles Now." Among the work exhibited were photos by Dennis Hopper, a method actor who had taken up photography during a hiatus from acting. "London was such a concentrated thing," remembered Hopper. "If you went to hear music in a club, you'd see everybody. . . . You'd go into Annabel's and you'd see musicians, actors, lords, and ladies. I remember seeing Peter O'Toole and Richard Burton trying to drink each other under the bar."[13]

And there were other famous Americans on the London scene: Lenny Bruce appeared at the Establishment Club, Andy Warhol displayed his work at the Tate Gallery, Allen Ginsberg was a regular on the London party and literary scene, William Burroughs lived in St. James and Earl's Court, and Baby Jane Holzer gushed about Ad Lib (club) to New York magazine writer Tom Wolfe, who did several London stories during the period. After long, dormant years, London had again become the epicenter of the world.

Bob Dylan first came through town in 1965 with his air of smoke, mystery, and vituperation as a folk-singing poet and sneering whelp with his own entourage that included Joan Baez and filmmaker D. A. Pennebaker. He partied with the Beatles, Ginsberg, and Marianne Faithful. Scottish singer/songwriter Donovan attended a nonstop party Dylan hosted at the Savoy Hotel and played one of his tunes, "To Sing for You," which Dylan liked, and then Dylan took the guitar and played "It's All Over Now, Baby Blue," a new song he had written.

Dylan returned to London again in the spring of 1966 and confronted an English audience as earnest about folk purity as the Americans who booed him in recent concerts after he had made the leap from solo acoustic performance to fronting an electric band. His performances this time evoked not the swooning, attentive passion of the previous tour but opposing waves of anger and adoration. But nothing anyone had ever done compared to the next American sensation to hit London.

The Beatles in the Cavern

Brian Epstein

Carnaby Street

The Rolling Stones

The Experience

London was the perfect launching pad for Jimi Hendrix. Chas Chandler believed that putting him together with English sidemen and getting him booked into the right London clubs could lead to a recording deal. But first he had to get a work permit. Terry McVay, road manager for the Animals, accompanied Jimi and Chandler to London and carried Jimi's guitar when they passed through customs "because we didn't want anyone to know he was going to work." Arriving at Heathrow Airport on a Saturday morning, they were met by Tony Garland, the press officer from Jeffery's office, who spent two hours sorting out a work permit. "I had to invent a story that Jimi was this famous singer who'd come to England to collect his royalties," he recalled.[1] Jimi received a one-week visa and was cleared to enter the country.

Chandler reassured a nervous Jimi that he would be comfortable in London. "On the plane he had been worrying how his American style of playing would fit with the English guys," Chandler said. "So I decided when we got to London Airport to drive to Zoot Money's, which was on the way into town. I thought if he met Zoot it would dispel his fears about English musicians. We arrived at Zoot's house at 11 A.M., and Jimmy started jamming for two or three hours. The house was full of musicians, and it made him feel he could settle in England. He took to Zoot like a fish to water."[2]

Zoot, a keyboard player steeped in rock, jazz, and blues, was one of a half-dozen London musicians whose influence far outdistanced his affluence. He never had any hit records but was admired and recognized as one of the primary musical tastemakers of the London scene with some of the best musicians passing through his band. Playing a white Telecaster, Jimi, jamming with those assembled, reworked blues classics and soul hits. "When I heard him play it was evident that he had absorbed all forms of blues and black music," remembered Zoot. "He was able to play all forms of blues, gospel, whatever you want to call it."[3]

Andy Summers, who later helped form the Police, was living in the basement, heard the commotion, and came upstairs to be the first great British guitar player to be awed and dazed by the technical skills Jimi Hendrix displayed on a guitar. As Chandler had hoped, being readily accepted by Zoot and his band lifted a weight off Hendrix. As they drove into London, Jimi was relaxed and more focused on pursuing his dream.

Kathy Etchingham, an attractive, brown-haired twenty-year-old who worked as a part-time DJ, had been sleeping upstairs at Zoot's that day when his wife, Ronnie, rushed in and exclaimed, "Wake up, Kathy. You've got to come downstairs and see this guy Chas has brought back. He looks like the Wild Man of Borneo."[4] Kathy vaguely recalled the bed shaking from the commotion downstairs but was tired from the previous night's party and continued to sleep. Later, when she went for a drink at the Scotch of St. James, Jimi was playing guitar on stage. The Scotch was a club in central London between Piccadilly and St. James Park, an area that had once been the residences of British aristocracy, and attracted musicians and people who worked in the business to a large, open room downstairs with a stage at one end and booths and tables in the back and along the walls.

Unlike many clubs in the United States, being black was an advantage in London, where there were so many fans of American rhythm and blues and nearly all the musicians were white. Jimi was welcomed immediately, playing blues standards with gimmickry as the crowd watched in silent rapture.

"He was just amazing," Etchingham recalled. "People had never seen anything like it."

Eric Burdon, the singer for the Animals, was in the club that night. "It was haunting how good he was—you just stopped and watched."

Chas Chandler called Kathy to the booth where he sat with Linda Keith and Ronnie Money, and though buoyed by the crowd's response, he was concerned about Jimi violating his temporary visa. "I'm going to get him off," he announced. "He's not supposed to work, even without pay."[5] So, yanked from the stage, Jimi settled in the booth next to Linda Keith. Linda left, and when she returned, Kathy and Jimi were sitting together. According to Kathy, a fight broke out between Linda and Ronnie when Linda spoke badly about Kathy, and Chas, not wanting Jimi in the middle of a bar fight, told Kathy to take him by taxi to the hotel.

When they left the club, Jimi, unaware that traffic ran opposite to America, stepped onto the narrow street in front of a moving taxi. Etchingham grabbed and pulled him back, the taxi just brushing him. At the bar in the Hyde Park Towers Hotel, Jimi asked if Kathy would come to his room. She agreed, and they began an affair that would last on and off for the next two years, the longest Jimi ever experienced. Kathy's friends included The Who, the Rolling Stones, and many other bands, and they soon became his friends, too.

Chandler had many contacts in London's music press. The *New Musical Express*'s features editor, Keith Altham, felt rather bewildered after seeing Jimi perform at the Scotch: "To me it was like listening to some great jazz guitarist like Wes Montgomery. I said, 'Quite honestly, Chas, I can see this stuff going straight over the heads of most rock fans because he's almost too good.'"[6] And when Jimi named all the legendary R&B bands that he had played with to Tony Garland for future press releases, from the Isley Brothers and Sam Cook, to Ike and Tina Turner and Little Richard, Tony was so incredulous that he feared if he listed them all the journalist might think it was bogus.

At one point they were listening to a King Curtis record. When Garland asked if he knew who the guitar player was, Jimi replied with a big grin, "I played that, muthafuckah."[7]

Over the next couple of days, Chandler took Jimi to the hippest clubs. That first week, Jimi saw Paul McCartney, Ringo Starr, Pete Townshend, Eric Clapton, and John Mayall. Chandler wanted to sell Hendrix as an authentic American bluesman. To do this he needed to get Jimi on stage in London's showcase clubs, which made a work permit a necessity. "The only way Chas could do that was through Michael Jeffery," observed Eric Burdon. Jeffery seemed genuinely excited over Jimi's potential and set about convincing government authorities that the guitarist had a talent that couldn't be duplicated by English musicians. Jeffery had ties to the bookers who ran the club circuit and knew the right strings to pull and the government officials to bribe. There were also vague hints of his connection to organized crime. "England was knee deep in that kind of manipulation in that era," noted Burdon. "It was like the whole thing was run by Frank Sinatra."

Jeffery spoke in a whisper and wore a camel-hair coat and "showed quite a skill at bullshitting people," remembered Eric Burdon.[8] He first met Chandler when he signed the Animals as his first musical act, using insurance money after the nightclub he ran in Newcastle mysteriously burned down.

Chandler's roots were Newcastle working class: He spoke like a Newcastle "Geordie," with phrases like "a right nebby bugga" to describe a nosy person. Jeffery was a Cockney from London who could speak several languages, including Russian, and had the manner of the public school upper class. Their office was up a flight of stairs in a warren-like building on Gerrard Street in the heart of the West End, a low-rent neighborhood filled with artists, actors, and people on the fringe of society. Chandler met people at the pub around the corner, while Jeffery did business in the office.

As Jimi continued to make the rounds while waiting for his work permit, Chandler phoned keyboardist Brian Auger. "I've got this really amazing guitar player from America," he told him. "I think it would be perfect if he fronted your band."[9] Knowing nothing about Hendrix, Auger didn't want him in his band, which was blues-based rock with heavy jazz influences, but agreed to let him jam onstage at Blaises Club in Kensington.

Guitarist Vic Briggs was setting up for the show when Chandler came in and asked if Jimi could join in. Briggs, using one of the first Marshall amplifiers, an experimental model that had four 6-foot speakers capable of yielding tremendous power, politely agreed.

Jimi plugged his guitar into the amp and turned the volume knobs to the maximum. "I had never had the controls up past five," Briggs recalled.

"Don't worry, man," said Jimi. "I turned it down on the guitar." He shouted four chords to Brian Auger and began "Hey Joe." The wall of feedback and distortion turned every head in the club. It was the beginning of his love for the powerful Marshall amplifiers, and his ease in playing complicated parts stunned the audience.

"Everyone's jaw dropped to the floor," Auger recalled. "The difference between him and a lot of the English guitar players like Clapton, Jeff Beck, and Alvin Lee, was that you could still tell what the influences were in Clapton's and Beck's playing. There were a lot of B. B. King, Albert King, and Freddie King followers around in England. But Jimi wasn't following anyone. He was playing something new."[10]

Chas Chandler had told Eric Clapton about Jimi Hendrix. Clapton and the band Cream were playing a show at Polytechnic in Central London on Saturday, October 1, and he told Chandler to bring his protégé. Chandler and Jimi arrived with their girlfriends and stood in the audience. After the set, Chandler asked Clapton if Jimi might jam. No one had ever asked to jam with Cream—it was too intimidating. Clapton, Jack Bruce, and Ginger Baker did not know what to think. Finally, Bruce said, "Sure, he can plug into my bass amp."

Jimi plugged into a spare channel and "got up there and played a killer version of Howlin' Wolf's 'Killin' Floor,'" recalled Tony Garland. "I'd grown up around Eric and I knew what a fan he was of Albert King, who had a slow version of that song. When Jimi started his take, though, it was about three times as fast as Albert King's version, and you could see Eric's jaw drop—he didn't know what was going to come next."[11]

Clapton remembered, "He did a Howlin' Wolf number or something, but he did his whole routine. He did all the things with his teeth, playing the guitar with his teeth, and layin' it on the floor, and playin' it behind his head, and doin' the splits, the whole thing. It was incredible."[12]

Jimi held nothing back on stage. His speed, tone, and flair were so overwhelming that Clapton ceased playing and exited the stage stunned.

Chandler immediately made his way to Clapton. "I went backstage and he was trying to get a match to a cigarette. I said, 'Are you all right?' and he replied, 'Is he that fucking good?' He had heard ten bars at most."

Clapton recalled in an interview, "I thought, 'My god, this is like Buddy Guy on acid.'"[13]

Jack Bruce thought about Clapton's reaction and some graffiti in London that proclaimed, "Clapton is God!" "It must have been difficult for Eric to handle," Bruce said, "because [Eric] was 'God' and this unknown person comes along and burns."

Jeff Beck was there, too: "Even if it was crap," said Beck, "and it wasn't—it got to the press."[14]

A European rock star named Johnny Hallyday was in the audience when Jimi played the Cromwellian. Hallyday's career had been overshadowed by the Beatles, but he was still hugely popular in France. His style was closer to Elvis Presley than to the sophisticated blues rock of Hendrix, but he was so thoroughly impressed that he offered Jimi two weeks of supporting dates on a tour of France that would open at the Olympia in Paris on October 15. This was the kind of debut Chandler was seeking. "From that moment we were in a whirlwind finding him a backing group," said Chandler.[15] Having spent most of his career in large, revue-style bands, Jimi thought he needed a large R&B band with horns. But Chandler wanted a small group with just a bass and drummer because it was cheaper and could be centered on Jimi.

A twenty-one-year-old former art student from the seaside resort of Folkestone named Noel Redding arrived first. Playing with obscure groups, he had read a "musicians wanted" ad in *Melody Maker* and came to audition for guitarist in the New Animals. "Chas asked if I could play bass," recalled Noel. "I said no, but I'd try."[16] Chas told him about Jimi. Noel picked up a bass and jammed with Jimi Hendrix in his hotel room. Jimi told him what chords to play, and, playing "Hey Joe" and "Mercy, Mercy," he played them well. Afterward they went to a pub to chat. Noel was rail-thin, wore big round glasses, and had a full head of frizzy hair like Bob Dylan. Jimi offered the job. Noel accepted: "I'll switch to bass. I don't see anybody else playing lead guitar with this bloke."[17] Having arrived in London broke, Noel asked for and was given ten shillings for train fare home. The drummer was selected a few days later.

John "Mitch" Mitchell came with more confidence and talent. He was only twenty but had been performing publicly since he was a child, having played the Artful Dodger in *Oliver* on the London Stage, and had considerable experience with touring and studio sessions. He had just left Georgie Fame's Blue Flames when he encountered Chandler in a club and said that he was available. A diminutive 5'7", Mitch was a powerhouse drummer and, after two auditions, was given the job. "The sound was clear, fresh, and exciting,"[18] recalled Chandler. No other musicians were needed, and both Chandler and Jeffery believed that Jimi's name should be in the band's name. After much discussion they settled on The Jimi Hendrix Experience.

"We all thought it was wild," said Noel, "but then we really were 'an experience.'"[19]

From their first time rehearsing, the Jimi Hendrix Experience was loud, but no one wanted to sing. Noel had a squeak, and while Mitch could sing, his voice wasn't the right one needed. Besides, no one expected drummers to sing. Jimi, still nervous about being in England, was too embarrassed to sing.

"Our first gigs were virtually instrumental," remembered Noel. "Finally, we broke down Jimi's shyness and persuaded him to sing. His voice had good bass fullness in it. . . . At first he would crank his guitar up really loud to cover his singing, but gradually he gained confidence and found the right balance between voice and guitar and was very pleased he could do it and so were we."[20]

The band members signed contracts with management giving Chandler and Jeffery 20% of all revenue. The band would split 2.5% of the royalties on record sales and were advanced a salary of £15 a week. A separate agreement was signed between Jimi and Chandler, giving them both 50% interest in Jimi's songwriting for six years. These contracts would later make management much richer than the band, but it was not then known if the band would make money. The members were happy to be receiving a salary. Any future money to be made by the band would be funneled into a shell company called Yameta, set up in the Bahamas to avoid income taxes in Britain, a ruse Jeffery had used with the Animals and which Chandler complained made accurate accounting impossible, benefitting Jeffery the most. To pay for the gear and travel expenses to France, Jeffery borrowed money from his parents and Chandler sold his bass guitars.

Jimi signed the contracts without reading them. He used his salary advance to update his wardrobe at the shops on Carnaby Street, where stores like Granny Takes a Trip and I Was Lord Kitchener's Valet specialized in vintage youthful clothing. Chandler had urged him to buy suits, but Jimi, done with that style, chose to wear outrageous clothing. In addition to the scarves, rings, capes, and hats he had incorporated into his Greenwich Village look, he added vividly colored, daringly patterned shirts, replaced his ragged overcoat with an ornately braided antique military jacket from the glory days of the British Empire, and bought velvet pants in bright colors. His dress became a hot topic among musicians.

"Even before we knew his name," remembered singer Terry Reid, "we called him 'that guy walking around who looks like he walked into a girl's closet and put everything on.'" The boy who had grown up wearing others' castoffs had blossomed into one of the first men to explore "vintage chic." With his crushed velvet pants, military coat, a gigantic black western hat, and long, windblown hair, Jimi turned heads as he walked down the street.

"People would just stop and stare," recalled Kathy Etchingham. "It wasn't because they knew his music; it was just because he looked so strange."[21]

Etchingham, a smart dresser, too, cut quite a look with the handsome Jimi in his extravagant wild clothing. Customers at Selfridge's department store snickered when they appeared: Some of it was because of their interracial relationship, but it was mostly because of Jimi's appearance. He and Kathy were living together in a cheap hotel. When Kathy encountered Ringo Starr at a club and complained about their room, Ringo offered his unused two-bedroom flat, and Jimi and Kathy, along with Chandler and his girlfriend, moved into Ringo's pad at 34 Montague Square. That the musician and his manager would be housemates suggested the fatherly role of Chandler.

Jimi discovered his own father had moved when he first tried to phone him. So, he called Ernestine Benson, who told Jimi that Al had remarried and that his new stepmother was Ayajo "June" Jinka, a Japanese mother of five.

When he reached his father, he called collect. "Al was furious at that kind of waste of money," recalled Etchingham. "Jimi kept telling him about England, but Al didn't believe it."

Jimi later said the first thing Al asked was, "Who had I stolen the money from to pay for the crossing." Finally, Jimi handed the phone to Kathy.

"Mr. Hendrix, it's true," spoke Kathy in an English accent. "Jimi's here in England."

His response surprised her. "You tell my boy to write me. I ain't paying for no collect phone calls," and hung up.

Jimi said to Kathy, "What's he doing adopting other people's children when he couldn't even look after his own."[22]

The Jimi Hendrix Experience debuted at the Novelty in Évreux, France, on Thursday, October 13. Opening for blond singer Johnny Hallyday, they played "Hey Joe," "Killin' Floor," Otis Redding's "Respect," and Wilson Pickett's "Land of a Thousand Dances." A French critic wrote that Jimi was "a bad mixture of James Brown and Chuck Berry, who pulled a wry face onstage for a quarter of an hour and also played with his teeth."

The band was under-rehearsed and ragged. "Jimi was still getting comfortable singing," remembered Noel. "We hardly knew each other."

When the tour hit Paris for a show at the Olympia, Brian Auger and the Trinity had been added and the date was sold out. The French could be a tough audience. "But if they loved you," Brian Auger recalled, "they went crazy."

Playing with more confidence and adding "Wild Thing" to the playlist, the Experience put on their first truly great show. "Jimi just wiped the floor with the crowd," Vic Briggs recalled.[23] Jimi's mixture of blues and rock had found an audience in France.

Chandler's plan was starting to work, but with no income so far—payment for the brief Hallyday tour did not cover the costs—he and Jeffery were beginning to worry about their nearly $25,000 expenses. And so, a month to the day after Jimi's arrival in England, the Experience was rushed into a studio to record a few songs Chandler could take around to record companies. The first single they cut was "Hey Joe," which Chandler had heard Jimi play in New York. For the B-side, Jimi suggested "Mercy, Mercy," but Chandler wanted him to write a new song. For Jimi to make money in music publishing (for which Chandler would get half of the proceeds), he would have to write his own material. He was unsure of himself as a songwriter, so Chandler suggested he simply put down his feelings. Jimi did and wrote "Stone Free" in one evening. The lyrics of the song are about not being tied down by any one woman: Jimi was "stone free to ride the breeze."

Making the rounds, Chandler was turned down at Decca: "I don't think he's got anything," said an exec (now adding Jimi Hendrix to the

Beatles on their list of rejections). But other companies were interested, and he received two offers the following week. The first was from Polydor, a label interested in pop and rock music, which, with great reserve, agreed to release "Hey Joe" in December. The second was when Chandler encountered old friends Kit Lambert and Chris Stamp and members of The Who, whose guitarist, Pete Townshend, was regarded as one of the best and a pioneer in "feedback guitar."

Pete had heard Jimi play at one of his early London jams and felt "threatened" by Jimi, but being a good businessman, Pete knew that the sensible thing to do was offer the "threat" a contract and at least make a profit. Lambert had also heard Jimi play that night at the Scotch at St. James and promised to have a record out by Christmas, "If I have to take it round the shops myself" on a new label he and others owned called Track Records.[24] Chas and Jeffery had committed "Hey Joe" to Polydor but decided to let Track have all future products.

"Chas Chandler has signed and brought to this country a 20-year-old Negro named Jim Hendrix," observed an article in the *Record Mirror* on October 29, "who—among other things—plays the guitar with his teeth and is being hailed in some quarters as a main contender for the title of 'the next big thing.'"[25] Though his name was incorrect and his age was wrong, and it mostly remarked on his gimmickry, the piece elated Jimi. He cut the clipping out and saved it in his wallet.

Journalist Keith Altham said, "It seems ridiculous on retrospect, but the gimmicks were necessary early on for publicity. You first have to grab the attention of the media before anyone will notice you."[26] Jimi liked the attention his flashy moves brought but would grow tired of performing them night after night.

From Munich, Germany, where Jeffery had arranged a four-night stand at the Big Apple Club, Jimi wrote his father, "We're in Munich now; we just left Paris, and Nancy, France. . . . I have my own group and will have a record out in about two months."

They played two shows a night in Munich. Jimi did his entire routine, and with each show, the crowds got bigger and more enthusiastic. "You could feel that we were just on the cusp of success,"[27] recalled Redding. Making use of a long guitar cord, Jimi walked into the audience as he played. Returning to the stage, he threw the guitar before him and cracked the neck. Upset about the damage, he grabbed the neck of the guitar, raised it above his head, and slammed it down with violent fury. The crowd applauded madly and dragged him off stage at the end of the show. Chandler determined then and there to have Jimi smash more guitars, especially when the other gimmicks failed to excite the crowd.

A wadded-up dollar bill Jimi used to carry in the sole of his boot when scratching for a living on the Chitlin' Circuit was replaced by a pound note placed inside the brim of his hat. "When you've been penniless," he told Kathy Etchingham, "you never forget it."[28]

His boots told of the years of struggle. "When you saw the soles," said Garland, "they were completely worn through."

Not only were they old, they were also out-of-fashion. "He had these black boots . . . with zippers on the sides," remembered Noel.

Some thought the old shoes caused Jimi's unusual gait—a kind of shuffle with his toes pointing in, but even after he bought size eleven Cuban boots with square toes, the pigeon-toed walk remained. "You could tell by the way he walked that he had had the wrong sized shoes on as a kid, and that his gait was all screwed up," said Eric Burdon. "It was like his toes made a triangle as he moved."[29] Much about Jimi seemed angular: his body was V-shaped with wide shoulders narrowing to a very small waist, and when walking down the street with Noel and Mitch, Jimi would be in front with Noel and Mitch following in a triangular formation.

Though the band was created quickly with members who were strangers, Jimi, Mitch, and Noel were soon playing as if they'd been together for years. The appearance of all three began to merge. They dressed the same and had similar blousy hairstyles, and, except for the pale skin of Noel and Mitch, they could have been taken for brothers. Jimi was the leader in both music and fashion. When he switched to bell bottoms, so did Noel and Mitch. Their hair was the feature that stood out the most: Noel's curly afro came naturally, but Mitch got a permanent, and as their afros grew, they began to resemble bobblehead dolls. Photographers emphasized their afros in pictures with backlighting. "With all that hair," remembered Eric Burdon, "their heads were as wide as their torso."[30]

With a friendship forged from the road and the studio, they were lighthearted about being rock stars. Since management took care of business, playing in the band was almost like an extended adolescence. With Noel as a jokester, humor and boyish pranks bonded them the most, along with a shared pride in their music. "It felt for a time," recalled Noel, "like it was us against the world."[31]

At this early stage, much of Jimi's repertoire comprised an arrangement of songs made successful by other singers: "Hey Joe" had been part of the repertoire of Love and the Byrds, yet from the opening crash of the guitar feedback on Jimi's version, the song was entirely his. He also paid tribute to Dylan with a carefully crafted "Like a Rolling Stone" that was masterful in its originality, and to the great blues guitarist B. B. King with a race through his "Rock Me, Baby" that strung a curtain of bluesy notes across the sound of a buzz saw gone amok.

When Jimi had first met The Who at a recording studio soon after his arrival, Pete Townshend was not impressed: "He looked scruffy." Keith Moon kept yelling, "Who let that savage in here?"[32] Townshend made some suggestions about amplifiers, wondering if he really needed top-rated equipment, but when he saw Jimi perform again a few days later, "I became an immediate fan," recalled Townshend. "I saw all of Jimi's first London shows. . . . [Jimi] took back black music. . . . I went away and got very confused for a bit. . . . I felt I hadn't the emotional equipment, the physical equipment, the natural psychic genius of someone like Jimi."[33]

The clubs they played were small venues that didn't pay much, but a buzz was growing about the band. The Rolling Stones and the Beatles began coming to his shows. After one show, Eric Clapton invited Jimi to his flat. Kathy Etchingham came along. The mood was friendly, but their girlfriends did most of the talking. "It was a very strained meeting," Kathy Etchingham recalled. "They were both in awe of each other. We had to center the conversation around music." When he left several hours later, Jimi remarked to Etchingham, "That was hard work."[34]

In late November, a press conference was held for the Experience at the Bag O' Nails, a legendary nightclub at the bottom of a long stairway in a basement on a narrow street in Soho. Word of what had happened at the Polytechnic had spread through the British rock scene, and Chandler invited all the local talent agents, concert promoters, and club managers to the concert and reception. When a promoter at the reception offered the Experience a paltry $65 to open some shows for the New Animals, they made the most of the opportunity.

"At Croydon, on the first gig, I think the audience was shocked," Chandler said. "They were numb. They weren't sure what it was about. Next we got a gig at the Roundhouse in Chalk Farm. Jimi got his guitar nicked and I was flat broke, so I had to sell my last guitar. I swapped my last bass for a new guitar for Jimi. Two days later 'Hey Joe' hit the chart. It was all done by the skin of my teeth. The DJs hadn't been playing it on the radio, but the word had spread through the ballrooms and it started to sell. I think we had about thirty shillings left between us."[35]

Though his reputation was growing, whether Jimi could actually make any money depended on the success of "Hey Joe." They had begun to record an album, but if "Hey Joe" failed, there would be no record deal. Kit Lambert and Chris Stamp put Jimi on their new Track Records imprint and booked the band on *Ready, Set, Go!* for some national exposure. The Experience appeared on the show the same day the single was released, December 16, 1966, and the song became a hit.

Jimi jumped for joy when the single reached the charts and kept climbing. "It was like 'fantastic! Let's go to the pub and celebrate,'" recalled Etchingham. Management had played a role in artificially inflating its ranking by buying up all the singles in record shops. "It's called payola," said Kathy Etchingham, "and I know it happened because I bought several of them myself."[36]

The music scene in the United Kingdom was awash with drugs, particularly hash and LSD. Though the band smoked hash and sometimes tripped on LSD, initially they favored cheap amphetamines, which helped them stay up all night to perform or record. That winter, trying to raise money for studio time, the band played dates all over England, sometimes playing a show several hours away and rushing back to London for a session in the middle of the night when studio time was cheaper. "We'd be playing in Manchester," remembered Noel Redding, "and then we'd drive back to London. We'd get back at three in the morning and put down the tracks. And then we'd go to bed at five and get up the next morning only to have to go back up north again for another show. And we'd be back in London that next night doing more recording. That was how we made the first album."[37]

When they went into CBS studios to cut "Red House," "Foxy Lady," and "Third Stone from the Sun," they brought in four stacks of twin

Marshall amplifiers, a total of eight speakers. When the band began to play, Mike Ross, the studio engineer, retreated to the control room because of the noise. "It was painful on your ears," Ross recalled.[38] Jimi stretched even further on his original songs. He all but dropped the vocals on his funky blues "Red House" and used it as his most traditional piece, establishing himself as an absolute master of the blues form. For "Laughing Sam's Dice," the initial letters standing for his favorite psychedelic, Jimi wrote lyrics that formed a travelogue through outer space. The songs he wrote came quickly. "Red House" was about his Seattle girlfriend, Betty Jean Morgan, whose house had been brown, not red, but Jimi knew that "Red" had more of a ring than "Brown." The theme was a basic twelve-bar blues about a man whose woman no longer loves him, but Jimi's brilliant electric solo made the song a classic.

"The Wind Cries Mary" was based on a fight that happened between Jimi and Kathy Etchingham when he insulted her cooking one winter night. Kathy's cooking was a common contention between them and usually she joked about it with him, but this time the scene turned ugly. "I started throwing pots," Kathy said, "and I stormed out."[39] Mary was Etchingham's middle name, and when she returned the next day, Jimi had written "The Wind Cries Mary."

With twenty minutes left in a recording session, Chandler asked, "Have you got anything else," and Jimi provided the song and taught the band on the spot.

"Jimi just basically played the chords," Noel remembered, "and being an ex-guitar player, I could pick up the stuff really fast, and we got the feel, and we put it down."[40] There was even enough time to include Jimi's guitar overdubs.

In De Lane Lea Studio on January 11, 1967, the band worked all day to produce several songs, including "Purple Haze," "51st Anniversary," and another take of "Third Stone from the Sun."

"Purple Haze" was inspired by a dream Jimi had after reading the novel *Night of Light* by Philip José Farmer. Written one night at the Upper Cut Club in London and recorded the following day, Jimi introduced deliberate guitar distortion and some of his early voodoo-cum-psychedelic lyrics. The song later became the Experience's second successful single. After the long, difficult studio session, during which they had spent more than four hours on "Purple Haze," they still had two shows to do at the Bag O' Nails. The crowd gathered that night to watch the Experience was the greatest among London's elite rock. Most accounts of those attending include John Lennon, Jeff Beck, Paul McCartney, Jimmy Page, Ringo Starr, Eric Clapton, Mick Jagger, Brian Jones, Brian Epstein, John Entwistle, Donovan, Pete Townshend, Georgie Fame, Lulu, the Hollies, and the New Animals.

Terry Reid remembered, "It was as if all the guitar players in the world had shown up."

Paul McCartney was sitting next to Reid. "Have you seen this guy yet," asked Paul, "he's amazing."

Jimi walked on stage and said, "Thanks for coming," and then proposed to do "this little song that I know is very close to your heart," and played "Wild Thing," a pop throwaway hated by nearly everyone. "He played it," observed Reid, "and banged the shit out of this bloody thing, and takes off into outer space. Imagine the most horrible song in the world turned into the most beautiful."

Returning from the bathroom, Reid bumped into Brian Jones. "It's all wet down in the front," Jones warned.

Reid replied, "I don't see any water."

To which Jones said, "It's wet from all the guitar players crying."[41]

In the crowd, too, was Roger Mayer, who, in the Royal Navy Scientific Service, had done vibration and acoustic analysis to help silence British naval boats for underwater warfare. Using his inventive knowledge, he had already supplied Jeff Beck and Jimmy Page of the Yardbirds with sound effects gadgets for their guitars. Two weeks later he introduced Jimi to a complex version of a frequency doubler, an electronic device Mayer called the Octavia, and helped him find stunning new sound effects. They would work together for the rest of Jimi's career to develop equipment to further extend his range of guitar sounds and effects.

A week at the 7 ½ Club followed, with Clapton, Townshend, and Jagger all coming to see him again. At one show, Townshend stood next to Clapton, clasping their hands together as frightened children might do. Stunned by his sudden appearance in London, both were concerned about what Jimi meant for their careers. The two developed a friendship based upon Hendrix and what they might do in response. "Jimi was the new guitar in town," said an observer, "and he was a threat to people like Clapton and Pete Townshend. All the birds were falling all over him."[42] Mick Jagger, unimpressed with Hendrix in New York when Linda had taken the Stones to see him at a Midtown club, had revised his opinion. Bringing Marianne Faithful to a club date, she recalled, "Mick told me he'd seen Hendrix in New York. I think his line to me was 'He's going to tear the whole world apart.'"[43]

Marianne was enthralled with Hendrix. "Mick was the king and Marianne was the queen," said an observer, "and Jimi was the jack of spades." During a set break, Jimi came to their table and flirted with Marianne. The party that followed the performance had Jimi and Marianne, Brian Jones, Linda Keith, Paul McCartney, Kathy Etchingham, Chas Chandler, Noel, and Mitch in attendance. "Jimi could do no wrong," remembered one present. "He had three women all fawning over him—Linda because she felt some claim from New York, Kathy because she was his 'old lady,' . . . and Marianne, who had been living with Mick for only a few weeks and was happy with Mick but still felt this incredible attraction. Jimi just sat there in the middle of it, smoking hashish cigarettes and grinning uncontrollably."[44]

Though Jimi was involved with Etchingham, Chandler presented him to the public as a bachelor. Whenever interviewers showed up at their flat, and some were females, Kathy was hustled out. More than a few times she returned to chase out half-naked girls. Meanwhile, like his father before him, Jimi suffered from jealousy, especially when he drank, and he loved the beer in English pubs and was drinking a lot more. He sometimes imagined that every man was after Kathy Etchingham, who was very attractive. One night at the Bag O' Nails, Jimi thought she was talking to another man on the phone and grabbed the receiver and began hitting her with it with a shocking and hurtful violence that seemed so out of character that she screamed. At just this time, John Lennon and Paul McCartney walked into the club and calmly took the phone away from the normally polite and gentle Jimi.

The same trait that made Jimi such a talented musician, the ability to improvise and be lost in the moment of a performance, also at times caused him to recklessly act on immediate desires and urges, a mercurial, almost childlike nature painful for anyone who cared about him. After a show in Manchester, Kathy, catching him having sex in the women's restroom with a girl he had just met, resignedly said, "Hurry up or we'll miss the train back to London."[45] She did not like his betrayals, and they began to fight so often that Chandler took her aside and urged her not to do so in public, where a spectacle might hurt Jimi's image. But they continued to quarrel, sometimes publicly.

The Jimi Hendrix Experience was on the road night after night, traveling from city to city with road manager Gerry Stickells driving a van full of equipment, the three musicians following along in a car that constantly threatened to quit. Often there were two shows a day. In an entire month they had only three days off. Twice they performed concerts in the hinterlands and then rushed back to London for a television show. "Hey Joe" was soon replaced on the British record charts by Jimi's second single, "Purple Haze," which went to number three. The Experience ended January with two shows at the Saville Theatre on the bill with The Who: Lennon, McCartney, George Harrison, and the members of Cream were in attendance. After the concert, inspired by Jimi Hendrix, Jack Bruce went home and wrote "Sunshine of Your Love."

That march, in an article in the *Express,* Jimi, listing his likes, dislikes, and hobbies, stated his favorite composers were Dylan, Muddy Waters, and Mozart. He cut three years off his age because management told him younger would impress more girls, and he listed only his father and his brother Leon as family. Most of the survey contained flippant remarks, but he did say he wanted to "have my own style of music," and that his real ambition was "to see my mother and family again," which only a few people in Seattle would have understood.[46] Tony Garland, who had put the *Express* piece together, didn't know if Jimi's mother was alive or dead. Few people ever heard him talk about her. Kathy Etchingham knew she was dead. "He told me she drank herself to death," she said, "but he also said to me she was a goddess in the sky and an angel."[47]

Though his mother had been dead for almost ten years, Jimi was moved by her memory and still dreamed about her. He remembered a summer day when he and Leon were in the back seat of a car she was driving, the windows were down and he could smell her perfume in the breeze. It was rare for him to talk about these feelings. "He was usually not a touchy-feely guy," observed Kathy, who had also had a difficult childhood. He spent most of his free time practicing the guitar, but he liked to watch comedy on television, read science fiction books, and play board games. His favorite board game was Risk, the game of world domination. "He was very good at it and he played to win," remembered Etchingham.[48]

Touring cinema houses in the English hinterlands as part of a package, the Experience opened an act headlined by the Walker Brothers, with Engelbert Humperdinck and Cat Stevens also on the bill. Before the first performance, Altham, Chandler, and Jimi were discussing what Jimi could do to stand out. Altham suggested setting his guitar on fire. Jimi's eyes lit up. On stage that night before a couple of thousand people, when the Experience ended their five-song set with "Fire," Jimi poured lighter fluid on his guitar and threw a match. When the guitar burst into flames, he twirled it around like a windmill until a stagehand doused it with water. The flaming guitar stunt lasted only about thirty seconds but became legendary in the papers. But almost everything Jimi did made headlines. Advertisements for the shows touted, "Don't miss this man who is Dylan, Clapton, and James Brown all in one."[49] The tour brought Jimi many new fans, but he tired of the circus-like atmosphere backstage. On one date, a crazed fan chased him with a pair of scissors to cut a lock of his hair.

That spring, the Experience finished their debut album, *Are You Experienced?*. The album had been cobbled together in various studios over several months. To save time and money, Chandler sped up sessions by tricking the band into thinking they were rehearsing when he was actually recording. "Chas would always say, 'Okay, lads, let's run through it,'" recalled Noel. "And we'd run through the track and then Chas would say, 'Okay, do it again.' But he'd actually already taken the first take without us knowing. And then after the second take, we'd walk out, have a smoke, and he'd say, 'We got it.' And we'd say, 'What do you mean? We haven't even started it yet.' And he'd taken the first take."[50]

Chandler had risked his money and his personal reputation making the album, but early reviews were great. Keith Altham in the *N.M.E* wrote, "The LP is a brave effort by Hendrix to produce a musical form which is original and exciting." When the record came out, it went as high as number two on the British charts: the number one spot was held by the Beatles's *Sgt. Pepper's Lonely Heart Club Band.*

Are You Experienced? had a strong overall impact. Here was every threat in rock and roll wrapped in peacock finery: On the cover was a black man with scarves tied around his neck, Edwardian jacket fashioned from upholstery material, hair frizzed out, and on each side of this dark man stood two frail, white Englishmen also dressed from Carnaby Street. It wasn't unprecedented for whites and blacks to play together, the history of jazz is filled with such groups, but until the advent of Hendrix, such mixing in popular music was rare and its success was always limited.

On stage, Jimi not only sang about the sexual act, but he also performed it with his guitar, bumping and grinding his skinny hips, waggling his tongue, sticking his guitar neck between his legs and moving it to and fro vigorously. The vision was as violent as the sound. Don Menn in *Guitar Player* magazine noted, "The sounds of a neck shredding or an amp flying apart, of a string popping . . . of a dismembered pickup amplifying its own unraveling through a shattered speaker were sounds that Jimi did not invent, but . . . used to a particular musical degree. They fit in well with his more aggressive raw finales. . . . Jimi smashed many guitars, burned a few, and harpooned his speaker cabinets sometimes for show, sometimes out of frustration, and occasionally to create a raucous acoustical effect."[51]

Chandler and Jeffery planned to take the Experience worldwide. Touring with a live show, Jimi was a star in Europe and they thought it could happen in America. News of Jimi's recording success, his Wild Man image, and his smoking guitars reached the U.S. through the British music press: *Melody Maker,* the *New Musical Express, Music Week,* and *Record Retailer* were air-mailed to hundreds of record company executives who wanted to keep in touch with English pop successes. When Reprise Records of Burbank, California, offered Jimi Hendrix $120,000 for North American record distribution rights, Chas Chandler accepted the offer, and, on May 20, 1967, the Jimi Hendrix Experience was added to the growing Reprise roster, sight unseen, sound unheard, in a move that was a simple, expedient roll of the dice in a business in which making a $120,000 mistake was better than passing on an act that could later attract millions. Pop music was one of western culture's most exciting crapshoots in the '60s, and Mo Ostin, the man who ran Reprise, wanted a piece of the action.

The contract was signed just as producer Lou Adler and musician John Phillips were organizing a music festival in Monterey, California, happening in June. Andrew Loog Oldham and Paul McCartney were British advisers to the event. McCartney had written a review of "Purple Haze" for *Melody Maker*, calling Jimi "Fingers Hendrix: an absolute ace on the guitar."[52] Both Oldham and McCartney picked The Who and Hendrix as the most important UK acts. The gig would bring hardly any money to the band, but the exposure would be important. Copies of Jimi's debut album had made their way through America, and a few songs were being played on some radio stations, but he was still unknown in his country. After being so warmly embraced by Britain, going back to where he had struggled so long for recognition was not an easy thought. When Chandler announced that the Experience would soon head for California, Jimi only said, "I'm going home, home to America again."[53]

Following the release of *Are You Experienced?*, and still playing concerts, the band began recording another album. "We never stopped," recalled engineer Eddie Kramer. "Chas came out of the old school of 'We've got four hours, let's make the most of it.'"[54]

Jimi enjoyed playing so much that an all-day studio session was an opportunity to spend more time with his guitar. Using the Octavia on "Purple Haze" had changed notes an entire octave, creating an otherworldly sound he wanted to experiment with more to create new sounds, and, though complicated by experiments with phasing, guitar effects, and feedback, the sessions for their next album, *Axis: Bold as Love*, went quickly. "Jimi was always asking me 'Roger, what can we do?'" recalled Mayer. "We were trying to use sounds to create emotions and paint pictures. We had only crude technology at the time, but if we didn't have something we'd build it."[55] Jimi used Mayer's inventions to create extraordinary sounds never heard before.

Jimi loved that the Beatles were exploring the same psychedelic terrain in *Sgt. Pepper's Lonely Hearts Club Band.* Two of the most legendary shows he ever performed were the Experience's "Farewell, England" concerts at the Saville Theatre on June 4. The theater was owned by Brian Epstein, and with the possibility of the Beatles in attendance, Jimi wanted a great concert. Thirty minutes before they went on, Jimi stormed into the dressing room with *Sgt. Pepper's*, played the title track, and told his bandmates, "We'll open with this." Noel recalled, "We thought he'd gone daft."[56] They learned the chords as the song played on the record player, and then came on stage to thunderous applause. McCartney, Lennon, and Harrison were in Epstein's box. Eric Clapton, Spencer Davis, Jack Bruce, and Lulu were in the audience. Jimi thanked the opening band, Procol Harum, and then he thanked the audience for coming to his last concert in England "for a long, long time," and started into "Sgt. Pepper's Lonely Hearts Club Band" only three days after the album had been released.

If the Jimi Hendrix Experience had been less than inspired and brilliant, it would have been an insult to the Beatles and all their fans, but Jimi's technical skill and confidence were supreme. The title track played by the Experience became their own. "The Beatles couldn't believe it," Eddie Kramer remembered. "Here was Hendrix playing a song off their album that had just come out, and he'd taken the song and figured out a completely new arrangement, which was a killer."

Jimi found a new way of structuring the melody based upon his guitar parts rather than the horns the Beatles had used. "It was basically just done off the cuff," Noel recalled, "but that's how we did everything. We were fearless."[57]

Paul McCartney called the "Sgt. Pepper's" cover "one of the greatest honors of my career." At Brian Epstein's private party after the show, Paul McCartney opened the door for the Experience, holding a huge joint of marijuana in his mouth and passed it to Jimi saying, "That was fucking great, man."[58] In the storied history of British rock and roll, no single performer ever enjoyed as spectacular a rise as Jimi Hendrix.

The Beatles watching Hendrix at Saville Theatre

The Jimi Hendrix Experience – Noel, Jimi, and Mitch

Cream – Baker, Bruce, and Clapton

Chas Chandler and Jimi

Jimi with Eric Clapton

Zoot Money

Jimi and Kathy Etchingham

America

After the acceptance and success Jimi Hendrix experienced in London, returning to America felt strange, especially at first. When the band checked into the Chelsea Hotel after flying to New York, a woman, thinking Jimi was a bellhop, insisted he carry her bags, a reminder of racism in America. Later, decked in a floral jacket with a green scarf, no cab would stop on the streets. Attitudes improved when he explored the Village. The Mothers of Invention, aware of his fame in England, bought him a beer in a restaurant. At the Café Au Go Go, Richie Havens was excited to hear of his success, and, while watching the Doors at the Scene Club, he got a better idea of where rock was headed in America. The next day they flew to San Francisco, where Jimi's Carnaby Street flair looked strange and spectacular among the jeans, long hair, and beads.

"The Summer of Love" had descended upon the world, and its epicenter was San Francisco, exploding with youth, colors, new ideas, and the sounds of a thousand guitars. The discotheque was out and the cavernous dance hall was in. Indirect lighting was replaced by psychedelic blends of stroboscopic flashers, liquid color blobs, black lights, moirés, films, and slides. Victorian poster art was reincarnated to advertise dances held by homegrown groups such as the Grateful Dead, Jefferson Airplane, and Big Brother and the Holding Company. Two former Harvard professors, Timothy Leary and Richard Albert, announced a new religion, the League for Spiritual Discovery, using LSD as its sacrament. "Turn on, tune in, drop out!" became the catchwords of the time. Even journalism was being altered as the "underground" newspaper blossomed along with "underground" radio, a maturation in broadcast that seemed to come when Top 40 radio didn't grow up with its audience. As everything was changing in American youth, in June there stood at the apogee a gathering of singers and musicians by the California coast in Monterey.

The First International Festival of Music grew from the desire to raise the cultural awareness of rock and roll. John Philips, Paul McCartney, Lou Adler, and others talked about how rock and roll wasn't considered an art form the way jazz was. Derek Taylor, who had been the Beatles's press officer, was hired to handle publicity and made the statement, "no one would get any money at all for doing the festival, and all the profits would go to charity . . . just a flower strewn festival for love." John Phillips and Lou Adler were co-directors with a board of governors that included Donovan, Mick Jagger, Paul McCartney, Johnny Rivers, Smokey Robinson, Paul Simon, and Brian Wilson. They were delighted to have found a way of giving back to the industry. "Entertainers who have starved and become rich are forever haunted by guilt," said Derek Taylor. "They wanted to be generous, to make a gesture. The spirit around them became unbelievably cheerful. . . . Every major pop artist in the world was called. . . . No one said no."[1]

When Paul McCartney suggested the Jimi Hendrix Experience—"You can't do the festival without them"[2]—Phillips called Chas Chandler in London, offering no money for performing, but willing to pay for airfare and accommodation. With the Mamas and the Papas, the Beach Boys, Simon and Garfunkel, the Byrds, Dionne Warwick, and The Who already committed, Chandler could not say no. More bands came from around the world. From Memphis: Otis Redding and Booker T. & the MGs, including Jimi's old friend Steve Cropper; from Chicago: Mike Bloomfield with his new band, the Electric Flag, with Buddy Miles on drums, and the Paul Butterfield Blues Band; from Los Angeles: Canned Heat and Buffalo Springfield; from New York: the Blues Project and Laura Nyro; and from San Francisco: the Grateful Dead and Janis Joplin. From India there came the world famous sitarist, Ravi Shankar, and from England: The Who, Eric Burdon's New Animals, and the Jimi Hendrix Experience.

They came together in the sunshine just north of the long, wild coast of Big Sur, gathering in peace to listen to their new music presented from the big stage of a large, enclosed corral in the Monterey fairgrounds on the weekend of June 16–17. Promoters had planned for ten thousand fans, but at least ninety thousand came, and so they set up stages outside the gates for jam sessions. People wore costumes and antique clothing, cowboys and Indians were numerous, and they came on their best behavior to prove that love could work. Organizers brought in a hundred thousand orchids—everyone appeared to have flowers in their hair. The Experience arrived Friday, the day the festival began, and would not perform until Sunday night. Infamous chemist Augustus Owsley Stanley III was freely handing out LSD to musicians backstage. Owsley's favorite color for his self-produced LSD was purple, nicknamed "Purple Haze," Jimi was amazed to discover, by someone who had heard his English singles.

Jimi spent Saturday making his way among the crowd, hanging with Buddy Miles, Brian Jones, and Eric Burdon. The sun was shining. He wore his antique military jacket with an "I'm a virgin" button on it. Brian had on an antique wizard's coat. "They couldn't have looked more freakish," Eric Burdon observed.[3]

During the day, Jimi watched the Electric Flag, and then Big Brother and the Holding Company with Janis Joplin giving one of the defining performances of the festival. Saturday's highlight was Otis Redding with his masculine showmanship and voice backed by Steve Cropper's guitar. Jimi spoke to Cropper briefly and joked backstage with Jerry Miller of Moby Grape about their times together at the Spanish Castle in Tacoma. Late that night, Jimi borrowed Jerry's Gibson L5 guitar for a workout at an alternative stage surrounded by sleeping people.

"People in the crowd actually groaned when they saw him because no one knew who he was and they wanted to get some sleep," recalled Eric Burdon. "He started playing this beautiful, sad, melodic stuff and it developed into a happy jam."[4] During the night the drowsy audience witnessed Jimi playing with Ron "Pigpen" McKernan of the Grateful Dead, and Jorma Kaukonen and Jack Casady of Jefferson Airplane.

"Nobody was a legend then," remembered Jack Casady. "The most unique part of Monterey was that all these musicians got to meet each other." On Sunday, during the Grateful Dead set, Jimi led another jam backstage that included Janis Joplin, Mama Cass, Roger Daltrey, Eric Burdon, and Brian Jones, all singing "Sgt. Pepper's." They were so loud that Bill Graham came backstage and said, "Shut the fuck up! You're killing the other acts."[5]

No one knew then the historical importance of Monterey, but Jimi was aware that much rode on the U.S. debut of the Experience, and, wanting to stand out, he spent the afternoon painting his Stratocaster with psychedelic swirls.

No exact Sunday lineup had been set. Ravi Shankar was to open, and the Mamas and the Papas were to close the show. The Grateful Dead, also scheduled for that afternoon, agreed to play wherever they were slotted. It was not yet decided when Jimi and The Who would play. "We were both desperate to be noticed," recalled Pete Townshend. "I really did not want to go on after Jimi." Nor did Jimi want to follow The Who.

Finally, John Phillips tossed a coin and The Who won. "If I'm going to follow you," threatened Jimi to Townshend, "I'm going to pull out all the stops," and stormed off to find some lighter fluid.[6]

The music performed that day on the broad stage of the horse arena of the Monterey County Fairgrounds launched rock to the stars. The Who performed a tremendous show: At the end of their set, Townshend smashed his guitar with such fury that a bit hit D. A. Pennebaker, who was filming thirty feet away. While the Grateful Dead served as a buffer between The Who and Hendrix, giving the audience a breather between explosive acts while keeping spirits high, letting the folks fold their chairs and dance, Jimi went to the Mamas and the Papas's tent where Owsley showed up handing out acid. Jimi took some, timing his trip to peak during the middle of his performance.

When the time came for the Experience to perform, Brian Jones went onstage for their introduction. "I'd like to introduce you to a very good friend, a fellow countryman of yours," he told the crowd. "A brilliant performer, the most exciting guitar player I've ever heard: the Jimi Hendrix Experience."[7]

"It was a thin line-up, just three," remembered Billy Gibbons, who later formed the band ZZ Top. "But when the music started it was ten, it could have been twenty. It was that powerful."[8] They began with "Killing Floor" and "Foxy Lady." On the third song, when they played "Like a Rolling Stone," Jimi began to win over the crowd. He was wearing a jacket with psychedelic art, headband, tight red pants, a yellow ruffled shirt with a pink feathery boa wrapped around his neck, and acknowledged the audience with beautiful smiles. He played with his teeth, played behind his back, and played between his legs, but the gimmicks were backed by innovative songs played by a band tightly together for the past seven months. "We just nailed it," said Noel. "That made the band in America." Jimi plowed through "Purple Haze" using feedback, and then launched into "Wild Thing," calling the song "the English and American combined anthems."[9] Two minutes into the number, he grabbed a can of Ronson lighter fluid and set the guitar on fire, eventually kneeling over it and moving his fingers like a voodoo priest. When he walked off stage, Andy Warhol and Nico were the first to greet him, kissing him on each cheek. Nico later described Jimi's Monterey performance as the most sexual performance she had ever seen.

Pete Johnson wrote in the *Los Angeles Times* that "the Jimi Hendrix Experience owned the future, and the audience knew it in an instant. When Hendrix left the stage, he had graduated from rumor to legend."

Even the negative reviews created controversy useful to an unknown group. He was called a "psychedelic Uncle Tom" in *Esquire*, while Jann Wenner, who later started *Rolling Stone*, wrote in *Melody Maker*, "Although he handled his guitar with rhythmic agility and minor drama, he is not the great artist we were told."[10]

Pete Townshend thought Jimi relied on too many stunts. "When Jimi went on and started doing the same gimmicks we had done—and they were just gimmicks—I realized I had underestimated Jimi's readiness to play the fool to get attention."

Eric Burdon observed, "It was his coming-out party."[11]

The next day at the Monterey airport, attempting to deflate the tensions between them, Pete said, "Listen, no hard feelings. And I'd love to get a bit of that guitar you smashed." Jimi rarely used racist names, but when he did, obscenities could flow. Firing an icy glare, he called Townshend a "cracker." Townshend, surprised and upset, later recalled that in England they had frequently discussed the role of race in music: "We had talked a bit about the fact that he had taken back the black blues that artists like the Stones and Clapton had appropriated from the States, then sold back to the States as though it was British and White . . . that had always been discussed by us as a terrific and allowable irony."[12]

They eventually patched up their friendship, creating a lasting one, but at Monterey, they parted in anger.

The Experience contracted Michael Goldstein as their publicist in America and received an endorsement from Sunn Amplifiers, giving them free gear. Bill Graham asked them to open a few shows at the Fillmore in San Francisco, where they opened on a bill that included Janis Joplin's Big Brother. The crowd response was so great that they were moved into the headlining slot for the week. Jimi spent the next few days in Los Angeles at the home of guitarist Peter Tork in Laurel Canyon in the Hollywood Hills, partying with well-known friends and musicians.

Once he visited the offices of Reprise Records. "He came up and had an extraordinarily weak handshake," Stan Cornyn recalled, "and that shifting kind of voice and he was always answering questions a little more comically than you were prepared for . . . then he drifted on, probably wearing something purple and magenta."

One night, "Jimi and myself and Neil Young and David Crosby went to Stephen Still's place on the [Malibu] beach and jammed for three days," remembered Buddy Miles.[13] Meanwhile, the job offers were stacking up.

In July they had a show in Santa Barbara and then a gig in Los Angeles at the Whiskey A Go Go on the same bill as Sam and Dave. People lined the street outside the club. Sam and Dave thought the crowd was for them, but the place cleared when Jimi finished his set. Rock groupie Pamela Des Barres was at the Whiskey show. "No one in L.A. even knew who he was before the gig," she said. "Everyone knew afterwards." It was early in her groupie career, and when he tried to hit on her, she felt he was too strong. "There was an obvious magnetism he had. I just couldn't do it at the time."[14]

But Jimi soon met a groupie much more in tune at a party in Laurel Canyon. Devon Wilson was a tall African American who had been born Ida Mae Wilson but had picked up the name Devon while working the streets as a teenaged prostitute. She was beautiful and bright, ingested drugs like candy, and bonded with the biggest rock stars of the day. When she met Jimi Hendrix, she attached herself to him with a curse of love.

The Experience flew to New York for two club dates, and then to Jacksonville, Florida, as the opening act for the sold-out tour of the

Monkeys. The Monkeys had emerged from a television series that resembled the recent Beatles film, *A Hard Day's Night*, and had become a pop phenomenon. Their first two singles had gone to number one on *Billboard*'s record charts. By the summer of '67, their albums had done just as well, and they were earning $50,000 a concert. On the face of it, booking with the Monkeys looked like a great coup for the Experience, but the Monkeys's audience was prepubescent and Jimi's was far more adult.

In New York, Mike Jeffery told Goldstein and Chandler that it was a great deal. When Goldstein ventured that the Monkeys had a different audience, Jeffery said he thought the exposure was important. "I said it would be a fucking disaster," remembered Chandler. "But Mike had signed the deal and it was too late. I told the boys I wouldn't go with them on the tour. They went and died the death."[15]

"Our audience didn't exactly dig him," Peter Tork of the Monkeys remembered, but his band was enthusiastic. "We'd get there early and watch him from backstage. What he did was simply exquisite. I loved to watch the way his hands worked—it came so easily to him, it looked as if he wasn't playing at all." He thought the ease of Jimi's guitar playing could be repeated all day without strain. "Most guitar players have so much tension in their arms they hunch over," observed Tork, "but the easier you are—and Jimi was extraordinarily easy with it—the wider your range of expression."[16]

Opening for a teen sensation felt like backsliding, and Jimi had little enthusiasm for the tour. Chandler convinced the promoters to drop the Experience after only eight shows and fabricated a press release claiming the Daughters of the American Revolution complained that his show was "too erotic." The DAR probably weren't Hendrix fans, but getting kicked off a tour for being too erotic excited the public. The band returned to New York, where they got a last-minute booking at the Café Au Go Go. Jimi was now a star, and though the hall was small, there were lines around the block. He also tracked down Charles Otis and paid back the $40 he'd borrowed before leaving for England.

Several of the top clubs in Manhattan had closed their doors so the owners could attend the Monterey Pop Festival, and they returned with reports of Jimi's outrageous sound and style. The size and makeup of his band had changed since leaving the Village, but the powerful guitar playing was the same and so were the visual tricks. Hungry and searching for a break a year ago, great success was now upon him. When he visited the loft of Buzzy Linhart, he was treated like a celebrity. "We had a literal ton of red Lebanese hash that someone had flown in on a private plane," said Linhart. "Jimmy would come by all the time, as would Bob Dylan, Roger McGuinn, David Crosby, and others."[17] Jimi wanted to meet Dylan, who he always seemed to miss, and he liked to get stoned. Jam sessions often ensued. He played for eight hours on acid one night, wowing the other musicians with his stamina. However, when he went to Harlem it was much harder to connect.

"We didn't realize he had become successful," observed Tunde Ra Aleem, and so Jimi brought along a copy of *Are You Experienced?* for them to hear. The Aleems arranged for Jimi to meet influential black disc jockey Frankie Crocker, hoping the connection might give Jimi airplay on black radio, but Crocker hated the record and Jimi left the meeting downcast.

When he accompanied the Aleems to Small's Paradise, an old stomping ground, hoping to return as a hero, he was taunted instead. The fabulous mod clothes he wore sharply contrasted African American dress styles. "Jimi was wearing this giant witch hat," said Tunde Ra. "Everyone else was wearing little hats called 'stingy brims.' And he was wearing these giant bell-bottoms; everyone else had on tight-legged pants. Whatever he wore he had more. He had more hair, more pants, he had more of everything."[18]

Jimi still didn't fit in with Harlem, but the Village remained a groovy place where he spent evenings going from club to club with friends. He played with John Hammond at the Gaslight in the Village on two nights, bringing Eric Clapton along. Chandler held a press party at the Café Wha?, where he had "discovered" Jimi one year earlier, and at Steve Paul's Scene, the Experience blew an L.A. band called the Seeds off the stage.

Jimi also called up his old girlfriend, Faye Pridgon, and gave her some acid. While he swallowed two tabs, Faye and a dude swallowed a half. "I knew Jimi could take more of anything than we could," said Faye, "because he was already abnormal, so whatever he took just brought him back around to normal. So we knew if he could take a gallon, then we'd better take a pint."[19]

Jimi was drinking a lot, too. "At first," said Chas Chandler, "he never drank much—three whiskies and he was happy."[20] Now with the pressures of stardom, there were signs of strain and confusion as Chandler watched the alcohol intake accelerate.

Jimi, unable to put people from the past away, met with Curtis Knight and played him a demo from *Axis*. They wanted to go to dinner, but Jimi had no money. Knight suggested he borrow from Ed Chalpin, whom he had signed a contract with for a one-dollar advance in 1965. They dropped by Chalpin's apartment at two in the morning, woke him up, and the three went out to dinner. When Jimi became famous in England, Chalpin brought a court case that sought to halt any future recordings by the Experience, and yet Hendrix welcomed him as an old friend and appeared to hold no bitterness. Chalpin loaned Jimi a small amount of money and after the dinner, in a complete lapse of judgment, Jimi went into the studio in the middle of the night and cut six more tracks for Chalpin. Jimi's constant desire to play music canceled out other considerations, especially pertaining to business. On these recordings, he's heard warning Chalpin, "You can't, you know . . . put my name on the thing. . . . You can't use my name for any of that stuff." But Chalpin's spin was, "He loved how I recorded him in 1965 and he came back in 1967."[21] Chalpin released the session under Jimi's name, further complicating their legal issues. Unbelievably, as if in a trance, Jimi returned to do another session with Chalpin and Knight.

On August 21, the Experience flew back to London, where they had feature stories in two major newspapers and appeared on several television shows to promote their most recent single, "Burning of the Midnight Lamp." Hendrix, Kathy Etchingham, Chandler, and Chandler's girlfriend moved into a flat on Upper Berkeley Street. Jimi was a star, but Chandler was his boss and served as artistic director, mentor, friend, and employer. "They would talk about science fiction and they would play Risk together," recalled Eddie Kramer. "When Jimi walked into the studio, he trusted Chas to help him realize his dream." But, typical of a manager and temperamental artist, they often fought in the studio.

"Jimi was exerting his power," recalled road manager Neville Chesters. "By then, he knew what he wanted and what he wanted it to sound like. Chas liked songs to be tight and short. Jimi wanted the songs to extend and stretch out."[22] Now that success had found him, Jimi was taking more command.

In America, the reviews of *Are You Experienced?* were mostly positive, particularly in the underground press which recognized his revolutionary style, but some were bad. "The disc itself is a nightmare show with lust and misery," wrote the *New York Times*. The *Times* thought even less of the album cover, suggesting it "reinforced the degeneracy theme with the three sneering out from beneath their bouffant hairdos, looking like surreal hermaphrodites."[23] However, for the younger generation of Americans, outraged mainstream newspaper writers enhanced the value of a rock musician.

Far more important was the FM radio, where *Are You Experienced?* became one of the first staples. The album benefited from the cover photograph the *Times* had called degenerate. Jimi was photogenic and handsome, and the psychedelic image of this photograph gave a fantastic appearance to the band, suggesting that within the album a hallucinogenic world awaited. The combination of the cover and the groundbreaking music inside propelled the album to become one of the fastest sellers in the Reprise label's history, outselling Frank Sinatra, who Jimi had worshiped as a boy in Seattle.

Their return to England started badly. On August 27, when the Experience left the stage of the Saville Theatre to thunderous applause, they were told in their dressing room that Brian Epstein, the show's promoter, had died of an overdose of barbiturates and the second show was canceled. There was a scattering of concert dates, mostly in the north, and some were poorly attended. The office was paying many personal expenses of the band members and their girlfriends, and though money was coming in, the bills were larger than the income. "I had to pay the rent for their flats," recalled office manager Trixie Sullivan, "and they took taxis and limousines everywhere and charged them to the company."[24] To fill the coffers, the band made a short tour of Europe in September 1967 where, in Stockholm, Sweden, sixteen thousand tickets were sold. Back in London, Chandler took his three musicians into a studio to continue work on the next album.

Noel Redding remembers the sessions at Olympic Studio as exercises in great frustration. "We'd go in and learn a song. Jimi would tell us what he needed. We'd do about four bass tracks, then drums and vocals and rhythm guitar, and when it got to the thirty-sixth guitar overdub, I would lay down in the studio and go to sleep."[25]

Chandler remembered how Jimi "would split for a couple of days, and I realized he was on acid. At that time everybody thought it would sort out their problems. I took it eight times and was spaced out for eighteen months. Halfway through *Axis: Bold as Love*, he was dropping it every day. I told him he would have to be straight some of the time. At first I thought it would give him a new slant to his lyrics, but he'd lose his temper. . . . There were so many people hanging around him, he couldn't be himself. We had an argument about it and he said, 'Okay, no more.' Then someone would turn up at the studio with a bag of goodies and pour some more down his throat."[26]

By the end of October, the resulting album, *Axis: Bold as Love*, was finished and ready for release. It was self-indulgent, as had been *Sgt. Pepper's Lonely Hearts Club Band*, and began with the voice of Chas Chandler portraying an announcer on a radio station introducing an interviewee. The announcer's voice sputtered just as Jimi flew into his electric guitar with raucous feedback, electronic whining, and unidentifiable noise effects serving as an introduction to the first song, which casts Jimi in the role of an extraterrestrial space traveler who is astounded by and unable to comprehend the stench of a planet that seems to be burning.

When asked about the title song, "Axis: Bold as Love," Jimi explained the images that attracted him and the images he wished to project: "The axis on the earth turns around and changes the face of the world, and completely different civilizations come back or another age comes about. In other words, it changes the face of the earth and it only takes about one-fourth of a day. Well, the same with love. If a cat falls in love or a girl falls in love, it might change his whole complete scene."[27]

What Jimi had done was musically significant. The principal stylistic features of black soul music remained, the characteristic vocal and instrumental phrases, but the lyrics were basically "white." At first, Jimi disliked the Hindu-inspired design of the quasi-religious-looking art on the cover, "I'm not that kind of Indian," he said, but grew to appreciate the cover because it fit the trippy nature of the music inside. *Axis* was a more mature album that reflected a more cohesive sound by the group.

"Science fiction rock and roll" is how Jimi once described his music scene, and on this album the songs sound extraterrestrial and dreamy. In the studio, Jimi experimented with Mayer's many effect boxes, with panning and with stereo phrasing. "There was nothing that we wouldn't do, or that we wouldn't try for him," recalled Eddie Kramer. "The rules were there were no rules."[28]

Jimi still struggled with singing. Each song began with the band cutting instrumental tracks; vocals were added later. When Jimi sang, he insisted all groupies and hangers-on milling about had to leave the studio. He wasn't always pleased with his voice, muttering, "I can't sing a song," at the end of "Spanish Castle Magic," but he was fearless on the guitar parts like the delicate work required on "Little Wing."[29]

When *Axis: Bold as Love* was released in the UK on December 1, 1967, the Experience was on tour with Pink Floyd, the Move, and Nice that began in London's Royal Albert Hall, billed as "the Alchemical Wedding" because of the outlandish drug-soaked sound of the bands. Hugh Nolan wrote in *Disc* that Jimi's "hysterically exciting act provides what must be the most crashing, soulful, thrilling finale any pop bill could hope for—short of, perhaps, the Beatles." It was a typically brutal pace for the Experience, featuring two performances a night on a road trip that had them playing thirty-two shows in twenty-two days, but the reviews of the new album were glowing.

"A hit record with no doubts," wrote *Record Mirror.* "It's too much," raved *Melody Maker* in a review that was more like an endorsement of a new religion. "Amaze your ears, boggle your mind, flip your ears, do what you want, but please get into Hendrix like you never have before."[30]

Jimi's own explanation was "We tried to get most of the freaky tracks right into another dimension so you get that sky effect, like they're coming down out of the heavens."[31]

Fatigue and exhaustion were taking a toll. "I'd like to take a six-month break and go to a school of music," Jimi told *Melody Maker*. "I'm tired of trying to write stuff and finding I can't. I want to write mythology stories set to music based on a planetary thing."[32] He also suggested he wanted to supplement Mitch and Noel with other musicians.

To cope with their brutal schedule, the band had increased their drug usage, taking uppers and downers daily to go to sleep or wake up. Noel

Redding would write that drugs became a game of "I can take more than you."[33] Jimi had greater tolerance than anyone else in the band and crew and would take four tabs if Noel took two. Their reputation as drug users attracted more dealers and groupies who brought more drugs into their dressing rooms.

Money earned from Jimi's records and tours began flowing into the Bahamas, where dozens of banks in the capital city of Nassau served as tax havens for foreign investors. Mike Jeffery was paying huge sums into Yameta that had an account with the Nassau branch of the Bank of Nova Scotia. Designed to sidestep the exorbitant British income tax Jeffery would have had to pay on American earnings, Jeffery had formed and incorporated the company through a London attorney for the alleged purpose of finding, developing, and recording musical talent. This way, Jeffery could pay Yameta for these services and declare those sums as deductible business expenses, and because he owned the company, he could fly to Nassau, withdraw the money from the Bank of Nova Scotia, and put it in his pocket tax-free. He told his clients, first Eric Burdon and the Animals (all of whom remarked that when they wanted their money it wasn't there) and then Jimi, Noel, and Mitch, that their money would be safe and gather interest until they were old, retired, or needed it. Jimi took Jeffery at his word, although it was never made clear how the guitarist, as an American citizen, could benefit from a British tax haven. Jimi, unaware of any fraud perpetrated by Jeffery, focused his attention on his music and his rapidly accelerating success. On January 2, 1968, he was named the number-one musician in *Melody Maker, Disc,* and *Music Echo* polls.

They were soon on the road again with a tour of Scandinavia. On their first day in Sweden, "We all got rotten drunk," remembered Redding, and he and Jimi got into a fight.[34]

"I asked him what happened," said Chandler, "but he didn't know himself, and I never really got the full story. But I think Noel hit Jimi and Jimi laid out two cops and tried to jump out the window."

A newspaper quoted Gothenburg police as saying they arrested Jimi "after three of his colleagues sat on him to calm him down."[35] Jimi was taken to jail, where he spent the night, and charged with drunkenness. A photograph of him flanked by two policemen appeared in newspapers around the world the next day. Later, on January 12, following uneventful concerts in Copenhagen and Stockholm, he appeared in a Gothenburg court, where, in addition to paying for damages to the hotel, he was fined an amount equal to all his Swedish earnings.

Jimi was becoming a superstar in America, where his music was attracting a young, maturing audience of increased affluence. With the growth of FM radio stations playing album tracks rather than singles, causing long-playing records to sell in much greater numbers, *Are You Experienced?* was a smash, going to number five on *Billboard*. Another sign of Jimi's success was the increasing number of opportunists circling the Experience, the most notable being Curtis Knight and Ed Chalpin. Soon after Jimi's first album began selling for Reprise, Chalpin sold thirty tracks to Capital Records, which, in November, then rushed a Hendrix album of its own to the marketplace. The recordings showed early elements of the style Jimi later developed, but they were so badly recorded that the album's producer, Nick Venet, publicly admitted that only eight of the tracks were salvageable and even those had to be remixed. This record was an embarrassment to Jimi as a musician.

Except for Chalpin, Jimi's career became more carefully planned and executed. Since record sales rose following personal appearances, Chandler and Jeffery were determined not to repeat the mistake of the previous year when Jimi left the U.S. on the eve of an album's release. On a coming tour, they planned a media blitz with interviews everywhere. He went along with a concentrated effort from his London and New York publicists to get him into every magazine and newspaper on the European and North American continents. Their British publicist was a dapper, middle-aged man named Leslie Perrin, whose clients included the Rolling Stones. "Jimi Hendrix has put the fizz back in showbiz with his way-out brand of explosive showmanship," Perrin wrote in a release. "No one sleeps when the Jimi Hendrix Experience is on and no one wants to."[36] The release was sent to American publicist Michael Goldstein and then to everyone from radio disc jockeys to the editors of *Life* and *Vogue*. *Are You Experienced?* sold over two million copies, and advance orders for the second LP, *Axis: Bold as Love*, were climbing, too. When Mo Ostin had seen Jimi at Monterey, his face turned ashen; now his cheeks were flushed as profit soared.

At the end of January 1968, the Experience crossed the Atlantic for their first large-scale tour of the United States. Boarding the big BOAC jet liner from London's Heathrow Airport along with thirty other musicians with combined entourages of one hundred managers, girlfriends, and equipment handlers, Jimi sat resplendent in black bell-bottom pants, black boots, and a full-length black cape embroidered on the back with two doves in flight and lined with sky-blue silk. He wore a black bolero hat adorned with a purple plume. He had dropped acid before boarding, and, once in the air, he aimed an 8mm movie camera out the window at the fluffy clouds below. He had no idea how big he had become in America. When he had left New York six months before, his career had begun to accelerate but he had no way of knowing how fast, nor, until he walked onto the Fillmore Stage in San Francisco on February 1, how anxiously his return was awaited.

The reviews of *Axis* were mixed in America. *Rolling Stone* wrote, "Jimi sounded like a junk heap," and his songs were "basically a bore." Other reviews were better, but while most critics called Jimi "one of rock's greatest guitarists," his overall artistry and skill as a songwriter were hardly mentioned at all.

To kick off the tour, publicist Michael Goldstein included the Animals and Soft Machine in a press conference in New York City. A dozen magazines and radio stations were there. Michael Rosenbaum of *Crawdaddy* gave Jimi the space to expound. Jimi spoke using words and phrases like "groovy" and "you know" and "cool." When asked about the song "Bold as Love," he said certain colors matched certain emotions and he sought to play those colors. He said there were only three songs on *Axis* that he liked ("Bold as Love," "Little Wing," and "Little Miss Lover") and threatened, "Our next LP is going to be exactly the way we want it or else."[37] Impromptu remarks publicists wanted curtailed, these were not the words of an artist promoting a new record.

The tour started in San Francisco with shows at the Fillmore and Winterland, where Jimi was preceded by the blues band of Albert King, whose quiet, unhurried style of bending notes had done much to influence hundreds of guitarists. John Mayall, a British musician whose band the Bluesbreakers had, over the years, included such sidemen as Eric Clapton, Mick Fleetwood, and John McVie (founders of Fleetwood

Mac), also played. These bands were received with respectful but subdued applause, but the audience belonged to Hendrix.

There was a hush in the large, old ballroom as the Experience's equipment was moved into place. The room went dark as two thousand painted youths shuffled and murmured expectantly. The crowd pressed forward as Jimi, Noel, and Mitch took their places before twelve stacks of Marshall amplifiers with forty-eight speaker cabinets. There was a low hum and then a subtle whine. Building slowly, a single note from the cosmos, scaling, screaming now, and then falling into a rumbling, ear-popping crash—the sound of football field-sized sheets of steel falling from the tops of cliffs. The lights came on, revealing Jimi in his black and sky-blue cape, his white Stratocaster guitar held like a machine gun. "Comin' to gitcha, baby!" he shouted, and then the crowd began to dance.[38]

The next day Jimi met with young editor Jann Wenner and photographer Baron Wolman, giving them enough material for a flattering two-page spread in *Rolling Stone*, the national "underground" newspaper. In the interview, Jimi tried to explain what he felt when he played: "not depression, but that loneliness and that frustration and the yearning for something. Like something is reaching out."[39]

Bill Graham thought Jimi's appeal across racial lines was unique: "After Otis [Redding] he was the first black sex symbol in White America."[40] Jimi was drawing a growing number of female fans as much attracted by his sexual charisma as his guitar skill, but he was also being criticized when he didn't play the guitar with his teeth or set his guitar on fire. This bothered Jimi. "They want me to be a monkey on the stage," he told his friends.[41]

Changing the public image to more closely match the private one is always risky in the entertainment business and Jimi began to wish he'd never heard of pouring lighter fluid on guitars. A year earlier, Jeff Beck of the Yardbirds had warned of this problem in an interview with *New Musical Express*: "Jimi's only trouble will come about when he wants to get off the nail he has hung himself on. The public will want something different, and Jimi has so established himself in one bag that he'll find it difficult to get anyone to accept him in another."[42]

Album cover for *Axis Bold as Love*

Backstage with Michelle and Mama Cass

Jimi performing in Monterey

Monterey Pop poster

Cheap Thrills on the Road of Sameness

When on tour, most of Jimi's time offstage was spent together with the band in the backseat of a rented station wagon. On the first U.S. tour of '68, the Experience played forty-nine cities in fifty-one days, with road manager Neville Chesters driving about 18,000 miles, which was the first of three tours they undertook that year. Needing to make more money, Jeffery felt they couldn't turn down any dates, even if a last-minute booking required them to travel all night. They often traveled a long distance to one show and would have to backtrack for the next one. For the '68 Seattle show, the band flew from Santa Barbara to Seattle for a show on February 12 and then back to Los Angeles the next morning.

Not since his furlough from boot camp six years before had Jimi been in Seattle. He had left facing a prison term; now he returned as a famous musician playing to a sold-out show and was the last person off the plane when they landed. He hadn't seen his family in years. Leon, who had grown into a handsome twenty-year-old street hustler working out of a downtown pool hall, was surprised at his brother's appearance. "He had on this giant hat and a red velvet shirt. He had all this hair and he looked just wild."[1] Al, who had shaved off his moustache and was wearing a tie for one of the few times in his life, looked much older. Marriage appeared to have softened Al, and Jimi liked his new stepmother, June. Their reunion was warm. Al put his arm around Jimi and said, "Welcome home, son."[2]

Promoter Pat O'Day had asked if Jimi wanted to do anything special; Jimi said he wanted to play a free show for the students at Garfield High

School. O'Day tried to set that up. Promised a ceremonial key to the city, Jimi told the *Sunday Mirror*, "The only keys I expected to see in that town were of the jailhouse."[3]

The band went to their hotel while Jimi spent the afternoon with family, old friends, and neighbors at his father's house, telling stories of Swingin' London. "He looked so grown up," recalled Aunt Delores, who came by to see him, "he was like a hippie." Leon informed Jimi that many old friends from the neighborhood were now serving in Vietnam.

As the time for the concert neared, he asked Ernestine Benson to help curl his hair. "The problem with my life today," he admitted to her in a rare confession, "is that I have to take a pill to sleep, and a pill to perform."

When he complained of touring, she thought he might weep, and advised him, "You got to take some time off."[4] Ernestine felt he seemed just as lost as the poor, motherless child she had once watched over.

At the Seattle Center Arena that night, "There were maybe eight thousand or nine thousand there," remembered Leon. "Most of them looked like businessmen, and they didn't seem to get it. There were a lot of black people and they weren't into that kind of show, that kind of music."[5]

The band played a nine-song set with the greatest reaction coming on "Foxy Lady" and "Purple Haze." Reviewing the show for the *Helix*, Tom Robbins called Jimi "a black dwarf cowboy Oscar Wilde in Egyptian drag . . . with a voice like raspberry preserves—thick and sweet." Still, he liked his showmanship. "Despite the shallowness of much of his sound, Hendrix is a hotly exciting performer. What he lacks in content he makes up in style. He is, in fact, a master stylist; an outrageous exponent of high black showmanship."[6] Most of the audience applauded him simply for walking on stage as a hometown boy who had made good. Jimi's family sat in the front row, putting them directly before the speakers. Al watched some of it with his fingers in his ears.

Partying after the show in rooms at the Olympic Hotel, Jimi ordered steak from room service and insisted his family do the same. He gave Leon fifty dollars and told Al that if he needed anything to let him know. Around midnight, his manager reminded him that he was scheduled to appear at Garfield High at eight the next morning. Disregarding sleep, he returned to Al's, played Monopoly, and drank Al's bourbon with Leon.

Jimi was disappointed that Leon was a street hustler and wanted him to straighten out, but he knew Leon's childhood had been as rough as his own but without a wonderful obsession like music. At daylight, journalist Patrick McDonald arrived to take Jimi to Garfield High, where Pat O'Day met them with an empty limousine.

Pat was surprised to see Jimi wearing the clothes from the night before. "He was not capable, or able, to play, or really to speak," observed Garfield principal Frank Fidler, who had known Jimi since junior high. They abandoned the idea of a performance in favor of just speaking and answering questions from the students. The assembly was held in the 1,200-seat Garfield gymnasium. O'Day introduced Jimi as a former Garfield Bulldog who had gone on to international fame.

"Many obviously had no idea who Jimi was," said Peter Riches, who photographed the event. Some thought his dress was wild and inappropriate.

There was heckling, and some of the hecklers were African American students who hadn't heard Jimi's music, which was not played on black radio even in Seattle. "Garfield was highly politicized, and the Black Power movement was blooming," recalled student Vickie Heater. "To have this strange, hippie musician come along bothered kids."[7]

Hungover, nervous, and hardly able to speak, Jimi lost his bearing. From the stage, he mumbled, "I've been here and there and everywhere and it's all working." He stopped and paused, then declared he had written "Purple Haze" for Garfield, whose colors were purple and white. The audience began to whistle.

O'Day took the mic and encouraged questions. One boy raised his hand. "How long have you been gone from Garfield?"

Jimi appeared stymied and said, "Oh, about two thousand years."

Another asked, "How do you write a song?"

Jimi looked at the floor again. "Right now," he said, "I'm going to say goodbye to you and go out the door and get into my limousine and go to the airport. And when I get out the door, the assembly will be over and the bell will ring. And when I hear that bell ring, I'll write a song. Thank you very much."[8]

The assembly lasted five minutes. There was some booing at his departure.

When the students returned to class, Jimi was nowhere to be seen. O'Day and McDonald searched the limousine and the gym but couldn't find him. Then McDonald, spotting him hunched over alone in the coach's office, asked if he was okay. "Yeah," replied Jimi. "I just can't face an audience without my guitar. I don't feel well."

Climbing into the limo, Jimi apologized for his behavior at the assembly. "It was so strange how bad the whole thing turned out," said O'Day. "It had all been his idea. He had wanted so badly to go back to the school he had gone to. It was supposed to have been a homecoming. When he got there, he was scared shitless."[9] His high school years had been too difficult to contemplate, and trying to return as a hero turned into a bitter, disappointing spectacle.

Jimi left Seattle physically and emotionally drained, but America had embraced him and he had to keep working. *Axis: Bold as Love* had entered the *Billboard* album chart and quickly cracked the top twenty. The concerts in Los Angeles were sold out, and in Dallas, expecting to make about $7,000, Chandler and Jeffery walked away with almost four times that amount.

Along the way, many young women offered themselves to Jimi. "The groupie scene developed around Jimi so quickly," said Pat Costello, a publicist employed by Goldstein, "because he satisfied so many fantasies."[10] *Rolling Stone* devoted an entire issue to the subject of groupies, giving two pages to girls known as the "Plaster Casters," illustrated with photographs of the girls and their handiwork, which was making plaster casts of rock stars' genitalia. Word spread quickly about them.

On February 25, the Experience flew into Chicago for two sold-out shows at the Civic Opera House. After the matinee, driving back to their hotel along North Michigan Avenue in a limousine, a car pulled up next to them and a young woman leaned out the window pointing to words on her briefcase that read "Plaster Casters of Chicago." Jimi motioned them to follow.

At the Chicago Hilton, standing on the sidewalk, the three young women ran up to them excitedly. "We want to plaster cast your Hampton Wick," one of them announced.[11] The younger one was carrying a black attaché case. "We have all the equipment here. It won't hurt and it'll only take a few minutes of your time."

"Oh, yeah," replied Jimi. "I heard about you. Come up to the room."[12] Jimi agreed to be the first subject, Noel volunteered to go second, and Mitch politely declined.

Upstairs in his suite, Jimi peeled off his skin-tight bolero pants while the girls set up their equipment. In the bathroom, Cynthia, the leader of the group, mixed the dental plaster used in the castings, while in the other room, one of the girls orally stimulated their subject. "We were not prepared for the size of it," Cynthia wrote later about Jimi's member. Once aroused, they put a vase filled with plaster around his penis.

The process "was more clinical than erotic," Noel said. The room was silent during the molding.

"It wasn't very sexy, really," Cynthia recalled.

Jimi began bumping and grinding the mold for self-stimulation. Tour manager Gerry Stickells opened the door, and, so used to wild behavior on the tour, didn't raise an eyebrow. "Just, ah, let me know when you're ready," was all he said.

A few minutes later the vase was removed, leaving a perfect mold. Jimi inquired about Cynthia's plans for the casts. "I told him I wanted to put them on display," she said. "And he was cool with that."[13]

The story of Jimi's plaster "rig" was making media rounds. At a small gathering of music and publishing people, Ellen Sander, who wrote about rock music for the *Saturday Review*, had the Plaster Casters's casts on display. "There were six or eight of the casts, most of them rather small and shrunken," remembered Larry Dietz, editor of *Cheetah* magazine. "That is, they seemed so because of Hendrix's, which was eight or nine inches long and really big around. I went over at one point and actually touched it. There was absolute silence in the room. I mean, it was impressive."[14]

The sameness of life on the road was a drain on inspiration. Jimi's diary entries were usually "S.O.S." meaning "same old shit." But some days stood out. In Ottawa, Ontario, the Experience played two shows at the 2,300-seat Capitol Theatre. Joni Mitchell, who Jimi had met in the Village, was playing in a club down the street. "Went down to the little club to see Joni," he wrote in his diary, "Fantastic girl with heaven words. We all go to party."[15]

On the stage, Hendrix referred to the Vietnam War: "Instead of all that action happening over there, why doesn't everyone just come on home, and instead of M16 machine guns, hand grenades, and tanks on their backs, why don't they come back with feedback guitars on their backs? That's better than guns."[16]

The next day he wrote in his diary: "We left Ottawa City today. I kissed Joni goodbye, slept in the car for a while . . . in Rochester . . . thugs follow us. They probably were scared, couldn't figure us out: Me with my Mexican hat and Mexican moustache, Mitch with his fairy-tale jacket, and Noel with his leopard band hat and glasses and hair and accent."[17]

In March, on the night before the concert in Cleveland, Joe Esterhaus, a Hungarian-American journalist, convinced Jimi to jam at a local club. Leonard Nimoy was present. Jimi showed Nimoy the buttons on his hat that read "Make Love Not War," "Peace at any price," "LBJ is a Bag," and "Stoned," and, later that night, hooked up with a Cleveland groupie. "After a while, you remember the towns you've been in by the chicks," Jimi told a reporter, "except that lately I've been confusing the chicks and the towns."[18]

The band played two shows at Cleveland's Public Music Hall. After the early show, Jimi took a cab to Blaushild's Chevrolet, where he peeled off $8,000 in cash and bought a new 1968 Corvette Stringray. Jimi was nearsighted and had no driver's license, nor a garage or residence other than his flat in London, but he convinced a salesperson to drive the car to New York City, where he could have it stored, and then took a cab to the concert hall to play the second show.

On stage, as he was preparing to light his guitar on fire, a bomb threat halted the concert. No bomb was found, so he returned to the stage and announced, "Nobody but Jimi burns a house down," and the band tore through the rest of the set. Spending eight grand was remarkable, but Jimi, imagining each day might be his last as he had when he lived pennilessly, quickly embraced a life of excess. In his diary that night, he wrote "S.O.S."

Meanwhile, Ed Chalpin, with a piece of paper claiming Jimi's work, released albums from "bits of tape they used from a jam session," Jimi told *Rolling Stone*. "Capitol [Records] never told us that they were going to release that crap."[19] In England the high court ordered Decca Records not to release the controversial Hendrix/Knight *Get that Feeling* album.

A lawsuit declared that Jimi was merely a member of the group backing Curtis at the session when the album was cut, but that the record jacket gave the impression that Jimi was the leader. However, in New York, a district court judge refused to grant an injunction that would have restrained Capitol Records from selling or distributing the album. Because of Jimi's popularity, *Get That Feeling* sold nearly 100,000 copies of which Jimi received no earnings. The bandits took this court decision as a green light to produce and distribute as many more records as they could, all drawn from the early tapes. Some of the individual tracks were excellent, but the albums, as a whole, were not.

Martin Luther King Jr. was assassinated in Memphis on April 5, 1968. The next day, two shows were scheduled for the Experience in the three-thousand-seat Newark Symphony Hall. Dr. King's message of racial unity and nonviolence had resonated deeply with Jimi, who preferred to avoid direct confrontation in any area of life. "When the power of love overcomes the love of power," Hendrix once said, "the world will know peace."[20] At the first concert only about four hundred people were there. Jimi told them, "This number is for a friend of mine,"[21] and broke into a long, mournful blues instrumental in honor of Dr. King that moved some of the audience to tears. An hour into the show Jimi put down his guitar and walked off the stage. Fearing riots, the police canceled the second show. On the week that followed, Jimi privately sent $5,000 to a memorial fund in Dr. King's honor.

America's military presence in Vietnam, a buildup that had started within two years of Jimi's discharge from the army, had reached almost 500,000 soldiers, many of them poor and black like Jimi. That spring, his songs began to reflect a social consciousness. In "House Burning Down," he urged people to "learn instead of burn," a sentiment of Dr. King.

He planned and worked on songs for his third album, *Electric Ladyland*, at the Record Plant recording studio in New York in April and early May. Even after a full eight hours of recording, Jimi would jam at clubs at night. Living at the Warwick Hotel, he used his room as an informal studio to cut demos of songs. After throwing a wild party for guitarist Mike Bloomfield, with Truman Capote in attendance, the Warwick kicked him out and he moved to the Drake on Fifty-Sixth Street, which put him within a five-minute taxi ride to one of his favorite haunts: Steve

Paul's Scene on Forty-Sixth Street between Eighth and Ninth Avenues. If Jimi wasn't at the nearby Record Plant, he was at the Scene.

The Scene was dark and crowded every night, and when Jimi sidled in at about midnight, usually Devon Wilson or Jenni Dean, another no-nonsense super-groupie of mixed Jewish and Negro ancestry, were there along with many others. Some of the chicks would prepare themselves in the bathroom for half an hour before coming to the table, where Jimi would turn and say, "Hi, my name is Jimi, who are you?' These were the ones Jimi took to his hotel room for one-nighters.

"Everywhere he turned he was getting 'young tender ones,' as he used to call them," remembered Curtis Knight, who said Jimi told him that many times he would be "falling asleep from some all-night orgy and I would hear a gentle knock on my door. I'd stagger to the door naked and peep out and there would be some sexy, cute little thing standing there and she would ask if she could come in, and most of the time I'd say yes."[22]

Jimi was also spending money as fast as it poured in. Bills from the Record Plant came to $5,000 a week. His hotel rooms, chauffeurs, and generosity cost even more. "Money was no object to him. He had wads of money and he just gave it away to strangers," remembered Buddy Miles, who was with Jimi in New York.

Michael Goldstein said, "Hendrix spent money like a sieve. It ran through his fingers. . . . He bought a tremendous amount of clothes and then left them all over New York in various girls' apartments. He bought a house for his parents. And on the road it was even worse." In Los Angeles they stayed at the most expensive bungalow in the Beverly Hills Hotel, ordering room service. "I mean," Goldstein said, "those guys knew how to use room service."[23]

There was pressure to finish the next studio album, which was coming along slowly. Jimi didn't think the first two albums had captured the sound he wanted, and he began to insist on multiple takes on every song and was no longer willing to listen much to Chandler or the rest of the band. "Jimi had attempted to take over," Noel Redding recalled. "The pressure from the public to create something even more brilliant each time, while basically expecting us to stay the same, was crushing."[24] Jimi became increasingly unhappy with Noel's bass playing and began insisting that he, himself, play all the bass parts as well as lead guitar. Noel said that Jimi made the sessions impossible. "He was always trying to do it his way. There were times when I would go to a club between sessions, pull a chick, come back, and he was still tuning his guitar. Oh, hours it took!"[25]

Chas Chandler was growing disillusioned, too. "There was a dreadful atmosphere in the studio, which was full of hangers-on . . . nobody was ready to compromise anymore. All I was doing was sitting there collecting a percentage [as producer]."[26] The sessions were very different from the tightly controlled productions Chandler had run for the first album; the strong work ethic that had carried the band through their early records was replaced by a laid-back, jam-heavy approach to recording. The spontaneity fit Jimi's evolving muse, but Chandler began to retreat from his role as producer.

In early May, Noel stormed out of a session and missed the recording of "Voodoo Child." This session sprang from a jam at the Scene Club earlier in the night. When the club closed, "Jimi invited everyone back to the studio," recalled Jack Casady of Jefferson Airplane. "There were at least twenty people and most of them didn't belong there."[27] The formal recording for the day started at about 7:30 A.M. with a lineup of Jimi on guitar, Mitch Mitchell on drums, Traffic's Steve Winwood on organ, and Jack Casady on bass. The song took only three takes, but they were lengthy. The released version was fifteen minutes: Jimi's longest official studio cut. The recording sessions at the Record Plant kept going on and on. It was to be Jimi's first double album and gave him the room to stretch musically and break away from the two- to three-minute single format.

Negotiations were concluded with the bothersome Ed Chalpin and PPX Enterprises. The lawyers for Hendrix had lost their fight. What happened was unfair but not illegal. Chalpin was given a 2% "override" on Jimi's first three albums and complete rights to Jimi's fourth with a guarantee of $200,000. He also kept the rights to market the tapes from the sessions with Curtis Knight. In exchange Chalpin turned over the 1965 agreement, which had only four months remaining, and agreed to drop all further claims against Jimi in the U.S. It was a resounding victory for Chalpin, eventually paying him more than a million dollars, and a crushing defeat for Jimi. When told that the awful tapes from his past would continue to haunt him, he felt betrayed, and when told he owed Chalpin another album, he was furious. (In his next album for Reprise he included a song recorded in England the previous year, a cover of Bob Dylan's "All Along the Watchtower," taking it into the Record Plant to remix it, in which Dylan castigates businessmen who don't understand him but gleefully run off with all the profits they can make.)

Besides the "settlement agreement" with Chalpin, the lawyers also negotiated a new recording contract that increased Jimi's royalty rates to 5% and eliminated payments to Yameta, the trust company that had been receiving his royalties. In return, Jimi promised to deliver two albums and four singles each year for four years—a standard demand of musicians at this time. Yameta was paid well for this: Reprise had to pay Yameta $250,000 in cash with additional payments of $50,000 for the next four years. Reprise president Mo Ostin said, "Value is value, even if you're getting screwed."[28] Jimi turned the pages of the new contract, pretending to read them, but the convoluted language of lawyers never made much sense to him. He did not see the words and affixed his hasty, sprawling signature, signing the contract as he signed most papers put in front of him—without really knowing much about it.

Jimi, whose entire life revolved around music, was adrift without a guitar, or a concert stage, or jamming at clubs, or recording in a studio. When a performance was rained out in Miami, Jimi organized a jam in the hotel bar that included Frank Zappa, Arthur Brown, and John Lee Hooker. "It was probably the best music I've ever heard in my life," said Trixie Sullivan.[29]

Jimi had to climb through a bathroom window to escape the hotel management because the band, despite earning half a million dollars on the tour, didn't have the money to pay the bill. The Experience commanded as much as $50,000 a night, but there had only been five such nights since February, and so, after headlining at the Fillmore East in New York on May 15, they flew to Europe for a series of five high-paying concerts in Italy and Switzerland. They returned to New York to begin a second tour in the summer.

When concerts were infrequent, Jimi could do whatever he wished however he wanted. No one could predict his daily routine because no one knew where he slept. He had a suite of rooms in an East Side hotel, occasionally moved his guitars and clothes into a motor lodge near the Record Plant, but more often he was with one of his ladies, who sewed and cooked for him, and took drugs and slept with him. He usually woke in the early afternoon, ate something, smoked marijuana, and went shopping or drifted somewhere in a limousine or cab to visit friends. He didn't eat often, keeping a flat, muscled stomach that made him look like he needed a meal. At night he often visited Colony Records, the twenty-four-hour record store on Broadway. Day or night, he liked to browse at Manny's Forty-Eighth Street musical instruments store, where the owner, Henry Goldrich, catered to his whims. "Any new kind of toy or sound effect he bought immediately," Goldrich said. "Whenever he walked in, he was good for fifteen hundred to two thousand dollars."[30]

Most of his evenings were spent at clubs like the Scene or at the Record Plant, where he invited friends to sit in. One visitor was Al Kooper, who had played organ for Dylan's *Blonde on Blonde* album. In the studio, Jimi laid down track after track after track, using songs the way an artist applies layers of paint to canvas to create an effect that requires all the hidden levels below. He always worked with Eddie Kramer, the engineer who was with him in London when he had made his first records. It wasn't easy for Jimi to explain his recording process: "The mystique should remain," he would say, "analyzing it to the point that you want . . . is not a good idea," but Kramer was patient and seemed to understand him.[31] Like many musicians, Jimi was extremely articulate with his instrument but not always so eloquent talking about his music, though he was always ready to try.

"We're making our music in electric church music," he told a writer for New York's *East Village Other*, "a new kind of bible, not like in a hotel, but a bible you carry in your hearts, one that will give you a physical feeling. We try to make our music so loose and hard-hitting, so that it hits your soul hard enough to make it open. It's like shock therapy or a can opener."[32] Slowly the album came together, becoming a musical collage of old-style finger-picking and space-age sound effects, cruel and gritty words spat out at the establishment, and escape from this world and into another. The sessions may have been chaotic, but Jimi remained in control, creating a unifying energy that held sixteen tracks spread over four sides together in much the same way bits and pieces of magazine clippings are held together in a collage by the artist's well-defined vision. Jimi called himself the "producer and director" of the album, which meant it was Jimi's album and his alone.

In the July issue of *Eye* magazine, an article stated, "Hendrix is a master of ceremonies. He saunters on stage, looking like a buccaneer Othello come to Camelot, in velvet and lace and boots of Spanish leather, a Mexican bandit's hat on his head with a feather in the gold chain band, his silk blouse open to the navel, a shiny gold medallion sparkling on his chest, his crotch grimly outlined. He's the black sheep all wrapped up in the golden fleece."[33]

At the end of the month, the Experience began their second U.S. tour in Baton Rouge, Louisiana. Jimi was nervous returning to the Deep South. Stopping for lunch in Shreveport, Redding had to convince him to accompany them into a restaurant where he was the only black man. They were served but received many stares and quickly left. "I didn't believe that was possible, even in Louisiana," remembered Noel.

Pat O'Day promoted many of the concerts and recalled racial tensions being very high at several Southern shows. At one concert, when Jimi walked through the backstage door with a blond on his arm, a police officer, hired to protect him, pulled a gun and screamed, "The nigger has no right to have his hands all over that girl." Two other officers arrived and drew their weapons. Eventually, the police put down their pistols and walked off the job in protest.

O'Day was furious, but Jimi remained calm. "Fifty years ago," he told O'Day, "I couldn't have even walked into this auditorium. And fifty years from now no one is going to care."[34]

There were conflicts all around him. Business affairs were becoming messier. Letters were signed and sent to their booking agents, music publishers, and record companies that all future money should be sent to Jeffery and Chandler and not to Yameta. The accountants were also authorized to pay $75,000 in attorney fees for the Chalpin lawsuit. Chalpin had filed lawsuits against Jimi and his two London-based record companies, Track and Polydor. Instantly, both companies put a hold on all future royalties due the Experience and sued Jimi for getting them into this mess. For this reason, the accountants had the three musicians sign an agreement protecting the accountancy firm from any future legal damages. Chandler had told Jimi he should get a different lawyer than Henry Steingarten, who he shared with Jeffery, because since Jeffery managed Jimi, there was a clear conflict of interest.

Jimi was also fighting with Noel and Mitch. Noel did not like Jimi using Jack Casady as a bassist on the new album, and Mitch didn't like him using Buddy Miles for drums. Both musicians felt threatened. Then, frustrated by their slow progress in the studio, Chandler quit as Jimi's producer and co-manager. Chandler had been the true mastermind who created the Jimi Hendrix Experience and his loss was significant.

"Chas was one of the only people who told Jimi a straight story," observed Kathy Etchingham. "When Jimi lost him, he was then only surrounded by yes men."[35] So, Jeffery, who did not involve himself in creative decisions so long as Jimi was willing to record and tour, became Jimi's sole manager, buying Chandler's interest for $300,000 in cash and a percentage of future earnings.

Both Jeffery and Jimi were spending increasing amounts of time in the United States, where the arenas were large and bands could generate more money touring. "America is where the big money is," Mitch Mitchell told *Melody Maker*. The Experience was making more money, but expenses had also ballooned.

The entire operation seemed about to collapse. "We never even knew how much money we had," observed Trixie. "And the way they all lived, including Mike and Jimi, was 'let's spend it all now.'"[36]

When Jimi heard that the gate for a concert was $10,000, he spent that much on jewelry or clothes without taking into account the cost of putting on the concert or the percentage that went to Jeffery for management fees. Their bills for limousines ran thousands per month. The band's tab at London Speakeasy, where they ate most of their meals, was four thousand dollars a month, and litigation with Ed Chalpin was costing thousands as well.

On August 23, 1968, Jimi's road crew moved his big Marshall amplifiers and boxes of sound-warping gadgetry to New York's Singer Bowl to perform with the Chambers Brothers and Janis Joplin. Jimi and Janis talked and drank together backstage while the Chambers Brothers rocked through a set that included an extended version of their hit "Time." Janis then took the stage and excited the crowd with a torrid performance that lasted an hour and a half. The audience was exhausted when Jimi finally appeared, and he seemed annoyed. "He'd get highly upset on the stage if people wouldn't give him their attention," said Willie Chambers of the Chambers Brothers.

One member of the band remembered, "Between the first act of the evening and the last act before him—Janis—the energy of the audience was totally drained. There was no hope for him to express anything and he left the stage . . . dragging his guitar behind him."[37]

In September, Jimi played a sold-out concert at the 18,000-seat Seattle Center Coliseum. He and Leon were close this time. "I could talk to him," recalled Leon. "I'd dropped acid by then. He said acid was the beginning of the end of the world. He said he couldn't talk to nobody. Nobody understood him."[38] Al, who had wanted to show off his famous son, was infuriated when they arrived late. "The house was still full of people waiting for Jimi to show up," remembered Leon. "My dad was waiting in the doorway holding his belt in his hand. He said, 'You boys go in the room, you're getting a whipping for this.'"[39] Jimi and Leon were incredulous. Neighbors intervened and Al put the belt away but stayed angry the rest of the night. With their next show in Vancouver, Jimi, Al, and Leon, along with seven-year-old Janie, June's daughter whom Al had adopted, piled into the new car Jimi had bought Al and drove up and across the border.

The concert was held at the Pacific Coliseum. Jimi dedicated "Foxy Lady" to his grandmother, who was in attendance. "The way he was picking that guitar," Nora told a reporter, "oh, my gracious, I don't see how he could stand all that noise."[40] While in Vancouver he met with his cousins, Faith and Bobby Hendrix, his Aunt Pearl, and her young son, Henri Brown.

He turned to Pearl as he would to a mother and complained about his hectic schedule. "Jimi was already in a funk then," Faith Hendrix recalled. "He was crying to my mom. He wanted out. He didn't want to go back on the road."[41] He told his aunt that he had no choice. There were now thirty people on the payroll, counting on him for their livelihoods: management, crew, and band. He would often make this complaint, but he seemed incapable of ever saying no to work or a tour.

Two days later in Spokane, a critic for the *Spokane Daily Chronicle* wrote, "Hendrix steals the show. . . . He's so physically beautiful and such an accomplished musician that it's impossible to take your eyes off him."[42] After the concert, eighteen-year-old Betsy Morgan was invited to a post-show party at the Davenport Hotel, where she rebuffed Jimi's advances. When he asked, "Does the fact that I'm black have anything to do with it," and she replied, "Of course not, but I just met you," his mood lightened, and he invited her into his room where they tried on clothes and giggled.

"He had this boa, and he would sashay across the room wearing it like an old movie star," remembered Betsy, and when they sat on the couch and talked, "he wanted to know everything about what it was like to go to an all-girl Catholic high school," and he remained nice and gentle. "He was better behaved than the boys I was dating from Gongaza Prep," she said. Though pot was openly smoked at the earlier party, Morgan didn't see Hendrix take a single drink of alcohol or use any drugs. He drank only coffee, holding the cup like a gentleman. She recalled him as seeming "lonely" and with "a deep sadness" despite his outward levity. In the morning, after eight hours of chaste talking, Jimi walked her to the lobby and gave her $20 taxi fare. Her friends wouldn't believe she'd met him, so she asked for his autograph: He wrote, "To Betsy, what a wonderful evening we spent together."[43]

During a tour break in Los Angeles, Jimi rented a mansion in the affluent neighborhood of Benedict Canyon. He slept late and went out every night to play at the clubs on Sunset Boulevard. At the Whiskey A Go Go he met a beautiful waitress named Carmen Borrero, who became a steady companion. Leon, who had recently joined the army, went AWOL to be with his brother in Los Angeles. Backstage at a show, he found "a pile of cocaine, Johnny Walker, weed, and all kinds of shit right out there." Leon, only twenty, but an experienced hustler, took full advantage of the groupies. "Every model in L.A. was after Jimi," he recalled, "and if they couldn't get to Jimi, they'd come to the little brother. And afterward, they'd say, 'you tell your man that was the best pussy you ever had, and tell him about me.'"[44]

The bevy of groupies continued to be a logistical annoyance. "They would show up at all hours of the night," recalled Carmen. Jimi slept with some, but even his legendary sexual appetite wasn't as large as the army of women wanting to bed him.

The music scene in L.A. was awash with cocaine, Seconal, Quaaludes, and heroin. When Jimi mixed drugs with alcohol, madness set in. "Jimi was drinking, and he could not drink," recalled Carmen, and he was jealous of Carmen's friendship with other men. Thinking she was involved with Eric Burdon, he threw an empty bottle at Carmen and hit her above the eye. She was rushed to the hospital with fear of losing her eye.

Eric was shocked to see his normally peaceful friend turn violent. "It was the beginning of a seed of tragedy because he started lashing out at other people," recalled Burdon. "He apologized later and he told me a bit about how he'd grown up with brutality."

Despite all the drugs he consumed, alcohol, as it was with his mother and father, was more damaging to him. "He just couldn't drink," Herbie Worthington observed. "He simply turned into a bastard."[45]

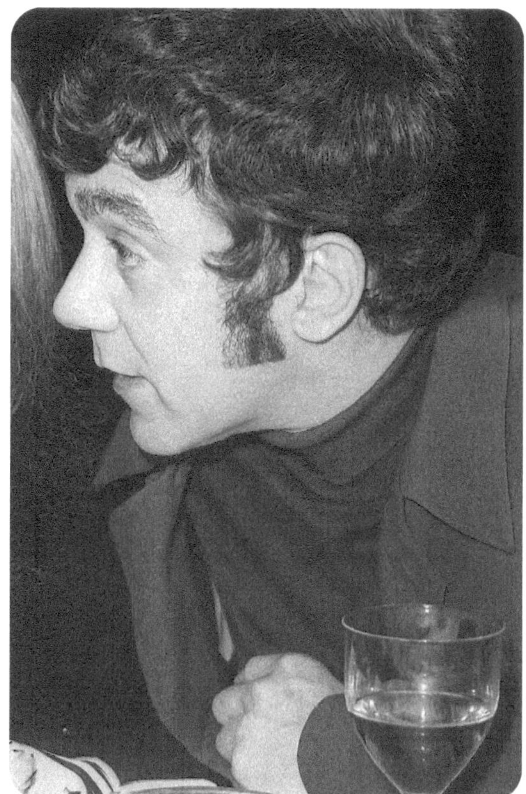

Ed Chalpin

Limo backseat with Carmen Borrero

Seattle reunion – Leon, Janie, Al, and Jimi

At Home with Handel

***Electric Ladyland* was** released in the U.S. on September 17, 1968, and went almost immediately to number one on the *Billboard* charts. Buoyed by Jimi's extraordinary rendition of Dylan's "All Along the Watchtower," which, ever present on the radio, many critics ranked as one of the only Dylan covers that topped Dylan's own version, the album stayed at the top of the charts for most of the rest of the year. Some critics challenged the length of the sixteen-song double album. Frank Kofsky in *Jazz & Pop* wondered if it was "absolutely essential that we be given a long and sometimes monotonous double album."[1] (Jimi would have preferred a triple LP set, saying, "We really got about half of what we wanted to say in it."[2]) But in the *New York Times,* Bob Palmer called the album a "genuine cultural event."

The album was loved by critics and fans on both sides of the Atlantic. "Jimi Hendrix's new album, *Electric Ladyland,* is a musical freeway," wrote Richard Goldstein in the *Village Voice.* "Hendrix's phrasing is as powerful, his musical presence as persistent as ever. . . . It comes at you whining, sighing, or curling its lip in arrogant dismay. . . . I suspect the reason why his all-star lineup [the use of Buddy Miles, Stevie Winwood, Al Kooper, and others on several songs] works is the firmly established subservience his backup musicians must inevitably accept. . . . Backed by even the most distinctive rock stylists, it is his guitar we hear first—loud and together. . . . Dig how this works in 'Voodoo Child,' the album's strongest cut and probably the finest rock appreciation of blues you'll ever hear. Hendrix is always out there, like an electronic minotaur, flaying away at the business of being absurdly black with the kind of groovy contempt the English call Flash."

In *Rolling Stone*, Tony Glover wrote, "Hendrix is the Robert Johnson of the sixties and really the first cat to ever totally play *electric* guitar."[3]

Jimi was in constant movement, settling into a suite of rooms at the Beverly Rodeo Hotel in Beverly Hills for a few days, and then moving east for a concert in New York on November 23 at the Philharmonic Hall. He celebrated his twenty-sixth birthday on November 27, and, on November 29, the Experience played at the Westchester County Center in White Plains, New York, a rich suburb of New York City. To the outsider, to the public, and to the media, the Jimi Hendrix Experience was entrenched as perhaps the most popular and prosperous band in America. Dozens of concerts lay ahead with fees now pushing $75,000. They had singles on record charts on both sides of the Atlantic, and *Electric Ladyland* was the number one bestseller in both England and America, and despite Jimi's profligate spending, there was even money in the bank.

It was at just this time the band began to break apart.

Insiders were not surprised. Noel and Mitch had been complaining openly for months. "After Chandler left, things began to drift apart," said Noel Redding. "We were so overwhelmed by the money and the glamour of being so-called pop stars, we all forgot we were people."[4] Jimi and Noel were often hostile, while Mitch tried to stay out of the way. Together and individually, they told friends that Jimi was impossible to work with. "Screw 'im!" said Noel. "I'm going home to me 'umble estate in County Cork."[5] Mitch said he was going to do the same at his estate outside London. The beginning of 1969 was the beginning of the end for the Jimi Hendrix Experience; the three who had once traveled together started going their separate ways. When the 1968 U.S. tour ended, Mitch and Noel flew to the UK for the holidays, while Jimi stayed in New York, jamming nightly in clubs.

However, the band was committed to dozens of appearances, and all through Christmas and New Year's, Jeffery talked to each one, crossing the Atlantic thrice in two weeks, trying to keep them together. A lot of rock and roll bands broke up in 1968—the Byrds; Blood, Sweat, and Tears; Big Brother and the Holding Company; Cream—and Mike Jeffery cajoled and begged and finally resorted to threats to bring the

Experience back together. "You have contracts and it won't just be me suing you," Jeffery screamed. "Everybody in the business will be suing you . . . I swear it! Don't be fuckin' stupid."[6] Though angered by the threat of decreased income for himself, Jeffery was correct in his appraisal. Jimi and Mitch, both close to broke, agreed to continue for the money. Noel had his money, but it was diminished by producing an album with Fat Mattress, a band he had founded, and he agreed to return only after Michael agreed to use Fat Mattress as the opening act in all the upcoming Experience dates.

Television exposure had helped launch the Experience, but by 1969 Jimi had little patience with the artificiality of the medium. On January 4, on the TV show *Happening for Lulu*, the Experience was supposed to play two songs with Jimi, ending the show in a duet with Lulu. The band opened with "Voodoo Child," but when Lulu tried to make an introduction, a shriek of feedback silenced her. Lulu finished the introduction, saying they were going to play their first hit, "Hey Joe." Two minutes into "Hey Joe," Jimi paused and said, "We'd like to stop playing that rubbish and dedicate a song to Cream, regardless of what kind of group they may be in, we dedicate this to Eric Clapton, Ginger Baker, and Jack Bruce," and then broke into a lengthy version of "Sunshine of Your Love."[7] Off camera the stage director signaled Jimi to stop. Jimi raised his middle finger, and they played the song through the rest of the show. The producer was furious. "You'll never appear on the BBC again," he threatened.

The event looked spontaneous, but Jimi had planned it. "I'm not going to sing with Lulu," he told Kathy Etchingham. "I'd look ridiculous."[8]

Still together, the trio took off to the Continent for a grueling tour of nineteen shows in sixteen days, starting in Gothenburg, Sweden, where Chas Chandler, in attendance, thought the band no longer played as a unit. The next evening at the start of the show in Stockholm, Jimi told the crowd, "We haven't played together in about six weeks, so we're gonna jam tonight . . . just mess around and see what happens." Aside to Redding and Mitchell, but heard by many in the audience, he added, "You wouldn't know the difference anyway."

Jimi complained that his audience didn't understand him and only wanted to hear hits. "He said he was sick of playing the hits and that he wanted to evolve," remembered Kathy Etchingham, "but he'd still always play the hits."[9] He cursed his audience but crafted his show to please them, for even as crowds mushroomed, he remembered his early struggles and feared hard times might return.

"Hendrix was listless and tired," wrote Ludvig Rasmusson after the Stockholm show. "The joy of playing was gone. He played his guitar carelessly. . . . All the other things were gone—liveliness, engagement, impudence, and poetry." Rasmusson was even harsher on Noel and Mitch. "It is strange that [Jimi] has put up with these two unimaginative musicians for this long."[10] Noel and Mitch were strong musicians, but on stage they relied on Jimi's energy to drive a show forward or sink it.

Noel attributed their poor performance to the difficulty of finding drugs. "I went out between shows and with much persistence managed to score a leaper,"[11] a methamphetamine pill the band crushed and snorted.

Throughout the Netherlands and Germany, the big, smoky halls were sold out. Their never-ending touring had turned them into road zombies, and the escape drugs provided became their strongest bond. Noel's diary, once detailing their musical achievements, now read like a pharmaceutical guide. Jimi had abandoned his journal.

Jimi pursued a university student named Eva Sundquist, whom he had previously met in a train station. He dedicated a concert to her, saying, "She's a goddess from Asgard," and spent the night with her at the Hotel Carlton in Karlstad, Sweden.[12] The night had lasting repercussions, as Eva became pregnant from this tryst. A few days later at a hotel bar in Dusseldorf, Germany, he met Monika Dannemann, a tall, blond ice skater who had gone to the hotel hoping to meet him. He spent the afternoon talking to her.

The band returned to London in February to play two concerts at the Royal Albert Hall that would be filmed by two American filmmakers, Jerry Goldstein and Steve Gold, who had formed a joint venture with Jeffery to produce a documentary on the Experience.

Kathy had found an apartment in the expensive neighborhood of Mayfair on the top floors of 23 Brook Street, one of a pair of well-preserved eighteenth-century townhouses a short walk from Carnaby Street and the Claridge Hotel. The adjoining house had once been the home of George Frideric Handel, the German-born composer who, like Jimi, had fled to London where his genius could be appreciated. Handel had died in that house in 1759. Jimi was fascinated that Handel had lived next door and bought albums of Handel's *Water Music* and *Messiah* and played them often. The thick walls of these two-hundred-and-fifty-year-old houses muffled almost all the noise from outside, and, though they lived in the heart of the West End, Jimi could play his guitar with the amp turned up as high as he liked.

He did interviews in these rooms, offering the kind of access few performers of his stature allowed. "He was always open, maybe too open," observed Kathy Etchingham. "If somebody knocked on the door, Jimi would be the first person to open it and a crowd of people would pile in." Their phone number was so widely circulated that Kathy put in a second line, which became so busy she started leaving the receiver off the hook. "We'd get calls all morning and all night."[13]

There were calls and visits from groupies and journalists. Sometimes Jimi would kick them out, but sometimes he wouldn't. When *International Times* writer Jane de Mendelssohn arrived for an interview, Jimi answered the door naked. He climbed into his bed, where there was pot, hash, pills, and bottles of alcohol, and lay there stoned for the three-hour interview, answering all questions except about his family. He hinted at his own true self when he said, "If I wasn't a guitar player I would probably be in jail."

On the questions of his songs, he replied, "On the first LP I didn't know what I was writing about. Most of the songs . . . were about ten pages long, but then we were restricted to a certain time limit, so I had to break them all down, so once I've broken the songs down, I didn't know whether they were going to be understood or not. Maybe some of the meanings got lost by breaking them down, which I never do any more." He commented on his schedule. "I've had no time off to myself since I've been in this scene. . . . Most people would like to retire and just disappear from the scene, which I'd love to do but then there's still things I'd like to say. I wish it wasn't so important to me. I wish I could just turn my mind off."[14]

Jimi, who often sidestepped the political and social movements of the day, told Mendelssohn, "in the Black Power Movement, they're using it wrongly . . . protest is over with. It's the solutions everyone wants now, not just protest." He compared the Vietnam War to D-Day: "The

Americans are fighting in Vietnam for the complete free world. As soon as they move out, they'll be at the mercy of the communists. For that matter, the yellow danger [China] should not be underestimated . . . war is horrible, but at present, it's still the only guarantee to maintain peace." His attitude on Vietnam would soon shift, but at this time, even with an anti-war bent in his songs, his views were surprisingly hawkish.

Eric Burdon remembered sitting on the roof of the Brook Street flat one day when a massive anti-Vietnam demonstration took place in the street below. "His reaction was quite a surprise to me," Burdon recalled. "He said he was still a soldier and still trained to think like one. He was pissed about the protests."

As the demonstrations grew louder, Jimi became angry. "When the reds come down from China and they take over North Vietnam and South Vietnam and then they go for Japan and beyond, then [you are] going to understand why the U.S. is there fighting these guys."[15]

The Experience had concerts at the Royal Albert Hall in London on February 18 and 24. When the first concert was played, Jimi had been snorting too much cocaine. "He was so stoned he was legless," recalled Trixie Sullivan. "I had to push him on stage."[16]

Jimi applied the improvisational style of his club jamming and the show was a let-down, but an impromptu jam in his bedroom later that night was inspired. When he played "Hound Dog" on acoustic guitar, sitting on his bed, his song had the warmth, humor, and energy that had been lacking onstage at the Royal Albert Hall.

At the second show a week later, Jimi was back on his game and thrilled the audience with a collection of his familiar songs and a new song written over the holidays, "Room Full of Mirrors," after which he went into an experimental instrumental of "The Star-Spangled Banner" that he had been playing with in the studio off and on for several months. Distortion verging on violence filled the rich, red hall, but, unlike in America where the audience would gasp, no one in London seemed to care.

The Royal Albert Hall shows were Jimi's last shows in Britain for eighteen months and were billed as "Farewell" performances. Many of London's best musicians attended, some joining the Experience onstage. The Experience rarely encored, but they did the night of the 24th, playing

"Purple Haze" and "Wild Thing." Fans trying to climb on stage nearly caused a riot.

Afterward, walking back to his nearby apartment with Kathy Etchingham, they were stopped by several men in black suits asking what he had in his suitcase. "A machine gun," he joked, and just as one of the men pulled a pistol from a shoulder holster, one of the others recognized Jimi Hendrix. Amid much laughter, identifying themselves as members of the U.S. Secret Service, they explained that Richard Nixon was staying at the Claridge Hotel and that Jimi was stopped merely as a precaution. "Well, you give ol' Tricky Dick mah best," replied Jimi. "Tell him . . . Jimi's comin' to gitcha!"[17]

On March 13, the Experience flew to New York City for a month of studio sessions before starting another tour. Kathy Etchingham soon joined them. Meanwhile, Devon Wilson had fastened herself to Jimi. She bragged to him about all the other stars she had bedded, which included women, too, and Jimi told her about all his groupies. The way Devon ordered people around during his concerts made some think she was his special girlfriend. But she also scored drugs for Jimi, which became more important than sex. Devon was increasingly strung out from cocaine and heroin, and Jimi increasingly joined her.

"They were these two birds of a feather," recalled Herbie Worthington. "She was this major groupie, but she was also very smart and very loyal to Jimi. And if you want to control somebody, there's no better way than to get high with them."

On at least two occasions, Devon followed Jimi to England. "She was the type who would ring on the doorbell and she would keep ringing until you answered," recalled Kathy.[18]

On Tuesday, March 18, Jimi entered the Record Plant to lay down the tracks for "The Star-Spangled Banner." The cost was $200 an hour. Jimi sat hunched over his Stratocaster, tuning meticulously to slowly create an aural tapestry, beginning with apocalyptic crashing chords and transitioning into the familiar melody with notes so high they hurt the ears. There followed four minutes of inspired noise, a triumphant electronic exercise that was simultaneously an assault on both hearing and patriotism. There were incredible highs and reverberating lows layered one on top of the other, sounding like signals from outer space. It was every war weapon and machine in America all risen together in song, conveying an image of beautiful violence even more vividly than the original composition by Francis Scott Key. Many performers in the anti-war movement had recorded protest songs, some of them quite famous, but, until Hendrix, no one had taken the national anthem itself, turned it inside out, and made it the ultimate protest song. When Jimi played "The Star-Spangled Banner" on April 19 in the Dallas Memorial Auditorium, the audience rioted, breaking chairs, rushing the stage, and engaging in hand-to-hand combat with the police.

Electric Ladyland was still high on the charts and praised by the most respected critics and magazines. Tom Phillips in *Jazz & Pop* made references to Brahms, Ravel, Berlioz, and Beethoven and said Jimi's story about mermaids and mermen in "1983" was reminiscent of Jules Verne: "Hendrix's genius lies in yoking the past and the future and making them work together." Phillips concluded, "He is all at once primitive, classical, and farther out than anybody else."

The music editor for *Rolling Stone*, Jon Landau, in a year-end critique, praised Eric Clapton's band, Cream, but added: "For all their instrumental expertise, they never approached the excitement of Jimi Hendrix. . . . He is the authoritative lead guitarist, the coolest showman, an excellent songwriter, and a constantly improving vocalist." The same issue declared that "For creativity, electricity, and balls above and beyond the call of duty, he has won for himself the *Rolling Stone* Performer of the Year Award."[19]

When Kathy arrived in New York, Devon wisely vacated. Kathy thought Jimi seemed a different person. He was "trailing an enormous entourage like the colorful leader of some circus freak show. . . . There never seemed to be less than twenty people." The women were "obviously whores" and the men appeared to be pimps and drug dealers. Some had little spoons hanging around their necks. Jimi called them "my friends." When an older man with a limp and a duffel bag full of cocaine packets and a .45-caliber revolver entered their hotel room, she decided to return to England. It was the end of their romance. "There was no way I was going to tame him," she said. "I wanted a decent family. Jimi wanted a family as well—he just didn't know how to get it."[20]

For the spring tour of 1969, the Experience played twenty-nine shows over the course of ten weeks before 350,000 fans, taking in over $1.3 million. Most of Jimi's time was spent with travel, the press, and trying to cram in the odd studio session on a day off. He soon complained of exhaustion and was irritable in interviews. There was crowd violence and gatecrashers at many shows. Black Panthers appeared backstage and criticized Jimi for using white musicians and a white promoter.

"They called him an Uncle Tom," recalled Pat O'Day. "I reminded Jimi that we worked for him, not the other way around."[21]

Growing up in a diverse neighborhood in Seattle, Jimi saw people as raceless, but in the public spotlight, the fact could not be escaped that he was black and most of his fans were white. At the Oakland show on April 29, Diana Carpenter, his old girlfriend whose prostitution had helped support him, had a note delivered backstage to him. He sent word to follow his limo to the airport, where they talked for the first time in three years. Diana handed him a snapshot, saying, "This is your daughter, Tamika. She's two years old." Holding her picture, Jimi remarked, "She has my eyes," and though he carried the picture onto the plane, he did not ask about the daughter; instead, he had talked about how tired he was of touring. [22]

Business ran smoothly at the office in New York, from where Mike Jeffery held meetings with accountants and lawyers and publicists and haunted small clubs looking for new talent. Jeffery was a man consistent in his contradictions. He was raised as part of the establishment, but smoked grass, snorted cocaine, and drifted toward astrology. He soon met a model named Lyn, who had come south from Canada with Levon Helm to the upstate New York village of Woodstock, where Helm and other members of The Band rehearsed and recorded with Bob Dylan. Dylan's manager, Albert Grossman, had a home there, too, where another of his clients, Janis Joplin, often came and went.

Woodstock, with open fields and woods and cows, was like an aging rural bohemian colony and the perfect mix for Jeffery. Outside of town, he bought a big white clapboard home surrounded by a white picket fence where he and Lyn became lovers.

25 Brook Street, London – Jimi lived on the left, Handel on the right

Album cover for *Electric Ladyland*

Jim with Devon Wilson

Inside London pad
on Brook Street

Bu$t and Boom

Pop music had become a big business with annual sales of more than a billion dollars and concerts grossing another $500 million. Jimi was contributing his share to the success story. His first three albums were certified "gold" by the Record Industry Association of America, each with retail sales of more than a million dollars, and the Experience was the highest-paid act in the world, getting $50,000 to $100,000 or more for each concert. Then on the morning of May 3, after stepping off the plane flying from Detroit into Toronto, Ontario, Jimi Hendrix was asked to open his flight bag. A customs officer saw a small glass jar containing four cellophane packets of white powder. Jimi, used to customs checks from his trips to Europe, knew not to carry drugs from one country to another and was surprised at the discovery. The Royal Canadian Mounted Police arrested him, and the tour almost fell apart.

A mobile drug testing lab was called to the scene, and while Jimi sat bored in a folding chair, a chemist went to work and determined the packets held heroin. Jimi was arrested and rushed to police headquarters, charged with possession of narcotics, and released on $10,000 bail, posted by a Toronto attorney. When the bust happened, Gerry Stickells called Mike Jeffery, who called Mike Goldstein, who took a cab to the offices of UPI, and then to the Associated Press. "I stopped the story from going out on the wires," said Goldstein, who bribed an AP editor with a case of liquor. "I never minded stories like that being in *Rolling Stone* or in our own [underground] newspaper. Where it would hurt you was not there, it was in the daily papers across the country, which would make large concert hall promoters close down all your concert dates. I knew a million dollars was riding on that story not getting out on UPI and the AP wire."[1] The incident was reported in only a few Toronto newspapers. A few hours later, before 12,000 fans in the Maple Leaf Gardens, many of whom had heard of the arrest on the radio or in conversation, Jimi walked onstage and said, "I want you to forget what happened yesterday and tomorrow and today. Tonight we're going to create a whole new world."[2]

Steve Weiss, who did legal work for Jeffery, flew from New York to represent Jimi at the arraignment two days later. Jimi wore a pink shirt open to the waist, an Apache-style headband, a multicolored scarf around his neck, and beads. When the judge called his name, "James Marshall Hendrix of New York," he rose and delivered a lips-pursed sneer. A few words were exchanged, and after posting a $10,000 bond, Jimi was allowed to continue the tour. A preliminary hearing was set for June 19. There had been dozens of rock and roll arrests for drugs in the preceding months, but usually for marijuana. A little pot was one thing, but heroin was something else. During the waiting period, Jimi lived in fear of a conviction, facing as many as ten years in prison.

The only detailed account of the arrest was soon printed in *Rolling Stone*. The story made it clear that some of those involved suspected a setup. It was usually customs agents who made arrests, not Mounties. "The Mounties . . . customarily do not wait at the airport to make dope busts," wrote the writer. "Another item is that all the inquiry and searching at the airport was done right out in the open at the custom's gate. The more usual procedure is for officers and those being detained to retire from public view, in respect for the privacy of the accused. But Hendrix and company were forced to stand for hours under the gaze of scores of onlookers. . . ." The reporter also noted that someone might have been out to "get" Jimi by "laying a surprise stash on him," placing the drugs in his suitcase in Detroit just before he left for Canada, then telephoning ahead to tip off the police. "The populace of Toronto are a very conservative lot and tend to look with suspicion upon anybody who looks and dresses a little different from themselves. Hendrix looks a lot different. Make an example of this freaky, frizzy-haired psychedelic spade (if you go by this reasoning) and maybe you can scare the freaks out of Yorkville."[3]

Back on the road, drawing 18,000 fans to a sold-out show in Madison Square Garden, where he made $14,000 a minute, Jimi had become the highest-paid rock musician in the world. The higher paydays increased expectations from the audience and critics. When Jimi complained about the revolving stage at Madison Square Garden, the *Village Voice* rebuked him: "He should bitch with all the bread he walked off with."[4]

Yet on most nights Jimi could be seen for free at New York clubs, on one occasion jamming with Stephen Stills and Johnny Winter. "He wanted to play the songs he grew up on: Freddie King, Earl King, Muddy Waters," recalled Johnny Winter. "I deferred and let Jimi play lead."[5] This jam lasted until 3 A.M. when they moved to the Record Plant where Jimi cut Guitar Slims's "The Things I Used to Do" with Johnny Winter on bottleneck guitar.

The band flew to Seattle on May 23 for a concert at the Coliseum, which Jimi dedicated to his family and Garfield High. As the show ended, there was a loud thunderclap and a downpour of rain outside. Alone backstage with Carmen Borrero and a few lingering fans, Jimi was suddenly seized with nostalgia and wanted to revisit the poor pockets of his youth. "You got a car," he asked a startled youth, and they walked in the rain to the kid's car.

Carmen didn't like the idea: "We were both still tripping from acid, so I'm not sure Jimi was thinking straight."[6] The kid apologized for his vehicle, a Volkswagen Beetle with springs sticking out of the seats and rusting holes on the floor. Jimi sat in the back with Carmen and gave the teenager directions.

Over the next few hours, Jimi retraced the poverty years of his estranged youth as they drove from house to house, spotting the ramshackle homes and clubs he knew and the lawns he had helped his father mow. At Garfield High he pointed to the windows of his classes. When they stopped at a drive-in hamburger stand on Madison Street, where he had once lacked the funds to buy a girlfriend a ten-cent hamburger, he had no cash on this day either, so the star-struck teenaged fan bought the burgers that they ate in the car. Carmen had heard much about Jimi's childhood, but she was surprised at the number of apartments, hotels, and boardinghouses he had called home. "On every block there was some place he had stayed," she recalled. "He had stories about everyone."

At three in the morning, they drove down the stretch of Jackson Street that had been the main stem for black entertainment. The street was puddled and quiet; the storefronts and clubs were now closed. Jimi pointed to boarded-up buildings that had once hosted Ray Charles and Quincy Jones. By an old hotel that still stood on a corner, Jimi said, "That's where my mother lived." Carmen had heard Jimi talk about his mother many times; he had even told her he wanted a daughter named Lucille, but she didn't realize she had lived near or in the same places as he.

"He had so idealized his mother," she said, "I had forgotten she was a real person."

He brought up the idea of visiting his mother's grave in Renton, south of Seattle, a thirty-minute drive, but everyone was tired, even Jimi yawned, and so the kid drove them back to the hotel. "We were flying out in just a few hours for a show Jimi had in San Diego that evening," recalled Carmen.[7]

News of the bust finally broke when the tour neared completion. Jimi, denying the drugs were his, told Jeffery that the bottle had been planted. Jeffery wanted to believe Jimi but had doubts and asked for advice from Louis Armstrong's publicist, Jerry Morrison. "I want Jimi away from it. . . . I want him away from those people," Jeffery said, expressing his concern about Jimi's occasional use of heroin and the friends around him who used it regularly, like Devon Wilson.

"Mike believed Jimi couldn't get his trip together in the city because of the leeches," remembered Morrison. "He wanted me to find a house that was isolated and insulated."[8] Jerry had introduced Jeffery to Woodstock and suggested that Jimi get a house there, too. Jeffery agreed and told Jerry to find one for Jimi, making sure he had everything he wanted in the house. Budget was not important—keeping Jimi out of trouble was very important.

Jimi and Jeffery entered into an arrangement to take over the lease of the recently closed Generation Club at 52 West Eighth Street, formerly a favorite jamming spot. They initially thought of reopening the club, but when Jeffery totaled the recording costs for *Electric Ladyland* and was alarmed to find they'd spent nearly $200,000 at the Record Plant alone, and another $20,000 to $30,000 at studios in London and Las

Vegas, he decided instead to convert the site into their own studio. Jimi approved of the idea and wanted to call it Electric Lady Studios. Mike went to Reprise Records for a $250,000 advance against future royalties to get the project underway. When construction began, costly problems emerged: The Minetta Creek ran under the ground, requiring stronger foundations, and a subway station fifty yards away made soundproofing much more expensive than anticipated. In a meeting, Jimi wanted to dump the whole project. Jeffery dropped his head into his hands, and then looked up and said to Jimi, "You tell me you don't like the Record Plant because you can't just show up when you want to. You say you want total control. This will be your studio. You can go in there any time you want and stay there all night." Jimi remained silent. "The damn place is almost ready," continued Jeffery. "We'll be open in a month, two months at the most. You can't back out now!"[9]

Jimi was beginning to look at Jeffery suspiciously. A friend told him that Jeffery, who had not been able to develop another successful act, had become economically dependent and was paranoid about losing him. Jimi went to his friend, journalist Sharon Lawrence, and told her nothing was going right: the bust, the studio, Noel, and Mitch. "Jimi and I used to have a lot of talks about things," said Sharon. "Jimi liked Noel a lot, loved him really, and I said, 'Well, you are doing things that are making Noel and Mitch unhappy. You are not communicating with them.'"

Jimi was also worried that his taxes weren't being paid. "I don't want to end up like Joe Louis," he told Sharon.

"He was very concerned his money was not being taken care of," said Sharon. "They kept telling him that his studio would be a great investment, and I said, 'Well, Jimi, you had better find out if your taxes are being paid before you go into such an expense. You have an investment with a man that you are not sure you trust.'"[10] It was difficult for Jimi to voice his complaints, and while in Los Angeles, he asked for Sharon's help when he met with Henry Steingarten, the attorney who represented both he and Jeffery.

Jimi was staying at the Beverly Rodeo Hotel; Steingarten was at a hotel miles away. For several days the two men traveled back and forth, generally with Sharon Lawrence present. Sharon persuaded Jimi to tell Steingarten how unhappy he was and how he wanted to be released from his contract. She remembered, "He wanted to be bought out of the studio if Jeffery would reimburse him for his investment, and Steingarten, at that time, said he would take it up with Jeffery." Jimi also told Steingarten that he thought Mike was taking money that belonged to the Experience. "Steingarten asked Jimi and me to gather as much evidence as we could in ways that Mike had been crooked, or had not Jimi's or the Experience's best interests at heart, and he asked us to find documents, to make notes, to tape anything, and to talk to Gerry Stickells and see how helpful he could be."[11]

Steingarten must have known that was an impossible task. He must have also realized the conflict of interest for his own firm. Since he represented both Jeffery and Hendrix, he was probably just humoring Jimi, knowing that all musicians claim their managers are dishonest and that it would all come to nothing.

The pressure continued to mount. Reprise Records had been demanding a new album for more than six months and resorted to what most record companies did when the artists failed to provide the contracted number of albums per year—they produced a "greatest hits" package. Called *Smash Hits*, this one had eight previously released songs and four never released in America. It was a good album and the reviewers had kind things to say, but, for Jimi, it was his musical past, not the present or future. In an interview, Jimi insisted the Experience would remain together for the remaining concerts of the summer but said he wanted a new band with Billy Cox as bassist, the Buddy Miles group backing him, and three soul sisters, saying his future direction might be toward "symphonic things. So, then the kids can respect the old music, the traditional, you know, like classics. I like to mix that in with the so-called rock today."[12]

On June 16, he flew to Toronto to appear in court for a preliminary hearing. He was wearing a suit. The judge determined that the appropriate tests were conducted on the suspected drugs and announced that Jimi would stand trial on December 8 on the two possession charges. Bail was set at $10,000 and Jimi flew back to Los Angeles. The next day he headlined the first night of a three-day festival at Devonshire Downs. Upset from the Toronto hearing, and frustrated by the lack of response to his new songs, Jimi played a short, listless set, left the stage to a smattering of applause, and collected $100,000, more than a third of the entire talent budget for the festival, causing resentment in some of the other performers, among whom were the Byrds, Creedence Clearwater Revival, Joe Cocker, and Marvin Gaye. To redeem himself, he returned the following day unannounced and jammed for forty-five minutes with Buddy Miles and Eric Burdon. But the audience wanted the old Jimi Hendrix, and according to friends, he hated to revert to his old style of performance.

A week later, on June 29, he, Noel, and Mitch flew separately to Denver to play at Mile High Stadium. The pattern of uninspired shows and dynamic jams repeated itself in Colorado, where, the day before the music festival, he showed up unannounced and jammed at a wedding reception in a Denver park with Herbie Worthington and Billy Rich. "Everybody in the park ended up coming to the wedding to see Jimi play," remembered Rich.

The Denver show was the final Experience show. Before the show, a journalist, having heard rumors that Jimi had hired a new bass player, asked Noel Redding, "What are you doing here? I thought you had left the band."[13] It was the first time Noel had heard about any changes, and he was upset. Rioting fans outside the stadium demanded that the festival be free. Jimi dropped acid with Herbie Worthington, took the stage almost levitating, and then his mood turned sour. He antagonized the crowd by changing the lyrics of "Voodoo Child" to "Gonna make a lot of money and buy this town / Gonna buy this town and put it all in my shoe," and announced at one point during the set that "This is the last gig we'll ever be playing together," spurring on the crowd of 17,000 people as rioting broke out inside the stadium.[14] Many tried to climb on the stage. When police shot tear gas canisters, the gas drifted onstage and engulfed the band.

The Experience put down their instruments and fled from the gas and the surging crowd. It was their last moments on stage together as a band. Gerry Stickells pushed them into a U-Haul truck, locked the door, and attempted to drive through the mass of people. Faces pressed flat against the windows, fans climbed on top of the truck, and their weight began to snap the roof supports. "They were pounding on the doors and the roof and you could see the sides of the van start to buckle," said Herbie Washington, who was with them.

Even in such fear, Noel joked, "That's my leg, mate, and I don't know you that well," to Worthington sitting next to him.[15] For three tumultuous years, Noel's sense of humor had helped hold the band together during difficult times, and again he joked that they would meet their deaths in the back of a U-Haul and would never get to spend their money or enjoy their fame. Slowly the van moved through the crowd; its roof was beaten flat, but they escaped.

Noel flew back to England the next day. "Jimi . . . was very hard to work with," he told *Rolling Stone*. "I think he suffers from a split personality. He's a genius guitarist and his writing is very good, but he whips himself. He gets everybody around him very uptight because he worries about everything."

Noel, Mitch, Jeffery, and others dependent upon the Experience's earnings thought it made no sense to abandon a winning formula, but that wasn't good enough for Jimi. "The recording sessions were chaos," Noel said, "and onstage it was getting ridiculous. The audience wanted us to play the old Hendrix standards, but Jimi wanted to do his new stuff. The last straw came at the Denver Pop Festival when Jimi told a reporter that he was going to enlarge the band . . . without even consulting myself or our drummer, Mitch Mitchell. . . . I went up to Jimi that night, said goodbye, and caught the next plane to London. I don't think Jimi believed I'd do it. Later on he phoned and asked me to come back, but I said 'stuff it!'"[16]

Jimi tracked down Billy Cox, offered him the job of bass player, and brought him to New York to rehearse with Mitch Mitchell. On July 3, 1969, news of the death of Brian Jones, formerly of the Rolling Stones, reached Jimi. Jones had been found floating in the swimming pool of his English estate. Jimi was visibly depressed over the loss of a friend and probably knew, too, it could happen to him.

The next scheduled performance date was August 17, 1969, as the final act in a three-day festival to be held in an alfalfa field in upstate New York. The young promoters of the festival were calling their event the "Woodstock Music and Art Fair . . . An Aquarian Exposition . . . 3 Days of Peace and Music." The roster of performers was impressive. The promoters were saying it would be the world's largest festival, a statement most people doubted. Three hundred thousand hippies in a cow pasture two hours' drive from New York City didn't seem too likely.

Jimi put his life on "cruise." He booked time at the Record Plant and jammed with the close-knit core of musicians gathering around him, which included Billy Cox and Buddy Miles, the fat, loud, fun-loving drummer who came and went, and a percussion player named Juma Sultan. It mattered little to Jimi who he played with, nor did he much care if the jams were taped as long as he was having a good time. He joined jams onstage at clubs, others he took into the studio. He often appeared at Steve Paul's Scene to play behind a "who's who" of musicians that included James Cotton, Johnny Winter, the Chambers Brothers, an early version of Fleetwood Mac, Led Zeppelin, Richie Havens, Buddy Guy, Jim Morrison (who did little more than scream drunken obscenities as Jimi played the blues), the McCoys, and a young Rick Springfield.

Jimi played with enthusiasm but was never competitive and soloed only when asked. "I feel guilty when people say I'm the greatest guitarist on the scene," he told a journalist. "What's good or bad doesn't matter to me. What does matter is feeling and not feeling. If only people would take more of a true view and think in terms of feeling."

For Jimi "feeling" was most easily expressed through music; in fact, it might have been the only way he could express himself with total candid honesty. Albums were "nothing but personal diaries," he said. "When you hear somebody making music, they are baring a naked part of their soul to you."[17]

During the summer of '69, Jimi became friends with Deering Howe, a young man he had met the year before by renting his yacht for a one-day cruise. A great-grandson of William Deering, a founder of International Harvester, great wealth ran through the branches of his family: Cornelia Vanderbilt was the maid of honor at his father's first wedding. He was a music fan but not involved in the business.

"I think part of the attraction [for Jimi] was that I came from money and there was nothing I wanted from him," Deering recalled. "We had almost nothing in common except for a love of music."

Jimi also befriended two women who ran a boutique selling leather fringe: Colette Mimram and Stella Douglas. "He was simply a charming gentleman," Colette recalled. "I think he gravitated to us because we were outside his world. In his world, everybody was after him for something." They were his first true adult friendships outside the music industry.

"We'd expose him to a certain refinement that he had never experienced before," said Colette.

The four dined together often that summer. "We were a group of people who would gather and eat together and talk," recalled Deering, who taught him how to order wine and meals in fine restaurants.[18] The dinners were relaxed and served as breaks from the stress of Jimi's career. With these friends, Jimi could relax and enjoy the refined culture of their company and talk about art, philosophy, religion, and politics.

Socially, Devon Wilson was still in charge. "She was a pretty wild lady," remembered a friend, "but she loved Jimi and he loved her and she ran the show. She told people where to sit in clubs."

Few knew where or when Jimi slept; mostly he stayed with one of his ladies. "He'd call in the middle of the night," said Alvenia Bridges, a young black model who had entered Jimi's New York entourage. "He'd come over to sleep. There were too many people at his apartment. . . . He called one night when I was living on the West Side and he came over and he slept for eighteen hours straight. . . . Sometimes he'd just show up. I'd leave the key for him. . . . He shared his dreams with me. He had a dream to bring together all the creative people that he knew."[19]

Mike Jeffery, desperately needing a finished album, rented an estate for Jimi near the village of Shokan, not far from Woodstock. It was an eight-bedroom, stone mansion on ten acres with a riding stable, swimming pool, and a cook and housekeeper, and, though the monthly rent was $3,000, Jeffery felt it was worth it if a new album resulted from the stay.

Jimi decided to fulfill his dream of building a larger, more diverse band. He hired Larry Lee, his friend in Nashville, for rhythm guitar, and added two percussion players he'd met in New York clubs, Jerry Velez and Juma Sultan, and along with Billy Cox, they all moved into the Shokan mansion to begin a mishmash process of forming into a band. They had no drummer—Mitch Mitchell was in England and it wasn't yet clear he would join. The situation became even more confused when Jimi suddenly left to go off with friends.

Deering Howe was traveling to Africa to meet up with Colette and Stella. Deering told Jimi there was no reason to earn money if you couldn't spend it and urged him to come along. Jimi, who rarely flouted management's orders, agreed and told Jeffery, who was furious but unable to stop him. Jimi also phoned the police in Toronto for approval to travel outside the United States. He needed the break and the RCMP approved the trip.

He spent nine days in Africa. "It was the best and maybe the only vacation he ever had," recalled Deering. They met up with Stella and Colette in Morocco, and the women were delighted to see him. The trip was spent buying rugs and clothes, eating, talking, and resting. "It was amazing to watch him, as a black man, experience Africa," Deering recalled. "He loved the culture and the people, and he laughed more than I'd ever seen him laugh."

Morocco was a place where race didn't matter and neither did fame. Jimi dropped his rock star persona and enjoyed life. "The vacation seemed to give him nourishment," said Colette. "It recharged him."

Deering remembered, "We talked about theater, art, Africa, but never music." Jimi had striven hard for fame on the Chitlin' Circuit and the streets of New York, but when he found it (or it found him) he wished to regain anonymity. The trip was so revitalizing that when he returned to America, inspired by the African music he had heard in Morocco, he wanted to play acoustic rather than electric guitar, and, in jam sessions in Shokan, he made recordings featuring only him and Juma Sultan. "They were only his acoustic guitar and my percussion," Sultan recalled. "It was phenomenal—a sound somewhat like Wes Montgomery or Segovia, but with a Moroccan influence."[20]

Colette Mimram's grandfather was a tribal leader in Morocco who had recently married a clairvoyant who worked for the King of Morocco. She was an old woman who spoke French, and, upon meeting Jimi and knowing nothing about him, announced that he had a forehead that indicated artistic genius. Later, as Jimi and his friends gathered around a table, she dealt a deck of tarot cards and read out Jimi's fortune. The second card dealt was the Death card. She explained to Colette in French that it might as well mean a rebirth. However, Jimi, staring transfixed at the card, cried, "I'm going to die." His friends tried to tell him that he should not take a random card dealt by an old woman as a serious omen, but over the next few months, Colette recalled, "he kept repeating that he was going to die before he was thirty."[21] The soothsayer also predicted that he would soon be in a large crowd.

In America, he put these visions on hold because in less than two weeks he was scheduled to play at the festival in upstate New York, and his new band needed rehearsing. Jimi had played in a dozen festivals over the last three years, and this one wasn't expected to be as large as some he had already done. This music and arts festival would take place on a long, sweeping pasture in Bethel on August 15–18. Originally billed as "An Aquarian Exposition," it came to be known as "Woodstock." Sixty thousand advance tickets had been sold; at most, the promoters predicted one hundred thousand attendees. When the organizers approached Mike Jeffery about booking Jimi, they settled on $32,000, less than what he often received but more than anyone else playing the event. A solid two hours from New York, Jeffery also didn't think many fans would make the trip.

The big stone house outside Shokan at the end of Taver Hollow Road was surrounded by miles of uninhabited hill country. The house was fully furnished with many antiques, but Jimi seemed oblivious to his environment so long as there was electricity for his guitar, food and sex whenever wanted, and a regular and varied supply of drugs and companions to accompany his music. The region's long-time reputation as an artists' colony provided a hands-off attitude toward celebrities. "We tried to keep the groupies away from the place," Jerry Morrison remembered, "but Jimi went into Woodstock and brought a few girls back. That let it out, and after that they were always infiltrating."[22]

Jimi began rehearsals in earnest. Mitch Mitchell arrived from London to find the tight ensemble of the Experience a thing of the past. "The band was grim," he remembered, "a shambles."[23] Mitch said the band didn't get better with practice. Juma Sultan and others argued that Mitch wasn't used to the Latin rhythms they were using. The group was called Gypsy Sun and Rainbows, and they had only a week of rehearsal.

Collette and Stella

Performing in concert

Toronto Trial

Deering Howe

Woodstock

For four days in the middle of August 1969, a young generation of Americans gathered together to listen to music on the rolling farmland in the Catskills of New York. The locus of their gathering was an alfalfa field with a broad, gentle slope forming a large, natural amphitheater above the stage where the musicians performed. The field was near the town of Bethel, a Hebrew name for "place of worship," on land owned by Max Yasgur, a local dairy farmer who believed in freedom of expression.

This was a searching generation of American youth, hard-bitten by an unjust foreign war, unlike the foreign war their fathers had fought in Europe and the Pacific for the liberation of humanity, and infuriated by the murders of their heroes Martin Luther King Jr. and Bobby Kennedy, who had fought for the equality and social justice in which they so fervently believed. They dressed informally in jeans, T-shirts, and flowing, flowery gowns; the men let their hair grow almost as long as the women's. Their music, too—a blend of rock, rhythm and blues, folk, eastern meditation, and African percussion and chants, with strands of gospel and jazz—was different from the music their parents had enjoyed. And yet, despite the setbacks, misunderstandings, and the ugly war in Asia into which many were drafted and died, they held onto their cherished ideals and believed they could change the world through love, peace, and music.

The Woodstock Music and Art Fair became a lasting testament to their belief.

The immutable chords of the festival were deliberately struck by four young businessmen who inadvertently created a juggernaut that almost instantly grew of its own gigantic volition into an exposition of peace and music that far outstripped the vision and preparations of the founders, whose initial idea was to start a recording studio in Woodstock, New York.

It was initially the brainchild of Michael Lang from Brooklyn, who had dropped out of NYU and opened a head shop in an affluent section of Miami, selling hookahs, pipes, and drug paraphernalia. Stout and competent, with a puckish face on a head full of long, brown, curly hair, Michael soon began promoting local concert events, tapping further into the burgeoning counter-culture movement. In the spring of 1968, he co-produced the Pop and Underground Festival at a horseracing track north of Miami with a lineup that included The Mothers of Invention, Chuck Berry, John Lee Hooker, and the Jimi Hendrix Experience. Lang admitted they were lucky to secure the Experience: "I think Jimi just happened to have an open date."[1] There were technical problems with the sound, and most of the second day was washed out by torrential rain, leaving the producers in a financial mess. But on Saturday night, Hendrix, in a bolero hat and red crushed velvet pants, had mesmerized the audience with breathtaking guitar solos.

Lang wanted to do more in music. Moving to Woodstock, New York, he soon befriended Artie Kornfeld, a young executive with Capitol Records. In February 1969, they made a proposal to John Roberts and Joel Rosenman, who owned a modestly successful recording studio in NYC, to build a recording studio in Woodstock to encourage recordings by residents such as Bob Dylan, Tim Hardin, John Sebastian, Janis Joplin, and the Band. The proposal suggested an opening-day press party with local luminaries playing a concert. Roberts and Rosenman had no interest in another recording studio but were excited about a concert, especially one featuring Bob Dylan. "Once they hear that Dylan is performing," thought Joel Rosenman, "we can get people from all over. . . . We can just sell tickets."[2] The four men soon formed Woodstock Ventures, a company to produce an outdoor festival, and agreed to use the profits to build a recording studio.

Large music festivals, having started in Golden Gate Park in San Francisco, where the Grateful Dead sometimes played for free, were still a new concept. Woodstock organizers wanted to avoid some of the problems that had plagued recent concerts by providing their own security and a beautiful setting rather than a horse track like the Pop Festival in Miami that drew a small, stoned crowd that conflicted with police. For security, they hired Hog Farm, a large traveling hippie commune adept at keeping the peace and caring for those suffering from accidental drug overdoses.

After they had lost the original site when the town of Wallkill banned any gathering of over five thousand (the townsfolk didn't want long-haired hippies nearby smoking dope and listening to their strange music), they found the peaceful, bucolic bowl above a lake in July. It was only five weeks until the concert, and one hundred thousand tickets had already sold. They had to hurry construction. There wasn't enough time to build both the stage and an enclosed perimeter a mile in circumference, so they built the stage and sound system and did without fences, as young people began arriving from all over the country to hear the greatest lineup of rock bands and folk singers ever assembled in one place.

The chord that struck America's youth in August 1969 was greater and more resonating than the organizers had envisioned or planned: Instead of a large, lucrative concert, they made history. And, though unable to secure Dylan, they did get Jimi Hendrix.

They came by the hundreds of thousands in a pilgrimage of peace and love, more people than could be imagined. For miles, the roads were clogged with cars, but no one was turned away, and instead of anger and frustration, these children of God, some with flowers in their hair, laughed and talked and danced and sang, some dropped acid, they all smoked marijuana, and, gathering their satchels, blankets, and whatever food they might have brought, they left their cars behind and proceeded to Max Yasgur's farm for song and celebration. The folks of Bethel knew they were witnessing something extraordinary and wonderful, and from their porches and along the road, they greeted this great, happy throng with smiles and peace signs. They found their way to the garden and, like golden stardust, lighted upon the gentle slopes above the great, just-finished stage.

"As you walked in it hit you," remembered an attendee. "Suddenly, it just all came into view at once: this whole enormous bowl full of people."

Another recalled "coming over the hill and feeling the energy of the crowd. . . . There was so much power in it."

"I never knew there was that many people in the world," thought a young woman. "It was really beautiful."[3]

By Friday the organizers, who had invested over three million dollars, knew that with no fences there was no way to collect fees, nor could they ask the multitudes already assembled to leave. As a business venture the project was dead, but at the same time a curious calm came upon them. Before the first act came on the stage, Tim Morris announced to the multitudes, "It's a free concert from now on . . . we're gonna put the music up here for free . . . the people who are backing this thing . . . are gonna take a bit of a bath, a big bath . . . What that means . . . is that your welfare and the music is a hell of a lot more important than the dollar."[4] The crowd understood the gift they had been given, and a gentle, peaceful roar arose as many stood and applauded.

The show was late in starting; the bands couldn't get to the site because of the clogged roads. When Richie Havens soon arrived with backup musicians, he was the first to perform. He played for over two hours, creating "Freedom" while on stage, a song that fit well with the crowd who absorbed it on every level of meaning.

Performers rotated to the site aboard a helicopter. Richie was followed by Sweetwater, taking the stage at 6:15, followed by Bert Sommer and Ravi Shankar, and then Tim Hardin, followed by Melanie and Arlo Guthrie. The long day into night ended with Joan Baez; the spotlights shining upon her, she ended her set with the Civil Rights anthem, "We Shall Overcome." In the darkness beyond, as people struck candles, lighters, and small campfires, the great field looked to be filled with fireflies.

The attendance increased on the second day by more than a hundred thousand. There evolved all around the perimeter a two-lane highway of people moving along to see all there was to see, and there was a lot to see and do. The Hog Farm had its commune in the woods near the main stage, selling crafts and attending to those on bad trips. Their leader, a man nicknamed Wavy Gravy, called himself a "Please Force," as he kindly gave orderly instructions. Many discarded their clothing to go skinny-dipping in a pond—"It was beautiful," exclaimed one of the girls. There was marijuana and bare breasts everywhere, both male and female, and a panoply of medical emergencies as would happen in a city of nearly half a million. Governor Nelson Rockefeller sent army medical units in helicopters to give all necessary aid. When the food ran out, the people of Bethel emptied their pantries and stores, giving it all away for free, cooking and distributing hundreds of thousands of eggs. "Kids are hungry," said a townsman, "you gotta feed 'em."[5]

The second day of music was devoted to rock. The bands were fantastic. When Country Joe and the Fish performed "I-Feel-Like-I'm-Fixin'-to-Die-Rag" the crowd joined in with the lyrics, a protest anthem against the Vietnam War. The Fish were followed by Santana, John Sebastian, the Keef Hartley Band, and the Incredible String Band. Canned Heat took the stage as darkness fell, singing "Going Up the Country," and then Mountain and the Grateful Dead played a long set, finishing after midnight. Creedence Clearwater Revival and The Who performed through the night and into the dawn of Sunday. With most people asleep on the ground, the music still rocked with Jefferson Airplane on stage in the morning. Joe Cocker came on in the afternoon with a thirteen-song set ending with the Beatles song "With a Little Help from My Friends." Then great clouds moved in and washed over the festival, rain shrouding the stage while people had fun sliding in the mud.

They began to leave after the rainstorm, walking to their cars to go home and back to work, reentering the world of reality. But the party wasn't yet over.

The music began again in the evening with Janis Joplin, Ten Years After, and the Band. Johnny Winter took the stage at midnight, followed by Sly and the Family Stone, their songs moving thousands to dance, followed by Blood, Sweat, and Tears. Sunday ran into Monday with Crosby, Stills & Nash harmonizing beautifully through a sixteen-song set that began with "Suite: Judy Blue Eyes" and included "Marrakesh Express" and "Wooden Ships."

The great crowd had thinned—the people were tired and more headed home—but the music continued with the Paul Butterfield Blues Band and Sha Na Na.

Then came Jimi Hendrix.

From the Shokan mansion, Jimi and his band had watched TV reports of the crowds. Billy Cox recalled, "We thought it was just a gig where a lot of good musicians were going to be."[6] Offered the chance to play at midnight when the crowd would be livelier, Jeffery insisted they close the show, so they spent most of the night in a cottage a few hundred yards from the stage, smoking pot and playing acoustic guitar. Finally, at 8:30 on Monday morning, Jimi, wearing a white, beaded, fringed jacket, blue velvet pants with a red bandana around his head, and carrying his white Stratocaster, took the stage with his band. Most of the crowd had departed—only 40,000 were on hand.

As the crowd thinned as the show progressed, Jimi announced, "You can leave if you want to, we're just jamming, that's all. Okay. You can leave or you can clap," and introduced another well-performed instrumental, "The Star-Spangled Banner." For those who remained—and those who eventually saw the film—this song defined Woodstock.

"Everything seemed to stop," recalled Roz Payne, a nurse in the "bad" trip tent. "Before that if someone would have played 'The Star-Spangled Banner' we would have booed; after that it became our song."[7]

Al Aronowitz wrote in the *New York Post*, "It was the most electrifying moment of Woodstock, and probably the single greatest moment of the sixties. You finally heard what that song was about, that you can love your country but hate the government."[8] Encased with sounds of rocket explosions and ambulance wails, Jimi challenged the audience to hear the national anthem any way they wanted. Through feedback and sustain, he made one of the best tunes in America his own.

He never spoke of it as a political statement. At a press conference three weeks later, he said of the song, "We're all Americans. . . . It was like 'Go America!' . . . We play it the way the air is in America today. The air is slightly static, see."[9] Jimi followed "The Star-Spangled Banner" with "Purple Haze," which got a visible response from the crowd, and ended with "Villanova Junction." When called for an encore, he chose "Hey Joe." When he finished, so did Woodstock, and having not slept for days, he walked off stage and collapsed from exhaustion.

Chording guitar

Joyful throng of thousands

Woodstock poster

Kidnapped and Released

Jimi had been charismatic at Woodstock, and, building on that momentum, he took his new band into the Hit Factory and cut six songs. They also rehearsed for a free street fair in Harlem, a gig that grew from the Aleem brothers' idea that a Harlem show might finally get Jimi on black radio. The Aleems had originally hoped to do the show at the Apollo, but the historic theater rejected the idea. "They didn't want him," Tunde Ra recalled. "They were afraid that there would be too many white folks." Rooted in the multiculturalism he had learned in Seattle at Leschi Elementary, "[Jimi] believed that color was what was on the outside, not what was inside," said Colette Mimram. "He felt his audience was white, but he wanted the black audience."[1] Still, he was anxious about performing to an African American audience.

The show in Harlem was to benefit the United Block Association (UBA). "Jimi was conned into doing that show," observed Michael Goldstein. "It was a time when any black hustler who could get near him was saying, 'You shouldn't have any white people around.'" Jimi was not getting paid for his appearance, and Jeffery, feeling threatened by the growing influence of the Aleems, was against doing it.

At a press conference two days before the show, looking resplendent in a black robe purchased in Morocco, Jimi spoke to a dozen reporters about Woodstock, saying he had been impressed by the nonviolent nature of the music festival and hoped the UBA show would bring the same sense of unity to Harlem, where "they're tired of joining street gangs, they're tired of joining militant groups . . . they want to find a different direction."[2]

The festival was an all-day affair. Many of the five thousand people gathered were white. There was music by Sam and Dave, Big Maybelle, Jay Dee Bryant, and Maxine Brown, all playing on a small stage that faced Lennox Avenue on 139th Street. Jimi was scheduled to play in the evening. Before the show he told a *New York Times* reporter, "Sometimes when I come up here people say, 'he plays white rock for white people' . . . Well, I want to show them that music is universal—that there is no white rock or black rock."[3]

But his equanimity could not dispel the tension. "A lot of black people in the neighborhood didn't even know who Jimi was," Tunde Ra Aleem said, "but so many white people were in the street they became curious."

Standing with Carmen Borrero, watching the other bands, people chastised Jimi for having a Puerto Rican girlfriend. "They saw Jimi with what they thought was a 'white bitch' and they threw stuff at me," recalled Carmen, whose blouse was ripped in a tussle.[4]

Following Big Maybelle, the 250-pound rhythm and blues singer, Jimi took the stage at midnight. The crowd booed when Maybelle refused an encore and booed when Mitch Mitchell, a white man, walked on stage. "People were annoyed because Mitch was a white kid in Harlem," TaharQa Aleem recalled. When Jimi came on stage wearing white pants, his clothes earned catcalls. As he began to tune his guitar, a bottle smashed against an amplifier. By the time Jimi began to play, only about five hundred people remained in the audience, and some started throwing eggs. "He had to act really quick or a riot could have happened," recalled TaharQa.[5] He began with "Fire" and followed with "Foxy Lady." When he played "Red House," the tough crowd softened with the bluesy flavor. Fewer than two hundred people remained at the end of his set, but he had survived one of the toughest audiences he'd ever faced. Two weeks later he dismantled the Gypsy Sun and Rainbows, keeping only Billy Cox.

Jimi had been frequenting a discotheque called The Salvation, one of New York's most fashionable Greenwich Village night clubs, including among its patrons Paul McCartney and Jordan's King Hussein. It was owned by a man named Bobby Woods. When the club was charged with liquor law violations and had its license revoked, the glamorous clientele moved on and was replaced by a seedier element, many of whom sold drugs. According to a bartender named Richie, this group included "younger mafia guys from Brooklyn who wanted to be paid protection money. There were four or five of them, and they'd take turns hanging out at the club to keep track of how much business we were doing, what was going on. The way they worked, they figured out what it'd be worth to you not to be hassled. They didn't want to put you out of business—they only wanted all they could get without bankrupting you. . . . These were younger guys out trying to earn their own 'bones.' Bobby resisted them right to the end."

Bobby knew Jimi was rehearsing a new trio with Billy Cox on bass and Buddy Miles as drummer and suggested showcasing the new band at Salvation. He wouldn't have to play his old hits, but anything he wanted, and so Jimi agreed to play without payment. Bobby put the word out and charged a $25 cover and a three-drink minimum at $5 apiece. The club held only 250 people and the lineups were around the block. "There were a couple of cops at the top of the stairs leading down into the club," recalled Richie. "Bobby was at the door grabbing the money as people came in and stashing it away."[6] Jimi performed fifty minutes of what seemed like an extended jam. The audience was somewhat cool, and microphone problems made it worse, but Jimi was pleased at the end of the evening.

Then something strange happened. One night he left the club with two people he knew slightly, ostensibly to score cocaine, and found himself held at gunpoint in an apartment in Little Italy. The next morning, he was told to call Mike Jeffery. "It was serious," Jerry Morrison recalled. "When Jimi called, he told Bob [Levine] that he was being held by guys who wanted Jimi's management contract. Jimi said that if Mike didn't turn it over, the guys were going to kill him." None of this made much sense.

There is no record of the kidnapping in New York City Police files, nor the FBI's organized crime desk. Kidnapping wasn't really a mafia interest, and if Jimi had been a target, as one mafioso put it, "every crazy nigger in Harlem would've come after the Italians once the word was out."

Mike Jeffery and Jerry Morrison didn't think it was a practical joke. Mike decided not to call the police and waited for Jerry to arrive at the office. Jerry arrived at around noon and, after listening to a replay of the early telephone call, made some calls of his own, finally reaching "the son of a top godfather who owed me a favor."[7] According to Jerry, the Don knew about Hendrix and told Jerry he could bring Jeffery along to meet after dinner. At the meeting, Jeffery started babbling that he would give anything the gangsters needed to secure Jimi's release. The mafioso told them he'd call in the morning. They returned to the office and spent a restless night waiting.

The following morning Jerry's mafia friend called and gave them an address. Jerry went with two friends to this address where they were told Jimi had been taken away by two men and a driver only an hour and a half earlier. They were told that the men who kidnapped Jimi were "jitterbugs" and didn't have permission to do it. Jerry surmised that they had asked Jimi where to go and Jimi told them his place in Woodstock. And so, Jerry and his friends made the drive to the country, to the long, narrow road, to the big stone house, and stopped about half a mile from the gate. Jerry got out and went ahead on foot through the woods, trying not to make noise as he went through the fallen leaves and brush. His friends joined him, and they sneaked up to the silent house and entered through an unlocked cellar window, then stealthily crept up the stairs to the kitchen door where two armed men were drinking coffee. They tied them up and went upstairs to find Jimi in the master bedroom, sitting in the middle of the bed, apparently having a wonderful time. "I knew you'd come," said Jimi.[8] Nearby there was an ashtray with marijuana roaches and an assortment of coke paraphernalia. The hoodlums were sent back to New York where they got their just deserts from the chieftains.

There wasn't so much as a whisper about the kidnapping among police and newspaper reporters who devote their lives to investigating crime. Bobby Woods closed Salvation in November, telling friends it was because of the mob shakedown. His body was found three months later, lying in the middle of a street in Queens, his arms folded neatly over his chest. His jaw was broken and he had been shot in the chest and behind each ear. It was an execution that went unsolved. Many thought the kidnapping was arranged from beginning to end by Jerry Morrison to make himself look good and gain an advantage in future dealings with Jimi and Mike Jeffery. But something had happened, it made some people squirm, and once it was past, Jimi rarely referred to it, and when he did, he didn't share much detail. It seemed to be something he wanted to forget.

In a profile by Sheila Weller that appeared in *Rolling Stone* that September, Jimi was self-effacing, polite, and charming as he showed his extensive record collection, which included Marlene Dietrich, Wes Montgomery, and Blind Faith. He was especially enthusiastic about Bob Dylan as he played along on his guitar to a Dylan record. "I love Bob Dylan. I only met him once, about three years ago, back at the Kettle O' Fish on MacDougal Street. That was before I went to England. I think both of us were pretty drunk at the time, so he probably doesn't remember me."[9]

Deering Howe remembered a meeting with Dylan in Manhattan that fall. They were walking down Eighth Street when they saw a familiar figure across the street. "Hey, that's Dylan," said Jimi excitedly. "I've never met him before. Let's go talk to him." As Deering followed, Jimi darted into traffic yelling, "Hey, Bob!" Deering thought Dylan was concerned by someone shouting his name and racing across the street, but when Dylan recognized Jimi, he relaxed. Jimi was modest and shy: "Bob, uh, I'm a singer, you know, called Jimi Hendrix."

Dylan knew who he was and loved his covers of "All Along the Watchtower" and "Like a Rolling Stone," saying, "I don't know if anyone has done my songs better."

The meeting was brief, Dylan hurried off, but "Jimi was on cloud nine," recalled Deering, "if only because Bob Dylan knew who he was. It seemed very clear to me that the two had never met before."[10]

Deering had late-night jam sessions in his penthouse featuring Jimi and Mick Jagger. "There were some occasions at four in the morning when they all showed up at my apartment." Devon Wilson had added Mick Jagger to her list of conquests, which led to uncomfortable scenes at these jams. "Devon loved having Mick on her arm in front of Jimi," remembered Deering. "She had glee at rubbing it in." Hendrix wrote a song, "Dolly Dagger," based on an incident in which Mick pricked his finger, and, rather than a band-aid, Devon said she would suck the wound clean. Jagger had successfully wooed Devon but was not successful in the musical showdowns with Jimi at Deering's apartment. "When you saw Jimi play the blues on an acoustic guitar," Deering said, "he was never better."[11] Jagger was speechless.

On his twenty-seventh birthday, November 27, 1969, Jimi watched the Rolling Stones at Madison Square Garden. Backstage before the show, he and Keith Richards joked about their once-heated rivalry over Linda Keith. Jimi borrowed a guitar and began to play. While a filmmaker captured the scene for a documentary, Mick Jagger walked in front of the camera as if to draw attention away from Jimi. When the concert began, Jimi sat onstage behind Keith's amplifier, visible to all. An invitation to jam with the Stones on his birthday would have been a gracious gesture, but after the sessions in Deering Howe's apartment, Jagger knew Jimi's talent could silence everyone in a room, and he had no desire to be upstaged at his own show.

Jimi began to dress more conservatively, still wearing lots of jewelry and bright colors but fewer scarves. He even began wearing stylish suits. The groupie scene was less important and no longer was he a fixture in nightclubs. He talked about his music in an article in *LIFE* magazine with a deep-felt reverence: "A musician, if he's a messenger, is like a child who hasn't been handled too many times by man . . . hasn't had too many fingerprints across his brain. That's why music is so much heavier than anything you ever felt." In *Rolling Stone* he said, "I don't want to be a clown anymore. I don't want to be a rock and roll star!" But it was too late. Jimi had become rock royalty. *Life*'s editors called him a "rock demigod," while *Vogue* called him "cinnamon to a generation short on spice."[12]

That fall he leased an apartment at 59 West Twelfth Street in Greenwich Village, the first and only place of his own in New York City. He decorated it with help from Colette Mimram, covering the walls with bedspreads and prayer rugs and hanging a tapestry over his four-poster bed. He arranged three sofas low to the floor in the living room and put throw pillows around the room. "The place looked like a Moroccan bazaar," recalled Colette. "There were African textiles all over the ceiling."[13]

On Sunday, December 7, he flew to Toronto for his heroin possession trial with Jeanette Jacobs and Sharon Lawrence, the UPI reporter who testified for him. He had his hair cut and wore a blue blazer and gray slacks to court.

At the hotel was Chas Chandler, who had come from London to offer his testimony. Facing a possible seven years in jail, Jimi was visibly nervous when he entered the courtroom on Monday at 10 A.M. It was a twelve-person jury trial with a presiding judge in a white wig in the British tradition. The prosecution's first witness was Marvin Wilson, the customs officer who had searched Jimi's flight bag at the airport. He told his story much as he had before: When he found the vial of white powder, he asked Jimi if he knew what it was. Jimi said he did not know what it was and that someone must have put it in his bag. Wilson also mentioned how his supervisor took Jimi into a private room where he was searched and a lab test was performed on the powder. The second and third witnesses were the supervisor and lab technician, both supporting Wilson's testimony.

When Jimi took the stand, under questioning from the defense, he told the judge and jury that he was a musician with four gold records. His voice was soft, and while answering he gazed into his lap. When his lawyers asked about the fans, Jimi said they gave him gifts all the time. The lawyer asked if they ever gave him drugs. Jimi said again, "All the time," adding that he was usually too busy when he got the gifts to look at them. Generally, he just tossed them into his bags to examine later. If the gift was dope, he would get rid of it. When Jimi admitted he had experimented with drugs but had given them up, his lawyer looked him in the eye and asked, "Do you mean you've given up drugs entirely?" and Jimi replied, "I've outgrown it."[14]

It was a lie, but "mea culpa," followed by a denial of current guilt, was a common defense in the 1960s and early 1970s. Juries seemed to like to "forgive" entertainers charged with possession of drugs so long as they seemed repentant and had successfully cleaned up their lives. When Jimi testified again the following day, he mentioned a girl giving him the vial in his hotel room in Beverly Hills and that he assumed it was Bromo-Seltzer to make him feel better, so he just threw it into his flight bag. The Crown, in cross-examination, tried to make Jimi look like a practiced, habitual user. When the prosecutor asked, "Come on now, Mr. Hendrix, what could such a tube be used for?" Jimi replied, "I dunno maybe a peashooter." The courtroom exploded with laughter.

Sharon Lawrence testified after lunch, confirming Jimi's story to the last detail. Jimi's next witness was Chas Chandler, who told the court that when he was touring and making records with the Animals, fans gave him gifts all the time. When he managed Jimi, fans gave drugs as gifts all the time. His testimony worked, making it clear that in rock-and-roll circles it wasn't that unusual for people to gift drugs to performers.

On the third and final day, Jimi entered the courtroom in a pinstripe suit and a lurid purple shirt. His lawyer rested his case on a technical bit of Canadian law that stipulated that true possession of something meant there had to be knowledge of that possession. In other words, if Jimi didn't know he had the stuff, then technically he didn't have it. It seemed a rather vague issue upon which to hang Jimi's future, but, said Jimi's attorneys, the law was the law, and if there seemed a reasonable doubt that Jimi knew what he had in his flight bag, he could not be convicted.

The Crown's closing speech was brief and ineffective: Why, they wondered, had Jimi not tried to find the girl who gave him the jar. When the jury returned, the foreman read the verdict, declaring James Marshall Hendrix not guilty. Jimi was elated. For nearly twenty minutes people came up to him, shaking his hand and saying, "Right On!" On the way out of the courtroom, Jimi told newspaper reporters, "It's the best Christmas present Canada could give me."[15] And before getting on the plane to go home to New York, he smoked some grass that was a gift from a Toronto fan.

Electric Lady Studios was taking longer to build and costing more than planned. Jeffery and Hendrix had already spent $369,000 and had to borrow another $300,000 to finish it. Jimi had nearly forty songs in various stages of completion; in fact, he had miles of tapes sitting in hundreds of boxes around town. Gerry Stickells did his best to keep things organized, but the chaos increased as Jimi kept recording. And there were demands from Reprise, which hadn't had new material in eighteen months. Knowing his next LP would only benefit Chalpin, in early December Jimi decided to do a live-performance album from four year-end shows scheduled at the Fillmore East. Needing to form his next band, he talked about bringing in Jack Casady from Jefferson Airplane and Steve Winwood from Traffic, forming a supergroup of sorts, until deciding upon a trio with Buddy Miles and Billy Cox.

Buddy was a multi-talented drummer who could also sing. Jimi named them Band of Gypsys, an idea that came from Mitch, who once called Jimi's unusual backstage entourage "like a band of gypsies." (The misspelling of "gypsies" was Jimi's touch.) They spent ten days rehearsing in late December, writing several new songs, one of which was "Earth Blues," featuring vocals from Ronnie Spector of the Ronettes, who had dropped by Jimi's apartment to find him in bed with five women. "They were lazing around, fighting over who was going to light his cigarettes or bring him a drink," she recalled. "It was like he was a sheikh . . . lying there like a king."[16]

Jimi, rich, talented, and handsome, was swarmed by young women. The doorman of his building called when a girl showed up unannounced. Many women wanted to have a relationship, but mostly he attracted groupies, partly on the reputation of his plaster cast. To them, he was a sexual conquest, as they were to him, and he had had so many he had long lost count of the number. "There were so many women after him, it was like he was a king in the garden," recalled Buzzy Linhart. "He was being treated like an object, though. There wasn't much romance to it."[17] He may have been afraid of getting too close to anyone for fear of being abandoned, as had happened so often in his childhood. Quick and nearly anonymous sexual relationships offered little risk of being hurt.

20

Playin' Good Music

On Christmas night, 1969, Carmen Borrero accompanied Jimi to Deering Howe's penthouse atop the Hotel Navarro. The ten-room apartment had two living rooms, giant windows facing Central Park, and a huge Christmas tree framing the fabulous view. A light snow had begun to fall when they arrived. Jimi was dressed in a lizard-skin jacket and red velvet pants. They ate a fine meal and drank Dom Perignon out of crystal flutes. Jimi said it was his best Christmas ever. He gave Carmen diamond earrings and a diamond ring meant as an engagement ring, but Carmen said they had never seriously discussed marriage. "That marriage would have been with three people: Jimi, Devon, and me," said Carmen.

Devon had induced Jimi to snort heroin. "He liked creative drugs, but he couldn't stand heroin," recalled Colette. "He tried it, but it was not what he wanted to do."[1]

Jimi "was obsessed with his hair; he loved his little curls," Carmen remembered. He would have his hair done by James Finney.

"Finney introduced the 'Blowout' through Jimi," said TaharQa Aleem. "Prior to that, it had been 'the Afro' and before that 'the Conk.'" Legendary jazz musician Miles Davis liked Jimi's hair and began going to Finney, too. Jimi and Miles became friends and occasionally went out together with girlfriends. One night they traveled uptown to Small's Paradise in Harlem.

With Miles, Jimi finally got the reception he had always wanted. "They put us in a table in the corner," Carmen recalled, "and even put a small curtain around us so we could smoke a joint. They sent over wine and played Jimi's music over the sound system."[2]

Miles and Jimi admired each other's work. When asked by the Aleems what he heard in Jimi's music, Miles said, "It's that goddamn motherfucking 'Machine Gun,'" referring to the song recorded with Band of Gypsys. TaharQa said he heard similar styles in Miles's music. "It ain't what you hear," Miles replied. "It's what you bring from the subjective to the objective."[3] Jimi's musical tastes were so eclectic that he never limited himself to one genre, and, inspired by his friendship with Miles, he began buying jazz albums, frequently going into Colony Records late at night and buying up bins of rock, jazz, and the classical greats.

A recording session was planned to pair Miles and Jimi together. Jimi liked to jam first and worry about contracts, record labels, and payments later. But Miles, frustrated by how little money he made with jazz and jealous of Jimi's earnings, called Mike Jeffery a day before the recording was scheduled and demanded $50,000 up front. The drummer for the planned recording, Tony Williams, made an equally large request. Jimi was so certain the session would take place that he wanted a superstar bass player to join, and he sent a telegram to Paul McCartney, asking him to play with the group. But Jeffery refused the musicians' outrageous demands and the session never occurred.

However, Jimi and Miles did get together and play music in Jimi's apartment. English singer Terry Reid was present. Jimi told Terry that someone may be coming by and went into his bedroom to tune his guitar. The doorbell rang, and Terry peered through the peephole. "There was this purple person with these shades around his head," he recalled. "There is no other human being who looked like that on the whole bloody planet." Reid opened the door and greeted Miles with a warm smile.

Miles scowled. "I knew he hated white people," Reid remembered, "so I tried as hard as I could to be welcoming with my British charm." Miles would not come in. He grabbed the door handle and shut himself out. Reid opened the door and urged him to enter.

"I want fucking Jimi Hendrix to open Jimi Hendrix's door," replied Miles.

Reid went to fetch Jimi. "Did you let him in?" Jimi asked.

"He shut the door in my face. He won't come in unless you answer the door."

"Yeah, he's like that," Jimi said with a laugh.

Miles entered silently. He and Jimi went into the bedroom while Terry sat in the living room. Soon he heard Miles's muted trumpet accompanied by Jimi's unamplified guitar drifting out from under the door. "It was truly beautiful," he recalled. "It was tasteful playing, nothing showy or over the top. In the jazz context, Jimi was still pushing the limits, and all those jazz guys respected him like they respected no one else in rock."[4]

Jazz producer Alan Douglas focused his attention on Jimi. "Jimi was a virtuoso," explained Douglas, "and it was my intention to deal with him in a way that if he felt like doing the blues, well, I would get a dynamic blues group behind him, and if he felt like playing Flamenco music, I would get some Spanish guys in. . . . He was getting into [jazz], so I set up some jams with John McLaughlin, Dave Holland, Larry Young, people like that. Jimi was talking to Miles Davis on the telephone. We planned to record with Roland Kirk. . . . There was a lot going on."

Plans to work with some of the all-time jazz greats eased some of the stress Jimi felt during otherwise strenuous weeks. Although Douglas had Jimi's blessing, he did not have Mike Jeffery's, and, according to Douglas, there was friction. "I was pulling Jimi in another direction and Michael was very paranoid about everybody and everything who got near to Jimi."[5] Soon Jeffery began threatening to sue Douglas. Jimi was still complaining to friends about Jeffery, but doing little else, preferring to keep the peculiar sort of "peace" that goes with backing down. Jimi was not a coward, but he was not a proactive fighter, and, as Mike Jeffery knew, he was a man who couldn't say no.

Jeffery had to regain lost momentum. With no new recordings in two years and only a handful of appearances in the past six months, Jimi was becoming invisible. *Rolling Stone* wrote, "Jimi had a big year—A pretty neat trick for a musician who made no music."[6] Reprise released a 45 rpm single containing two original songs, "Izabella" and "Stepping Stone," that did not make the charts.

Jeffery fired the publicist, figuring he was an unnecessary expense, and began negotiating with young filmmakers to put Jimi in a movie. A deal was made with Peter Pilafian, a sound engineer who worked with the Mamas and the Papas, for a simple in-concert film. A second film planned was to be directed by Chuck Wein, an Andy Warhol "factory" associate, and conceived as a sort of cinematic phantasmagoria of psychedelic and occult philosophy and phenomena.

Chuck Wein came into the office traveling at the speed of light and speaking what Jerry Morrison called "Fluent Tarot." Wein told *Rolling Stone*, "I had known Jimi from the Scene, and I was living with Pat Hartley and Devon. I was into reading tarot cards, and I read the cards for Jimi and Mitch Mitchell and Billy Cox. Jimi started to tell me about being from an asteroid belt off the coast of Mars, so I said, 'Stop and I'll tell you about it because it's a place I've seen three or four times clear as a bell.'"[7]

At that point the deal was struck to make the movie, which eventually became *Rainbow Bridge*. The financial backers were Mike Jeffery and Mo Ostin of Reprise Records. Mike eventually contributed $500,000 and Mo pledged $450,000 toward the film's production in exchange for the rights to distribute a soundtrack album. Chuck and his partner, Barry Prendergast, received the green light to start filming in Hawaii in July 1970, when Jimi was scheduled to play in Honolulu. Jimi plunged into rehearsals for upcoming concerts and was recording with an enthusiasm his friends hadn't seen in a long time. Rehearsing in a Greenwich Village loft with his Band of Gypsys took on the feel of extended jams.

Jeffery agreed to provide Chalpin the album he was owed with a "live" recording at the Fillmore. Live albums were quicker and much cheaper to produce than studio recordings. Jimi was contracted to perform two shows at the theater each night on December 31 and January 1. Chalpin's album would come from whatever was recorded those two nights.

Playing in his first all-black band since Curtis Knight and the Squires, Bill Graham, the producer, wanted Jimi to give the most exciting shows of his career. In the first show, Jimi performed his old tricks, humping the guitar and playing it with his teeth, and the trio gave the kind of show they used to do on the Chitlin' Circuit. Backstage, Bill Graham was not satisfied, and Jimi wanted to know why. Graham took him into his office and told him, "I thought the show sucked!"

Jimi was stunned and then turned angry. "What the fuck do you mean, man," he said. "Those people ate it up."

Graham replied, "You did your coon act. Lemme tell you something: You can't play the guitar while you're fucking it. You're recording these shows, right? Well, when you listen to that first one, you're gonna fucking throw up. I bet you won't use a note of it. So why don't you go out there and play the next show! You're a musician, Jimi. Play music!"[8]

During the next set, Jimi satisfied Graham, the audience, and himself. He started by playing "a little thing called 'Machine Gun,'" which was played unlike anything Jimi had played before. At the end of a turbulent decade during which music and politics came together as never before, Jimi had tried to be apolitical, but "The Star-Spangled Banner" had been a significant shift and "Machine Gun" was something else. For twelve minutes the stage reverberated with feedback that sounded like dive-bombing planes and women shrieking at the sight of their children's deaths. The audience recoiled as if physically struck. This song and lyrics filled up most of one side of the album delivered to Chalpin the following week. The second side was less remarkable, largely blues-based songs.

Bill Graham wrote, "There will never be anything like that [second] show. . . . He just played. And he just sang. He moved his body but it was always in time to the music. . . . There was grace, but no bullshit."

Halfway through the set, Jimi went backstage and taunted Graham. "Good enough for you, Jack?"

Graham said it was great, and then Jimi did "Wild Thing" with all the gimmickry. "All the shtick," Graham wrote, "the fire, throwing, kicking, humping, grinding. But what he had given them before, that was the real thing."[9]

Jimi left the stage pleased but became angry when he remembered the record would benefit Ed Chalpin. (When released in the spring, the album, called *Band of Gypsys*, soared up the record charts, going to number five on *Billboard*'s list and generally earning good reviews.) For days afterward it was all he could talk about as he plunged into a deep depression.

Jeffery insisted on getting rid of Buddy Miles and Billy Cox: "It isn't really working with Buddy and Billy," he told Jimi in his office. "They're good musicians and all that, but I think the audience wants Mitch and Noel." Jimi slumped in a chair. Jeffery pleaded sweetly at first but ended his long rap with curses and shouts. "I have nothing against black musicians," he said, "but I do think I know what your audience wants. . . . I don't care who you record with, but when you're onstage, everybody wants to see some white faces!" Jimi's face was a silent mask. Finally, Jeffery held up a letter of agreement that he wanted Jimi to sign. "You and Noel and Mitch agree to get together."[10] The money was fabulous, but Jimi took the paper, looked it over, dropped it to the floor, and walked out of the room, slamming the door behind him.

Jimi then did what he always did when pressure built: sought refuge in music and drugs.

Later, Jeffery told Jimi that the Experience was being reformed, whether he liked it or not. Jimi still resisted the idea, but some financial statements were shown. Jimi hadn't delivered an album to Reprise in almost two years, and, according to his contract, he was supposed to deliver two each year; that meant he owed Reprise four albums, plus Reprise's $250,000 advance for Electric Lady Studios. Jimi also owed the lawyers for the Toronto trial, the current bill for the Record Plant was $15,000, and he was hiring limousines and having them stand by around the clock while he partied or slept, another $5,000 monthly. His European royalties were frozen, thanks to the lawsuit by Chalpin, and he had not worked much since Woodstock.

"Jimi," Jeffery then said, picking up the one-page agreement to reunite the original Experience, "there are a lot of unpaid taxes too."[11] And so, with visions of Joe Louis on the financial ropes, Jimi signed on the dotted line.

"Musically it wasn't going down well between Jimi and Buddy," Jeffery said. "Jimi was able to instill in his music all the four elements—water, fire, air, earth. When he played earth, Buddy was the best drummer in the world for him. But Jimi was getting less earthy, and when he got out there into air, Buddy just didn't make it. There were those large gaps that had to be filled by somebody with a different drumming technique than Buddy's. . . . This is what I expressed to Jimi, and this is what he agreed with. . . . So I had the difficult position of removing Buddy from Jimi. Jimi felt it, but Jimi could never say no. Buddy was a friend of his in a nonmusical sense. I told Buddy the trip was over. . . . We argued a bit and we shouted a bit. . . . He felt that he was a star, too, and I regarded him as essentially a supporting man for Jimi."[12]

In early February, Jeffery brought Mitch and Noel over from England and told *Rolling Stone* that Jimi was reforming the Experience and wanted to give an exclusive interview. Jimi didn't want the reunion. He had always liked Mitch and respected his drumming, but he fought with Noel and had come to think he was an inadequate bass player. Yet when Mitch and Noel arrived, it was like old times. They laughed and told stories about the early days.

Rolling Stone's managing editor John Burks came to Mike's apartment, where the interview was held. When Burks asked Jimi about his Toronto court claim that he had outgrown drugs, Jimi replied, "I don't know, I'm too . . . wrecked right now," and grinned, showing his long teeth in a smile reminiscent of Charlie Chaplin.

Burks wrote, "This was Hendrix the comedian. This side of Jimi is the one people love. He does it all with split-second timing, a shrug, an eye cast downward, a slight over-accented word. It's the essence of his charm, and figures in many ways in the way he makes music."[13] Jeffery kept tiptoeing around the room during the interview, wincing whenever Jimi joked about drug use. As tickets were sold for a massive Experience Reunion Tour, Jimi decided he didn't want Noel in the band. He phoned Billy Cox and asked him to play bass, leaving it for Jeffery to tell Noel.

The spring 1970 tour began at the Forum in Los Angeles on April 25. The show was billed as "The Experience." The band consisted of Billy Cox and Mitch Mitchell. The tour drew some of the best reviews of Jimi's career. "Hendrix is a powerhouse of sex and sound," wrote Robert Hilburn of the opening show in the *Los Angeles Times*. Jimi played a few old hits, but "Machine Gun" and "Message to Love" were from the live Band of Gypsys album released the day before. Hilburn noticed, "The newer material generated less enthusiasm." Jimi cut back on the guitar gimmicks, which made him feel more energized about his playing.

Some critics missed Noel, but Mitch was playing better than ever; his jazz-influenced style fit well with the new material. "Mitch was just one bitch of a drummer," said Bob Levine. "With his ability to improvise, he was the perfect drummer for Jimi."[14]

Ballin' Jack was on the bill in Los Angeles, a band that included old friends Luther Rabb (who had played with the Velvetones) and Ronnie Hammond from Seattle, and they were well paid and given a full set.

"Jimi would literally give you the shirt off his back," Hammond recalled. "One night he was coming off stage and I said 'nice shirt.' He ripped it off and handed it to me." He also gave Luther a festive coat he had bought in London because he thought Luther looked better in it.

Luther was concerned about Jimi's drug use. "He was over the line," Luther recalled. "He was aware that it was hurting him. He was making efforts, but somehow, through management or someone, people were always funneling drugs to him."[15]

Touring with his old Seattle friends gave Jimi a levity he rarely felt on the road. He told Luther that he wore outrageous stage clothes because he wanted crowds to come back the next time he passed through, if only to see what he was wearing. Playing music with his old friends was a great relief, too. On tour he was compelled to play more of his hits. "He hated singing those hits," said Luther, "but he felt he had to. Much of his act was rooted in 'The Show,' and he felt he had to do things like play behind his back because that's why people came to see him."

Between sets he visited Ballin' Jack's dressing room to jam. "He'd call that private show he did with us 'The Seattle Special,'" Luther said. "The people in the audience didn't get to hear it, but it was the best stuff he would do all night."[16]

To accommodate the demand for tickets, they traveled across the country, playing in mammoth halls and auditoriums. Jimi was soon struggling with the grind. He came onstage drunk in Madison, Wisconsin, joked about needing a joint, and explained that "Room Full of Mirrors" was about "When you get so high that all you see is you, your reflections here and there."

He also mentioned Christ. Juma Sultan recalled that Jimi was increasingly reading the Bible: "He kept it open in his house and he was reading it closely, probably for the first time in his life."[17] Jimi was grasping at many things—drugs, religion, and women—as he searched for stability in a life that was ever more on the edge. His stage rap in Madison, touching on mortality, had a tone of desperation.

The halls exploded when he played his early hits, but when he played the new songs like "Message of Love" or "Ezy Rider," the crowds applauded perfunctorily, except in Berkeley, California, where he arrived on May 30 for two shows scheduled in the small community theater holding only three hundred people. A film crew hired by Jeffery documented these concerts, capturing some of Hendrix's best concert footage. Protesters attempted to break through the roof of the theater, throwing rocks at attendees, but Jimi saw none of this when he arrived in a stretch limousine with Colette Mimram and Devon Wilson. Kissing Devon before exiting the limo, he entered through the back door. During the sound check, Jimi played a seven-minute version of "Blue Suede Shoes," a song he had turned into straight-ahead blues.

In the first show, he transformed Chuck Berry's "Johnny B. Goode" into a quick-tempo rave, playing part of the solo with his teeth. He introduced "Hear My Train A-Comin'" with detailed story imagery which was in essence a recounting of his own life story.[18] Using the wah-wah pedal, the fuzz-face effects box, extensive feedback, and sustain, he created the illusion of additional guitars when there were none. He also used his thumb to play echo-like riffs, creating a call and response with those put down by Cox and Mitchell. Cox and Mitchell, players with deep intuitive skills, followed his long improvisations through the winding route of the song, lasting twelve minutes, a powerhouse anthem that most performers would have used to close the show, but it was just the third song of a twelve-song set.

The second show was even better. He introduced "Machine Gun" by saying, "I'd like to dedicate this to all the soldiers fighting in Berkeley, you know what soldiers I'm talking about, and to the soldiers fighting in Vietnam, too."

Carlos Santana saw the shows and thought they were on the level of John Coltrane. "Very few people play fast and deep," Santana recalled. "Most play fast and shallow. But Coltrane played fast and deep, so did Charlie Parker, and so did Jimi." Backstage, Santana chatted with Jimi, but their conversation was distracted by all the groupies present. "He was around with those ladies," remembered Santana. "I used to call them 'monitors' because they would go to bed with everybody and tell you everything about everyone else."[19] The groupies were impressed by Jimi's evolving dress: He now wore headbands instead of a witch hat, and kimono-like shirts and brightly colored scarves had replaced the antique military jacket.

Despite touring, Jimi spent much of the spring and summer of 1970 in the studio trying to complete a new album. He had enough material for four albums but wasn't ready to publish anything new. He worked obsessively, spending entire days working on one overdub. "It was an expensive way of doing it," observed engineer Eddie Kramer, "but considering all the stuff that was happening, it seemed to be the only way."

Few of Jimi's sessions began with a plan. He'd make use of the musicians he'd met in a club earlier in the evening; he even once invited a cab driver into a session after he mentioned he played the congas. However, as Electric Lady Studios came to completion, the cost of recording was reduced because Jimi and Jeffery owned the facility.

"He was very proud of that studio," Eddie Kramer recalled. "Being a black man of his stature, making a lot of money, and owning your own studio in New York City, that was the pinnacle of success for him." It became his home away from home and contributed to his perfectionism: He cut nineteen takes of "Dolly Dagger" before achieving a master.

"He loved that studio and he spent night and day there," recalled Deering Howe.[20]

By the middle of June, Jimi had whittled down the songs for his new album. He never settled on a title or a list of tracks. Jeffery said a single album would sell better, but Jimi wanted a triple set. He wrote a list of songs that included "Room Full of Mirrors," "Ezy Rider," "Angel," "Cherokee Mist," "Dolly Dagger," and twenty others, and that was as close as he would come to a finished album.

In late July, Jimi flew to Seattle, where Jeffery had arranged a last-minute show to help keep up with their staggering bills. The show was scheduled for Sick's Stadium, a 26,000-seat ballpark in the Rainier Valley that Jimi knew well from his youth. He took a morning flight on Sunday, July 26. The concert started at 2:30 P.M., but he wouldn't go on until the evening. His hope for a few hours of sleep became impossible when his family converged.

"He was tied up from minute one," recalled Seattle promoter Dan Fiala. "They'd be calling our office ten times a day saying they were going to pick him up. . . . Meanwhile, management was telling us, 'We've got to isolate him because they are driving him nuts.'" Though a superstar everywhere else in the world, in Seattle he was still Buster Hendrix who deferred to his father.

Jimi spent a bittersweet afternoon at Al's house, visiting with family and friends. He had a few drinks and got into an argument with Al, which upset them both. Jimi was also sad because Leon was in jail for larceny and missed his visit. His spirits rose when Delores Hall brought his fifteen-year-old cousin Eddy to play guitar. Jimi was impressed. "Jimi asked my mom if he could take me on the road with him," recalled Eddy.[21] Delores loved Jimi but turned down the offer.

A fractured part of the past emerged when an eighteen-year-old woman came by and asked for Jimi's autograph, saying she was his sister, Pamela Hendrix, who had been adopted by a family living nearby. He had not seen her for seventeen years and gave her an autograph and a hug. Not long after the extraordinary visit from his long-lost sister, he phoned "Auntie" Dorothy Harding and invited her family to the show, arranging for a limousine to pick them up. He also made a surreptitious phone call to his old girlfriend, Betty Jean Morgan, discovering they no longer had much in common and ran out of words to say.

An unseasonable downpour threatened to cancel the concert that night. Some of the equipment wasn't grounded and the promoters didn't want their headliner electrocuted. But Jimi went on anyway as the rain briefly let up. Addressing the crowd, he said, "You don't sound very happy, you don't look very happy, but we'll see if we can paint some faces around here," and then the band launched into "Fire."

Someone threw a pillow onto the stage that Janis Joplin had autographed on the same stage three weeks ago when it was tossed to her. Objects hurled on stage upset Jimi. He warned, "Please don't throw anything up here," and, his mood turning sour, exclaimed, "Fuck you, whoever put up the pillow," then kicked the pillow off the stage and raised his middle finger to the crowd.[22] He left the stage briefly while Mitch handled a drum solo, and then returned and played "Purple Haze," "Red House," and "Foxy Lady," then left without an encore.

Returning to his father's house after the concert, where again a crowd had gathered, he looked exhausted. Freddie Mae Gautier, a woman whose mother had cared for him as an infant, said he was wistful and sad, "as if he were under a spell." They talked, and despite the earlier argument with Al, Jimi spoke warmly of his dad, saying he had come to understand his difficult life. "Al would be up all night sometimes working," Freddie recalled. "As Jimi got older he realized how much his dad had given up for him and Leon."[23]

At about midnight, Jimi left the house with three young women: his cousin Dee Hall, Alice Harding, and new stepsister Marsha Jinka. Dee was impressed by his concert. "He said he was ready to make some big changes in his life, and that his music would be changing, too."

When asked if he had explored jazz much, he replied that he was tinkering with it and that he planned on making another album in the fall, had written a screenplay, and wanted to go to school to learn how to compose music. They knew he was a dreamer.

After taking a hit of acid—"he called it Purple Haze," remembered Dee—they tripped through Seattle in search of his past as he had with Carmen Borrero and a boy in his beat-up Volkswagen. They went to Garfield High and the places where he had lived. They drove by clubs where he had tried to jam, and he mentioned the names of people who wouldn't let him join their bands. Dee had never seen him so nostalgic and was surprised how well he seemed to have resolved the painful parts of his life.

"They really treated you like dirt—they would laugh at you," she told him.

"Oh, sometimes you have to go through that," he replied.

They stopped by the Yesler Terrace Neighborhood House, one of the first places where Jimi performed, and the Harborview Hospital where Jimi was born and where his mother had passed away. Dee asked Jimi if he had seen his brother Joe. "Not for years," he said, "but I sure would like to." They even drove by the detention center where Jimi had spent several days after being arrested in a stolen car. He got out of the car and walked around the facility.

"It was like he was trying to come to terms with his past," recalled Dee.

"He wanted to look at everything, every place," Alice Harding remembered.[24] He hadn't slept for two days but refused to go home and rest. They drove the back roads around Lake Washington, and when they reached Renton, Jimi wanted to visit his mother's grave, which he had never seen. They never found the graveyard and finally returned to Seattle, where they passed a house on Yesler Way where Jimi had lived with Al and Leon. The house was vacant and rundown, which saddened Jimi, who got out and walked to the darkened structure. A light rain was falling. At the window of the room where he had once slept and played countless hours of air guitar with a broomstick, Jimi put his hands around his eyes, pressed his face to the glass, and peered into the shadows as if viewing a childhood reel.

Bill Graham

Miles Davis

Backstage with Mick Jagger

21

An Ending Too Soon

Jimi Hendrix was exhausted. "Everyone thought it was drugs, but he was really beat," remembered Dan Fiala. "He had been working way too hard, going in the studio when he wasn't touring, and it was really getting him."[1] People urged him to take time off, but he flew to Hawaii the day after the Seattle show to play another concert and film a movie. Arriving in Maui on July 28, the laid-back style of the island and the filming of *Rainbow Bridge* were restorative. Living in a dormitory for a week and eating vegetarian meals with the crew and cast, he reveled in the chance to talk about religion and mysticism.

"He seemed happy to be there," remembered cast member Melinda Merryweather.

"It was a spiritual cleansing for Jimi," observed Chuck Wein, who gave Jimi books to read—*The Tibetan Book of the Dead* and *Secret Places of the Lion: Alien Influences on Earth's Destiny*—the latter being a book about space alien involvement in human culture for centuries, a theory Jimi believed.

Along with his Bob Dylan songbook, Jimi also carried *The Urantia Book*, an alternative bible for UFO believers that mixed tales of Jesus with stories of alien visitations. Hawaii also had plenty of drugs. In the four years since becoming a star, he had become dependent on drugs to bear the pressure of touring, but when a cast member suggested they fly in Devon Wilson to bring drugs, Jimi was against it. "Devon knew how to hold on to him through the drug trip," said Melinda, but Jimi wanted distance from her.[2]

Jimi's original elation soon became tempered by mood swings. One minute he'd say how much he loved Hawaii—he told Melinda that he wanted to retire on Maui and grow grapes on the side of a mountain—and the next minute he was deeply depressed. He had made and spent millions and had no great wealth to show for his work. A paternity suit was brought against him by Diana Carpenter; her lawyers requested blood samples, which Jimi never gave. He never publicly stated Tamika was his daughter, although, in an unreleased song, he did sing about his child "Tami," the only acknowledgment he ever made.

Disturbed by this and other ghosts of his past, while shooting a scene for the film, Jimi suggested to Chuck Wein and actress Pat Hartley, "Why don't we all just commit suicide, the three of us." Wein didn't take him seriously, but another day, when he asked Jimi if he would be playing Seattle again soon, Jimi replied, "Next time I go to Seattle, it'll be in a pine box."[3] However, there was no despair when Jimi played music. For two hours one night, he and the pianist at the Maui Belle nightclub in Lahaina played jazz standards to a handful of astonished patrons.

Filming was chaos. Warner Brothers had insisted on a full union crew from Hollywood, few of whom could relate to anyone else on the scenes. Further damaging to communication was the abundance and variety of drugs. Members of the surfing community practically worshiped Jimi and brought him gifts of locally grown marijuana called Maui Wowie and sat around in the evening, sucking hashish smoke from elaborate water pipes. For a scene in a pasture near Makawao, a farm and ranch community, every hippie on the island showed up to romp in costume in the tall grass and drink Electric Kool-Aid (LSD-laced punch). Plot was virtually non-existent; improvisation was all. It got confusing as the camera captured the wide range of the hip 1960s experience, from yoga, meditation, and Zen, to flying saucers, clairvoyance, and ecology, to encounter group Tai Chi Ch'uan and Polynesian girls spilling out of their bikini tops.

In a free concert near the Rainbow Bridge Occult Center on the slopes of Maui's Haleakalā Crater, Jimi, Billy Cox, and Mitch played on a tiny stage in the middle of a field on the side of a crater mountain before eight hundred fisherman, surfers, and native Hawaiians, who Wein had seated in sections based upon their astrological signs. Initially disturbed by the audience's laid-back response, the band played a routine ten-song first set, retired to a teepee for forty-five minutes smoking pot and drinking beer, and then returned to the stage. The second set was more energetic. Jimi played like someone in love with the guitar again.

This concert formed the last half-hour of the film and much of the soundtrack. By the time Chuck and his expensive camera crew returned to Hollywood, they had more than forty hours of puzzling film and still more scenes to shoot. Warner Brothers was nervous. The original budget had been set between $200,000-$300,000. Now it was clear that a million dollars was disappearing into a purple haze.

The band flew to Honolulu and played the last show of the tour. The next day, Billy Cox and Mitch flew home while Jimi returned to Maui to spend the next two weeks on an extended vacation, a break achieved by subterfuge when Jimi cut his foot on the beach and pretended the injury was worse than it was to fool management. "We put on about twenty times the amount of bandages it needed and took pictures to make it look like he was seriously injured," remembered Melinda Merryweather. He rented a house where he spent most days writing music and poems. Melinda observed that the longer he stayed in Hawaii, the clearer his mind became, and the more contemplative and sadder he became. "He talked about his mother a lot and her Native American roots."[4] Jimi felt conflicted about Al, but told Melinda he felt no anger toward him. Melinda thought he was a man at a crossroads, wanting to change his life.

During his second week of vacation, drinking and perhaps tripping on LSD, he wrote his father a long, rambling letter that was nonsensical in parts, but reflective and sensitive. Near the end he challenged his father about his mother: "There are things I must know about her for my own strictly private reasons."[5] He apologized for their fight in Seattle and asked for his cousin Dee Dee and stepsister Marsha to forgive his stoned and melancholy trip through his Seattle past. He wrote his New York phone number, asking for his cousin Faith to call him (whenever he and Faith spoke, she got the impression he didn't want her involved in the lifestyle of a rock musician), and wrote "Love Forever" to his stepsister Janie.

"He didn't want to leave Hawaii," Chuck Wein recalled.

"You people are so lucky," he told those gathered at the airport. "You get to stay here."[6] But he wanted to complete work on an album he was tentatively calling *First Rays of the New Rising Sun*, and on August

14, Jimi Hendrix flew to New York and disappeared into Electric Lady Studios.

It was hot, humid, dirty, and noisy in New York, but as Jimi loped the short five blocks from his apartment to the studio, he found himself smiling. Jerry Morrison was calling jazz musicians to arrange meetings and schedule some possible jams, among whom were Dizzy Gillespie and saxophonist Zoot Sims; Alan Douglas contacted Miles Davis, Roland Kirk, and Gil Evans in further attempts to bring great jazz talent to Jimi. His friends thought he seemed more energized.

Descending the steps to the subterranean studio, entering the air-conditioned coolness, and walking past a huge, curved psychedelic mural, feeling his feet sink into the red plush carpeting and knowing it was all his, had to have been a wonderful feeling. The men's room had a shower, there was a full kitchen, and soft, sprawling couches were built into each of the control rooms, covered with tie-dye silks and velvets designed according to his Indian/Moroccan/hippie tastes. The control rooms resembled spaceship interiors, like the Jupiter mission in the movie *2001: A Space Odyssey*. Floating ceilings, multi-ramped floors, carpeted wall surfaces, and complex lighting systems replaced the conventional shapes, colors, and textures found in most recording studios. In this environment, Jimi began finishing more songs. Music was still his great escape, and lost in the ecstasy of sound and electricity, the hours slipped by like moments as spools of tape piled up.

Immersed in his studio, his eyes reflected the rows of red, green, and white lights as he spent hours adjusting the hundreds of switches and tuning knobs in search of the perfect mix. Once he called Les Paul, the great guitarist he almost met in a roadhouse, to help solve a problem with his knowledge of electronics. Les happily answered Jimi's questions. He had "an idea of miking a guitar amp from far away—across the room—while running the guitar directly into the board at the same time," remembered Les.

He also told Jimi about the time he and his son had seen him at the bar in Lodi, New Jersey, in 1965. "We tried to find you for months after that," said Les.

Jimi shook his head as he heard the story. All he could think after hanging up was, "Just think . . . I came that close."[7]

But life was complicated for Jimi: Owning a studio had been his dream, but the debt from building the studio forced scheduling another tour and he felt trapped. "He didn't feel things were going well career-wise or monetarily," said Deering Howe. "All his audience wanted to hear was the big four songs that they knew, and Jimi wanted to play other stuff. Artistically, it was like he was trapped back on the Chitlin' Circuit again, forced to play what someone else told him. He didn't feel he could break free of that."[8]

Jimi's conversations were also shot with discontent for Jeffery. Alan Douglas and Chas Chandler said they were repeatedly approached to take over Jimi's affairs, but his contract with Mike Jeffery was ironclad and they were partners in the new studio.

Jimi objected to many of Jeffery's decisions, such as the difficult tour routings, and became increasingly aware of financial exploitation. When Jeffery had given Track and Polydor Records the right to distribute the Experience records for 10%, he made 7% of record earnings, Jimi made only 3%—which he shared with two others—and then Jeffery told Jimi he wanted his 30% commission on Jimi's 3%. Though he had helped make his client the biggest star in the world, "There were things that Jimi did not like," recalled TaharQa Aleem, "but Michael was trying to talk things through. Jimi had a temper and he was reactionary. He was also a difficult client for Michael." As their clashes escalated, Bob Levine, Jeffery's assistant, began handling most interactions with Jimi.

"Jimi told me he would never leave Michael," Levine recalled. "He knew Michael was a heavy and it was popular to make him a villain, but Jimi knew Michael would make him the most money."[9]

On August 26, the night before flying to London for the next tour, Jimi spent the evening at the opening party for Electric Lady Studios. Mike Quashie helped host the party. (After spending a night on Quashie's couch, Jimi left $2,000 in cash on a coffee table for his rather despondent friend.) Arrayed in fanciful Caribbean styles, Quashie welcomed guests effusively at the door. Reporters and photographers and the "Beautiful People" of New York were in attendance.

"We arranged it in two stages," said Pat Costello, Jimi's publicist. "We had the record business people come at five-thirty or six-thirty and the music press come an hour and a half, two and a half hours later, to be sure that the straight biz suits and ties were gone so the rock writer could light up at will."[10]

Johnny Winter, Yoko Ono, Mick Fleetwood, and Noel Redding were there. Jimi, who remained in one of the second-floor offices most of the evening with friends, told Noel he would probably see him in Europe. Later that evening, he met up with Colette Mimram and Devon Wilson. Colette had talked about accompanying Jimi to Europe but couldn't renew her passport. Devon wanted to go instead, but Jimi rejected her. "[Devon] had a great rap," recalled Colette. "She could get blood out of a stone—but she was a junkie and he didn't want anything to do with that." Devon had once been one of the most beautiful women in rock and roll, but as her heroin addiction spiraled out of control, it ruined her looks. Even Jimi, who hated to say no to anyone, cut off their friendship.

"I want you to leave," he told her that night, and so she left.[11]

The next morning, without sleep, Jimi boarded a plane to England to play at the Isle of Wight Festival.

Arriving at Heathrow on August 27, the London press was out in force. "If I'm free," he told the *London Times*, "it's because I'm always running."

In a penthouse suite in the Londonderry Hotel, friends, musicians, and journalists queued up in the hall, waiting for an interview. Jimi talked about the possibility of ending his career. "I'm right back now to where I started," he told *Melody Maker*. "I've given this era of music everything. I still sound the same, my music's still the same, and I can't think of anything new to add." He thought he was ready for the large R&B ensemble band he had wanted since coming to London in 1966: "A big band full of competent musicians that I can conduct and write for."

He spoke of his current band in the past tense: "It was the greatest fun. It was good, exciting, and I enjoyed it." When asked about his hair, he said, "Maybe I grow it long because my daddy used to cut it like a skinned chicken."[12] Kathy Etchingham remembered how Jimi feared his father might grab him and cut his hair during visits to Seattle.

Kathy, now married, learned Jimi was in London when a friend called to say he had gone mad and kicked two girls out of his suite. Etchingham immediately went to the hotel and found the two nearly naked, frightened girls outside his bedroom. She entered to find Jimi in bed amid broken lamps and empty whiskey bottles. His complexion was pallid, he had a high fever, and the heat had been turned high. She turned down the heat, put a cool compress on his forehead, and he peacefully went to sleep. She thought he looked ill rather than crazed and wondered if his sickness was related to drug withdrawal.

Jimi miraculously recovered the next day when two other women visited the hotel. He was immediately besotted with one of the girls, Kirsten Nefer, and spent the afternoon with her. "He was more or less interviewing me," Kirsten recalled.[13] They even called her mother in Denmark, where his tour had a show, and spoke for an hour. The women slept in an adjoining bedroom, left the next morning at ten, and an hour later Jimi appeared at Kirsten's house. He was leaving the next day for the Isle of Wight and urged Kirsten to attend.

The Isle of Wight is a peaceful, diamond-shaped island off the south coast of England, where, in the summer of 1968, Ronnie and Ray Foulk held a pop festival with hardly a stir among the inhabitants. When the brothers invited Bob Dylan in 1969, nearly 150,000 people crossed the six miles of water from the mainland. They wanted an even bigger act in 1970, so they moved the site to sparsely populated West Wight, where rolling hills fall away into cliffs as sheer and white as those of Dover, and invited Jimi Hendrix to headline the festival, which included The Who, Joni Mitchell, Chicago, Joan Baez, the Moody Blues, John Sebastian, Leonard Cohen, Kris Kristofferson, Jethro Tull, Donovan, and the Doors. A great multitude of people, the best estimate is about 400,000, crossed the Solent to camp on Afton Down in a last hurrah for love, peace, guilt-free drugs, and sex on the grassy slopes overlooking the stage. Unlike Woodstock, the weather was sunny for the whole four days.

On the afternoon of August 30, exhausted from lack of sleep, Jimi swallowed a handful of Benzedrine for energy and flew by helicopter to the Isle of Wight, where the crowd had exceeded all expectations, making the logistics chaos. Hundreds of people tried to break down fences on the two-hundred-acre site, equipment malfunctioned, and the show was running behind schedule. When he landed, a friend named Vishwa, who taught yoga and transcendental meditation in L.A., cut through the crowd and led Jimi to a dressing room. Thousands were spread over a huge, sloping field permeated with odors of sweat and hash and surrounded by tents, banners, and sleeping bags. Vishwa was worried because Jimi looked sick. The speed he had taken in London had run its course, and now he was smoking hash. Jim Morrison made his way through the crowd to say hello. Jimi brightened for a moment, then fell back into exhaustion. The trousers of his elaborate butterfly stage costume split at the crotch, but Noel Redding's mother was there to help mend it. Richie Havens, who ran into Jimi backstage, was shocked at how ill his friend looked.

"I'm having a real bad time with my lawyers and my managers," he complained. "They are killing me, everything is turned against me, and I can't sleep or eat."[14] Havens told him to call when he got back to London and to get some rest.

Jimi finally got his cue to perform at 2 A.M., heading to the stage holding a Stratocaster in one hand and a can of beer in the other. He received an enthusiastic welcome and crashed into "God Save the Queen," giving it the same sort of distortion and improvisation as he gave "The Star-Spangled Banner." Next came the great Beatles hit, "Sgt. Pepper's Lonely Hearts Club Band," "All Along the Watchtower," and "Red House." The crowd gave old favorites like "Hey Joe" and "Voodoo Child" the greatest applause, but the English fans were appreciative of new numbers like "Hey Baby" and "Freedom." During his last song, "In from the Storm," protesters launched flares onto the wooden awning of the stage. Jimi was never in danger, but no one knew this at the time.

"The show just fell apart at the end,"[15] observed Kirsten, and Jimi was exhausted. As he headed for Scandinavia and the Netherlands, the tedium of touring began again as he moved from jet plane, to limousine, to dressing room, to stage throughout Europe.

On stage in Stockholm the next day, Jimi, appearing late and playing longer than scheduled, put on a good show that the announcer ended while Jimi was still performing to declare that the amusement park, closed during the concert, needed to re-open. Backstage, Jimi encountered Eva Sundquist. Eva had given birth to Jimi's child, James Daniel Sundquist, and had written to him several times about the baby to no response. She now asked if he wanted to meet his son. Amid the noisy crowd of journalists, groupies, and fans backstage, Jimi, already fighting a paternity suit with Diana Carpenter, gave no answer as he pulled away from Eva.

He never met his only known son.

In Aarhus, Denmark, witnesses described seeing Jimi take an entire handful of sleeping pills in the early afternoon, a few hours before a concert. (He often mixed drugs, taking downers and uppers to counteract their effects.) He was suffering from a bad cold and complained of not sleeping.

Kirsten Nefer flew in from London. When she arrived at the hotel, Mitch Mitchell was in the lobby. "You better go up there because Jimi's in a very bad mood," he said.

Kirsten was shocked at his condition. "He was talking about spaceships in the sky," she said. "He was staggering. There was no sense to what he was saying."[16] Insisting Kirsten sit next to him and hold his hand, Jimi attempted interviews with reporters. She was afraid he would get worse if she left.

Jimi stumbled out of the cab at the concert site. He ordered people out of his crowded dressing room and then ordered them to return. When he announced, "I can't do this gig," Kirsten told him there were four thousand people in the hall and many were stomping their feet.

A roadie helped him walk on stage, where his first words to the audience were, "Are you feeling all right? Then welcome to the electric circus." He began to strum his guitar without bothering to chord it. Mitch started a drum solo, hoping Jimi would join in, but after two songs, his fingers numb, his eyes glazed, he said to the audience, "I've been dead a long time," then dropped his guitar and collapsed.[17] The show was canceled; the audience received refunds. He had been on stage for less than eight minutes.

Jimi Hendrix was falling apart. He took a cab to his hotel with Kirsten, where journalist Anne Bjorndal was waiting in his room. Despite his condition, he attempted the interview. Talking wild, he quoted Winnie-the-Pooh and said he loved Hans Christian Andersen's fairy tales. His playing, he said, took too much out of him. "I sacrifice part of my soul every time I play." And, with the vision of the Death tarot card in Africa haunting him, he stated, "I'm not sure I will live to be twenty-eight years old. I mean, the moment I feel I have nothing more to give musically, I will not be around on this planet anymore unless I have a wife and children; otherwise, I've got nothing to live for."[18] Jimi felt as lonely and isolated as when he had lost his mother. The journalist departed, and, though in desperate need of sleep, he told Kirsten he would die if he closed his eyes.

"He was afraid something was going to happen because of all the drugs he'd taken."

Instead, they talked for several hours, and though she had known Jimi for less than a week, he asked her to marry him. She protested, but he pleaded, "I'm so fed up with playing. . . . They want me to do all these shows. I just want to move to the country. I'm so sick of burning my guitar."[19] He finally fell asleep at six in the morning.

When he awoke at noon, he seemed improved. On the way to the airport, hearing Kirsten sing a few bars of a Donovan song, his mood lifted. Kirsten thought he was rousing from his fog. In Copenhagen, Jimi's hotel was across from a loud construction site. Jimi said he wouldn't be able to sleep, so Kirsten suggested her mother's house. At Kirsten's mother's house, he had soup and slept for several hours in a bedroom. When he awoke, her brothers and sisters had arrived, and they all sat down to a dinner of spaghetti. Reporters who had gotten wind of him and Kirsten came to the house and interrupted the meal. Kirsten wanted to send them away; instead, Jimi invited them inside and announced his new love.

That night, in the dressing room at the concert hall, he serenaded Kirsten with an acoustic guitar and was late for the show. "You could hear the crowd screaming for him," she recalled. Then suddenly he announced he couldn't perform. Kirsten told him that her mother was waiting to see him perform and he had to go on. Jimi went onstage and, unlike the previous concert, put on a great show. "The concert of the year," one paper announced.[20]

Mitch came up to Kirsten afterward. "What have you done to him," he said. "Jimi hasn't played this good in years."[21]

Jimi asked Kirsten to his next few shows in Germany. When she managed to get time off from filming a movie, he said he didn't want her after all. "A woman's place is in the home," he said, and then changed his mind and remorsefully begged her to come. Worried that his erratic behavior was the result of drugs, she wanted no more of his wavering affections and decided to break it off. Parting at the airport, Jimi quoted a line from Bob Dylan: "Most likely you'll go your way and I'll go mine."[22]

"The pace in Europe," Billy Cox recalled, "was both exhilarating and exhaustive."[23]

After the concert in Berlin, a critic wrote that Hendrix "plays as if he's drunk."

A writer backstage witnessed Jimi sniffling and asked, "Do you have a cold?"

Jimi curtly replied, "That's from snorting, man."

Guitarist Robin Trower visited backstage and announced it was the greatest concert he had ever seen. "Uh, thank you, but, naw," responded Jimi, who even stoned knew when his playing was good.[24]

His next show was the Love and Peace Festival on the German island of Fehmarn on September 6. Riding there on the train, he broke into a locked sleeping car and was discovered by a conductor. Jimi said he was trying to sleep and avoided arrest only when an official who recognized him intervened with the police.

The Love and Peace Festival in Fehmarn was plagued by delays, violence between gatecrashers, the police, and the crowd inside. Hells Angels were there; some were armed with weapons. When Jimi went on stage, there were boos and chants of "Go home!"

"I don't give a fuck if you boo," called Jimi, "if you boo in key." During his thirteen-song set, a Hells Angel broke into the box office and made off with all the receipts. As he walked offstage, not knowing about the robbery, he told a reporter, "I don't feel like playing anymore."[25] Jimi caught a helicopter and then a plane back to London. Moments after he had left, Hells Angels burned the stage to the ground.

Someone had given Billy Cox an LSD-laced punch, and, exasperated by fatigue, he had a bad reaction. Normally the soberest member of the band, Billy began to rant incoherently and was taken to a hospital in London.

Jimi had a room at the Cumberland Hotel overlooking the Marble Arch just off fashionable Park Lane, but there were other places available to him where friends were staying, including the apartment of his German, sometimes-girlfriend Monika Danneman, in the Samarkand Hotel in the more bohemian Notting Hill Gate district.

In the final week of his life, Jimi slept in many beds, but he still had ideas about music. In an interview with *Melody Maker*, he said he wanted a big band in which his guitar would take a diminished role. "I want other musicians to play my stuff. I want to be a good writer." Expressing worry about his image, he said all the visual gimmickry was in his past, saying it was something he had used to get people's attention. He told Keith Altham of the *Record Mirror*, "I look around at new groups . . . and they're into those same things with the hair and clothes—wearing all the jewelry and strangling themselves with beads. I got out of that because I felt I was being too loud visually . . . I got the feeling maybe too many people were coming to look and not enough to listen. . . . I started cutting my hair and losing jewelry. . . . The freaky thing was never publicity hype. That was just the way I was then."[26]

Kirsten Nefer returned to visit him at the Cumberland Hotel on Tuesday, September 8. The door to his room was open, and she saw him prone on his bed. Fearing he might be dead, she checked his pulse and discovered he was sleeping. The phone rang, awakening Jimi. The call was about Billy Cox—the drugs he'd been slipped seemed to be staying in his system. They found Billy and took him for dinner at a curry house on Fulham Road. "Billy was talking in tongues and making all these strange noises," Kirsten recalled. They dropped Billy at the hotel with a roadie and went to see a movie, Michelangelo Antonioni's *Red Desert*. Leaving the cinema, Jimi danced along the curb. "He was so happy, he was skipping," Kirsten recalled.

He told her he wanted to take two years off and that "I only want to play the acoustic guitar from now on."[27]

Billy's condition worsened during the night. A physician was summoned who suggested sending him home to America. Jimi and Kirsten decided to spend time at a disco, but Jimi was too self-conscious to dance, and they returned to the hotel where their efforts to enjoy a romantic evening were constantly distracted by Billy. "Every time we were about to go to bed, he was there," Kirsten called. "Jimi was so good to him. He'd say, 'Remember when we were in the army together?' Billy kept saying, 'I'm going to die.'"[28] The doctor returned and injected Billy with a sedative. The next day Jimi and his hairdresser, Finney, coaxed a few words out of Billy Cox and put him on a plane to the States, where he could recover. Without Billy, the band had an uncertain future and Jimi seemed unnerved.

In his hotel room, he entertained writers, usually with women present, while drinking Chablis or rosé wines. Some of the girls said he was smoking a lot of marijuana and swallowing pills. He seemed nervous.

"He told me a story about being kidnapped and taken to upstate New York," said Alvenia Bridges. "He got really intense about his management. He said, 'Man, they'll just do anything with you.' He was real unhappy in London. He didn't seem like his old self."[29]

On Friday, September 11, he did a long interview with Keith Altham. Asked if he wanted to be recognized as a songwriter, Jimi replied, "I wanted to just lay back and predominately write songs when I can't go on a stage anymore." Drinking wine as he talked, he sounded optimistic, but many answers seemed nonsensical.

When asked what he'd change in the world, he replied, "The color in the streets," but when asked if he was a "psychedelic writer," his answer had a deeper meaning. "I think maybe it's more that than anything else. I'm trying to get more so into other things, you know, as of where reality is nothing but each individual's way of thinking." (This would be reflected in his next album with "Valleys of Neptune," "Between Here and Horizon," and "Room Full of Mirrors.") When Altham asked Jimi if he had enough money for the rest of his life, he replied, "Not the way I'd like to live," and the interview ended.[30]

Devon Wilson phoned on Saturday, September 12, to announce she was coming to London. A long argument ensued, with Jimi yelling into the phone, "Devon, get off my fucking back for Christsakes," and abruptly putting down the receiver.

Kirsten was in the room and felt discouraged. She had been cast in a film opposite George Lazenby and Jimi yelled at her. Convinced she was sleeping with Lazenby, "he shook me until I had blue marks all over."[31] When he insisted she quit the film, she stormed out of the room. She tried phoning later that night—he wasn't in—and left several messages over the next few days. She even stopped by his hotel looking for him but would never see him again.

Others were looking for him, too. Mike Jeffery was in London trying to find him, perhaps because Jimi had told Chas Chandler he wanted to rehire him and fire Jeffery. Meetings were planned with lawyers to settle the overseas claim from Ed Chalpin's PPX lawsuit, and Diana Carpenter's lawyers were trying to force him to take a blood test in her paternity suit against him. Out and about in London, Jimi managed to encounter old friends but avoided Jeffery and the lawyers.

He bumped into Kathy Etchingham at Kensington Market near Chelsea. "He came up right behind me and grabbed me," she recalled.[32] He was shopping for antiques and had a blond woman with him. Kathy had been the longest romantic relationship of his life. He told her that he was staying at the Cumberland Hotel. She quickly kissed him on the cheek and parted.

At the Speakeasy, entering while she was leaving, he encountered Linda Keith. They chatted for a few minutes. She was with a new fiancé and wearing an engagement ring; Jimi was with the mysterious blond. Their meeting was not a coincidence. Though they had not remained friends, Linda had recently been on his mind, and he sought her out. "This is for you," he told her as he handed Linda a guitar case. Inside was a new Stratocaster, a gift to acknowledge the help she had given in New York, which included a purloined guitar.

"You don't owe me anything," she told him, but Jimi insisted, "I owe you this," and walked away hand-in-hand with the blond.[33] The guitar was strapped to the roof of her fiancé's small sports car, and, when she later opened the case, she also found the letters she had written to him in the summer of '66 when they had romantic feelings.

The blond woman was twenty-five-year-old ice skater Monika Danneman. For several days, beginning on Tuesday, September 15, she was the main love interest of Jimi. That night, they showed up at Ronnie Scott's nightclub, where Eric Burdon and War were playing. Jimi had hoped to jam with his good friend Burdon but was stoned and staggering and ultimately turned away at the door.

"For the first time I'd ever seen him, he didn't have his guitar," recalled Burdon. "When I saw him without that guitar, I knew he was in trouble."[34] Eric remembered that Jimi had "a head full of something, heroin or Quaaludes." People felt embarrassed to see him turned away from the stage.

Steve Cropper also remembered Jimi on these nights. "I think the last time I saw Jimi, The MGs [Booker T. and the MGs] were at the Bag O' Nails, and at first he either didn't see me or didn't recognize me, so I quickly got up and confronted him. At that time he was totally out of it. So, I asked his friends that were with him to take care of him and get him home because we had a plane to catch to go back to the States the next day and I couldn't do it."[35]

On the evening of September 16, Jimi careened from flat to flat and from club to club with various people. Eventually he returned to the popular jazz club on the edge of Soho, Ronnie Scott's, entering the dark club with Monika Danneman. Alvenia Bridges and Finney were there along with Alan and Stella Douglas and Devon Wilson, who was angry with Jimi because she had been looking for him for two days.

Eric Burdon was onstage and invited Jimi to sit in. "At first he played like an amateur, real bad, using stage tricks to cover up," Eric said. "Then he came on with a solo which was up to scratch and the audience dug it. He went offstage and came back and played the background to 'Tobacco Road.' He wasn't just freaking. He was jelling nicely with the band."[36] Jimi chose his old role as band guitarist and not lead singer. When he and Monika left, they went to the Samarkand Hotel.

The next morning, Thursday, September 17, he awoke late. It was a beautiful, cloudless day in London, the sky a royal blue. Early mid-afternoon, he had tea in the little garden outside Monika's room, where she took photographs of him, some of him playing the black Stratocaster he called "the Black Beauty." In the photo, he's dressed well in a blue jacket with a scarf and black pants but looks tired and drained of emotions; his expression is sad and contemplative. During the afternoon they went to a bank, a drugstore, and an antique market, where Jimi bought a few items. Gerry Stickells and Mitch Mitchell reached him by phone at the Cumberland Hotel, where he said he was alone. Mitch made plans to meet him to play with Sly Stone in the late evening, a date Jimi would not make. Later, with Monika along, he saw Devon Wilson and Stella Douglas walking along King's Road. Devon and Monika exchanged icy stares; this time, Devon might have been right. They invited Jimi to a party that night and he immediately accepted.

Driving toward his hotel, while stopped in traffic, a man in a car next to Monika rolled down the window and playfully invited Jimi to tea. Jimi agreed, but they first drove to the Cumberland Hotel, where Jimi went inside and phoned Eddie Kramer about their next recording session in New York and then called Henry Steingarten to investigate ways of disentangling Mike Jeffery before their contract ended in December. Outside, they followed the car, which held the man and two women: Monika complained, but Jimi had always been spontaneous.

The young man was Phillip Harvey, the son of a wealthy member of Parliament. They arrived at his opulent home in Marylebone at around 5:30 P.M. A long, mirror-lined hallway led into a large living room decorated in a Middle Eastern style, much like Jimi's apartment in Manhattan. Jimi relaxed as they sat on pillows, smoked hash, drank tea and wine, and chatted about their careers. He said he would be moving to London again.

At about 10 P.M., Monika became agitated—too little of the conversation involved her. "I've had enough," she said, then stormed out of the house.[37] Jimi went outside to fetch her. Harvey and the two women could hear her yelling loudly in the street. Fearful of police, he went out and requested they quiet down. Their screaming subsided. At 10:40 P.M., Jimi apologized for her behavior and left.

He returned to Monika's hotel, took a bath, and then wrote the lyrics to a song titled, "The Story of Life." An hour later, Monika dropped him off at the home of Pete Kameron, who had helped start Track Records. Jimi complained to him about his business problems. Devon Wilson and Angie Burdon, Eric's estranged wife, were also at the party. Jimi ate Chinese food and took at least one amphetamine tablet. In thirty minutes, Monika rang the intercom, saying she was there to pick up Jimi. Stella Douglas told her to come back later. Monika soon returned.

"[Jimi] got angry because she wouldn't leave him alone," wrote Angie Burdon in a letter to Kathy Etchingham. "[Jimi] asked Stella again to put her off, Stella was rude to her, and the chick asked to speak to Jimi."[38] Jimi spoke to Monika and abruptly left the party around 3 A.M. Friday.

Only Monika witnessed his last hours, and the truth to her statements is doubtful. She said that around four in the morning, after drinking some wine, he asked for some sleeping pills: This is probably true—Jimi often swallowed barbiturates soon after amphetamines. "I persuaded him to wait a little longer," she said, "hoping he would fall asleep naturally."[39] They were both still awake at six, she claimed, when she secretly took a sleeping pill. Her prescription sleeping medication was a powerful

German sedative called Vesparax. Taking an entire pill would have put someone into a long, deep sleep. More likely, she took the pill earlier than six o'clock, probably around four, and ominously fell asleep.

Though exhausted and desperate for rest, Jimi could not sleep. He probably found the bottle of Vesparax after 7 A.M. and, not realizing how strong they were, put nine pills in his hand and swallowed them. There were fifty pills in the bottle. The nine pills he swallowed were almost twenty times the recommended dose for a man of Jimi's frame and weight, and he would have lost consciousness immediately. Very soon the Vesparax, the alcohol, and the other drugs he had consumed likely caused him to heave up the contents of his stomach. The vomited wine and undigested food were then breathed into his lungs and caused him to stop breathing. A non-inebriated person would have had a gag reflex and coughed out the material. But Jimi was totally unconscious and helpless.

If someone had been there and heard him gasp, they might have cleared his airway, as had happened in an incident before with Carmen Borrero. Monika Dannemann might have helped had she been awake, but there was no rescue on the overcast London morning of September 18, 1970. The young woman sleeping near him was almost a stranger: Jimi was alone with his fate, and though under heavy pressure, the circumstances and choices were of his making.

Jimi passed away in the early hours of Friday morning. He was twenty-seven years old, just five days short of the four-year anniversary of his first arrival in London. He had come so far, accomplished so much, and risen so high, and just as suddenly fell away into eternity.

The woman with him continued her story. "I woke up about 10:20 A.M. He was sleeping normally. I went round the corner to get cigarettes. When I came back, he had been sick . . . I saw that he had taken sleeping tablets. There were nine of mine missing." She saw vomit drying around his mouth and nose. She tried again to wake him. He failed to respond to her calls and touch. She wanted to send for help but said she feared Jimi would be angry if she sent him to the hospital and nothing was wrong. After several frantic phone calls, she finally reached Eric Burdon.

"I can't wake up Jimi!" she cried.

"Call an ambulance! Now!" replied Eric.[40]

Jimi was declared dead at the hospital. The body was identified by Gerry Stickells and then moved to the morgue. An autopsy was performed on September 21, 1970, three days after he had died, by Robert Donald Teare, a practicing physician and pathologist. He found Jimi to be a "well nourished and muscular young adult man." There were several drugs found in his liver, blood, and urine, and enough alcohol to fail a drunk-driving test.

Her Majesty's Coroner Gavin L. B. Thurston ruled that from the basis of the pathologist's findings Jimi had died "as a result of inhalation of vomit due to barbiturate intoxication."[41] What this meant was that Jimi had so depressed his central nervous system that he had paralyzed his gag reflex. Then, as his stomach rejected the poisonous overdose, the vomit was caught and couldn't be fully expelled, and because Jimi was unconscious and unable to move, some of what was expelled was inhaled into his lungs. Literally, he had drowned in his own vomit.

For those close to Jimi, it was a tough time. At his country house in Surrey, England, Eric Clapton later confessed he went out into his garden and cried all day. Even the enigmatic heart of Bob Dylan was touched as the young laureate burst into tears. Faye Pridgon, who had moved to Brooklyn, had a squad car outside her house relay the news just heard over the police radio. Leon was in a cell in Monroe Penitentiary when called to the chaplain's office where his father sadly broke the news in a telephone call. In Vancouver, Nora Hendrix painfully pondered, "that drug business is terrible . . . when I thought about it, I hoped he'd give himself a few years before he got into it himself, but he didn't give himself very long."[42]

The body of James Marshall Hendrix was buried in a cemetery in Renton, Washington, near the unmarked grave of his mother, Lucille, put to eternal rest by family and friends who had known him since childhood.

The soul of Jimi Hendrix lives on forever in his music.

Michael Lydon later wrote in the *New York Times* that "Jimi Hendrix was more than a star. He was a genius black musician, a guitarist, singer, and composer of brilliantly dramatic power. He spoke in gestures as big as he could imagine and create; his willingness for adventure knew no bounds. He was wild, passionate, and abrasive, yet all his work was imbued with his personal gentleness. He was an artist extravagantly generous with his beauty."

John Burks in *Rolling Stone* said, "The amazing thing is how rich a musical legacy Hendrix left in so short a time."[43]

His friend and studio engineer Eddie Kramer said, "I lost this wonderful musician friend, if you will, but the world of music lost a genius."

Behind the controls at Electric Lady Studios

Jimi with Kirsten Nefer

Hawaii

Pallbearers at funeral

The last photo

Legacy

The life of Jimi Hendrix could inspire an ambitious dramatist to write words to capture the moments of tragedy, triumph, and comedy that can happen within a singular body of humanity. Jimi's was the soul of a genius whose triumphs came through music—great music—that unfolded from within a gentle, sensitive nature. The heights he reached were spectacular: songs beloved by a generation and beyond, which are his greatest legacy, generating millions of dollars through recordings and performances and giving him worldwide renown as one of the greatest rock stars of an era.

Born into a family stricken with poverty and alcoholism, struggling with cohesion and lost equilibrium, the adversity Jimi Hendrix experienced as a child drove him to use his imagination to create an internal world much different and brighter than the brutal reality of parents fighting and separating, wearing ragged hand-me-down clothes and shoes with holes in the sole, not always having enough to eat, and the early death of his mother and the loss of younger siblings. He survived these years, and as he grew, nurtured by degrees within an understanding community in the central district of Seattle, his imagination never stopped creating.

Jimi Hendrix heard music everywhere, from the noise of a construction site, cars driving down the street, and records played by an aunt on an old phonograph. From the time he got his first guitar, a second-hand acoustic with a single string, he ceaselessly sought to replicate the sounds he heard into music. Some of these sounds no one else could hear until they heard him play the electric guitar using distortion and feedback to infuse a strange, compelling energy into the blues.

Then, they were enthralled.

Many have been inspired and still light up the electric guitar to jam along to Jimi's style, and experience the thrill of playing beyond the limitations of space and time; some songs with puzzles that remain unsolved until finally a piece comes along and fits perfectly, the timing couldn't be better, and all the sides become a perfect fit. His music really had no barriers.

His death was abrupt and tragic, dying at twenty-seven, leaving many who loved him stranded and heartbroken. Compared to all the money made by his records and concerts, there was little in his bank account, and he left no will. But people continue to listen to his music and there are tapes of songs he had recorded, demos and masters, still being found. Some of them are complete, or nearing completion, and have been released posthumously, generating royalties for the company owned and operated by the Hendrix family, members of whom manage his growing estate, which is now worth almost $200 million. There is also a foundation his father established in 1988, the Jimi Hendrix Foundation, for continuing his name and legacy for charitable endeavors.

But, of course, Jimi Hendrix's greatest legacy will always be his distinctive music, melodious electric chords that illuminate the heavens with the sudden thrill of lightning in a clear blue sky.

Bibliography

Boyd, Joe, John Head, and Gary Weis, dirs. *Jimi Hendrix.* Released December 21, 1973, by Warner Bros.

Burdon, Eric and J. Marshall Craig. *Don't Let Me Be Misunderstood: A Memoir.* Da Capo, 2002.

Conforth, Bruce and Gayle Dean Wardlow. *Up Jumped the Devil: The Real Life Robert* Johnson. Chicago Review Press, 2022.

Cross, Charles R. *Room Full of Mirrors: A Biography of Jimi Hendrix.* Da Capo, 2005.

Darcy. "Devon Wilson: The 'Dolly Dagger' in Jimi Hendrix's Life." *Rocks Off Magazine*, December 2, 2022, https://www.rocksoffmag.com/devon-wilson/.

Egan, Sean. *Jimi Hendrix and the Making of Are You Experienced.* A Capella Books, 2002.

Etchingham, Kathy. *Through Gypsy Eyes: My Life, the Sixties, and Jimi Hendrix.* Orion, 1998.

Graham, Bill and Robert Greenfield. *Bill Graham Presents: My Life Inside Rock and Out.* Da Capo Press, 1992.

Henderson, David. *'Scuse Me While I Kiss the Sky: Jimi Hendrix: Voodoo Child.* Atria, 2009.

Hendrix, James. *My Son Jimi.* Aljas Enterprises, 1999.

Hendrix, Jimi, *A Selected Press Anthology*, 1967 - 70

———. *Starting at Zero: His Own Story.* Bloomsbury, 2013.

Hendrix, Leon with Adam Mitchell. *Jimi Hendrix: A Brother's Story.* Thomas Dunne Books, 2012.

Hopkins, Jerry. *The Jimi Hendrix Experience.* Arcade Publishing, 1983.

James, Etta. *Rage to Survive: The Etta James Story.* Villard Books, 1995.

Knight, Curtis. *Jimi: An Intimate Biography of Jimi Hendrix.* Star Books, 1974.

Lauterbach, Preston. *The Chitlin' Circuit and the Road to Rock 'n' Roll.* Norton, 2012.

Lawrence, Sharon. *Jimi Hendrix: The Man, the Magic, the Truth.* Sidgewick and Jackson, 2005.

Levy, Shawn. *Ready, Steady, Go!: The Smashing Rise and Giddy Fall of Swinging London.* Doubleday, 2002.

Marlatt, Daphne and Carole Itter. *Opening Doors: In Vancouver's East End: Strathcona.* Harbour, 2011.

McDermott, John, dir. *Jimi Hendrix Experience: Electric Church.* Legacy Recordings, 2015.

Mitchell, Mitch. *The Hendrix Experience.* Da Capo, 1990.

Murray, Charles Shaar. *Crosstown Traffic: Jimi Hendrix and the Rock n' Roll Revolution.* St. Martin's, 1989.

Norman, Philip. *Wild Thing: The Short Spellbinding Life of Jimi Hendrix.* Liveright, 2020.

Pennebaker, D. A. *Monterey Pop.* Released December 26, 1968, by Leacock Pennebaker.

Pesant, Steven C. "Rainy Day, Dream Away: The Jimi Hendrix Experience: Miami Pop Festival." *Jimi Hendrix,* May 18, 2025, https://www.jimihendrix.com/editorial/rainy-day-dream-away-the-jimi-hendrix-experience-miami-pop-festival.

Redding, Noel and Carol Appleby. *Are You Experienced?: The Inside Story of the Jimi Hendrix Experience.* Da Capo, 1996.

Richards, Mick. *Creating Woodstock.* Virtue Films, 2019.

Roby, Steven, ed. *Hendrix on Hendrix: Interviews and Encounters with Jimi Hendrix.* Chicago Review Press, 2012.

Roby, Steven and Brad Schreiber. *Becoming Jimi Hendrix: From Southern Crossroads to Psychedelic London, the Untold Story of a Musical Genius.* Da Capo, 2010.

Scorsese, Martin, dir. "No Direction Home: Bob Dylan." *American Masters.* PBS, 2005.

Shapiro, Harry and Caesar Glebbeek. *Jimi Hendrix: Electric Gypsy.* Heinemann, 1990.

Shelton, Robert. *No Direction Home: The Life and Music of Bob Dylan.* Da Capo, 1986.

Smeaton, Bob, dir. "Jimi Hendrix: Hear My Train a Comin'." *American Masters.* PBS, 2014.

Wadleigh, Michael, dir. *Woodstock.* Released March 26, 1970, by Warner Bros.

Wein, Chuck, dir. *Rainbow Bridge.* Antahkarana Productions, 1971.

Endnotes

Chapter One: Crossroads

1. Charles R. Cross, *A Room Full of Mirrors: A Biography of Jimi Hendrix* (New York, 2005), 132.
2. Howlin' Wolf, in conversation with Peter Guralnick, www.peterguralnnick.com.
3. Charles Shaar Murray, *Crosstown Traffic* (St. Martin's Press, 1989), 27.
4. Murray, 35.

Chapter Two: A Struggling Musical Family

1. *Vancouver Sun*, 1937.
2. James Hendrix, *My Son Jimi* (Aljas Enterprises, 1999), 32.
3. Cross, 15.
4. Cross, 19.
5. Cross, 19.
6. Cross, 20.
7. Cross, 21.

Chapter Three: Battered Childhood

1. James Hendrix, 43.
2. Cross, 24.
3. James Hendrix, 44.
4. Cross, 25.
5. James Hendrix, 48.
6. Cross, 27.
7. Cross, 28.
8. James Hendrix, 52.
9. Cross, 28.
10. Cross, 29.
11. Cross, 29.
12. James Hendrix, 60.
13. Interview, *London Evening Standard*, October 1967.

14. Cross, 31–32.
15. James Hendrix, 60.
16. Cross, 32.
17. James Hendrix, 57.
18. Cross, 32.
19. Cross, 33.
20. Jimi Hendrix, *Starting at Zero: His Own Story* (Bloomsbury, 2013), 75.
21. Leon Hendrix, *Jimi Hendrix: A Brother's Story* (Thomas Dunne, 2012), 54.
22. Cross, 36.
23. Cross, 37.
24. Leon Hendrix, 138.
25. Cross, 40.
26. Cross, 41.
27. Cross, 41.
28. Cross, 42.
29. Cross, 42.
30. Cross, 43.
31. Leon Hendrix, 119.
32. Cross, 45.
33. Cross, 46.
34. Cross, 46.
35. Cross, 47.
36. Cross, 50.
37. Cross, 50.
38. Faith Hendrix, interview with author, Spring 2025.
39. Cross, 51–52.
40. James Hendrix, 97.
41. Cross, 52.
42. Cross, 53.
43. Cross, 53.
44. Leon Hendrix, 143.
45. Cross, 54.
46. Cross, 55.
47. Leon Hendrix, 146.
48. Cross, 58.
49. Leon Hendrix, 148.
50. Leon Hendrix, 149.
51. Cross, 59.
52. Interview, Ray Connolly, *London Evening Standard*, October 1967.
53. James Hendrix, 113.

Chapter Four: A Musician Begins to Emerge

1. Cross, 63.
2. Cross, 63.
3. Cross, 63.

4. Cross, 64.
5. Cross, 64.
6. Cross, 65.
7. Cross, 66.
8. Cross, 67.
9. Cross, 68.
10. Cross, 69.
11. Cross, 69.
12. Cross, 69.
13. Cross, 69.
14. Cross, 70.
15. Leon Hendrix, 156.
16. Cross, 70.
17. Leon Hendrix, 158.
18. Cross, 72.
19. Cross, 73.
20. Cross, 73.
21. Cross, 73–74.
22. Cross, 74.
23. Cross, 76.
24. Cross, 76.
25. *Jimi Hendrix, A Selected Press Anthology, 1967–1970* - from the private collection of Rob Frith.
26. Cross, 81.
27. Cross, 83.

Chapter Five: Marbles

1. James Hendrix, 132.
2. Cross, 87.
3. Cross, 87.
4. Cross, 88.
5. Cross, 88.
6. Jerry Hopkins, *Jimi Hendrix Experience* (Arcade, 1983), 42.
7. James Hendrix, 133.
8. Steven Roby and Brad Schreiber, *Becoming Jimi Hendrix: From Southern Crossroads to Psychedelic London, the Untold Story of a Musical Genius* (Da Capo, 2010), 16.
9. Cross, 91.
10. Cross, 91.
11. James Hendrix, 135.
12. Roby and Schreiber, 17.
13. Roby and Schreiber, 17.
14. Roby and Schreiber, 20.
15. Cross, 92.
16. Roby and Schreiber, 19.
17. Roby and Schreiber, 25.

18. Cross, 94.
19. James Hendrix, 137.
20. Roby and Schreiber, 28.
21. Roby and Schreiber, 30.
22. Roby and Schreiber, 30.
23. Roby and Schreiber, 33.
24. Cross, 97.
25. Roby and Schreiber, 35–36.
26. Roby and Schreiber, 31.
27. Roby and Schreiber, 32.
28. Cross, 97.
29. Cross, 99.
30. Roby and Schreiber, 18.
31. Roby and Schreiber, 35.
32. Cross, 100.
33. Roby and Schreiber, 34.
34. Cross, 101.
35. Interview, *Jimi Hendrix, A Selected Press Anthology.*
36. Roby and Schreiber, 36.
37. Roby and Schreiber, 38.
38. James Hendrix, 138.
39. Cross, 102.

Chapter Six: Chitlin' Circuit

1. Cross, 103.
2. Cross, 103.
3. Cross, 104.
4. Roby and Schreiber, 43.
5. Roby and Schreiber, 43–44.
6. Roby and Schreiber, 45.
7. Roby and Schreiber, 46.
8. Roby and Schreiber, 47.
9. Roby and Schreiber, 47.
10. Roby and Schreiber, 48.
11. Roby and Schreiber, 49.
12. Cross, 105–6.
13. Roby and Schreiber, 54.
14. Roby and Schreiber, 55.
15. Roby and Schreiber, 56.
16. Roby and Schreiber, 57.
17. Hendrix, *A Selected Press Anthology*.
18. Roby and Schrieber, 58.
19. Roby and Schreiber, 58–59.
20. Roby and Schreiber, 61.
21. Roby and Schreiber, 62.

22. Roby and Schreiber, 62.
23. Cross, 106.
24. Roby and Schreiber, 63–64.

Chapter Seven: Manhattan Rhapsody

1. Roby and Schreiber, 65.
2. Roby and Schreiber, 75.
3. Cross, 109.
4. Etta James, *Rage to Survive: The Etta James Story* (Villard, 1995), 142.
5. Roby and Schreiber, 75–76.
6. Cross, 111.
7. Phillip Norman, *Wild Thing: The Short, Spellbinding Life of Jimi Hendrix* (Liveright, 2020), 53.
8. Roby and Schreiber, 69.
9. Cross, 109–10.
10. Roby and Schreiber, 71–72.
11. Roby and Schreiber, 73.
12. *Jimi Hendrix*, directed by Joe, Boyd, John Head, and Gary Weis (A&E, 1973).
13. James, 146.
14. Roby and Schreiber, 74.
15. Roby and Schreiber, 78.
16. Norman, 55.
17. Roby and Schreiber, 78.
18. Roby and Schreiber, 79–80.
19. Roby and Schreiber, 82.
20. Roby and Schreiber, 85.
21. Interview, *Jimi Hendrix, A Selected Press Anthology*.

Chapter Eight: On the Road Again

1. Roby and Schreiber, 85.
2. Roby and Schreiber, 91.
3. Roby and Schreiber, 92.
4. James Hendrix, 139.
5. Interview, *Jimi Hendrix, A Selected Press Anthology*.
6. Roby and Schreiber, 89.
7. Roby and Schreiber, 92.
8. Roby and Schreiber, 91.
9. Roby and Schreiber, 93.
10. Steve Cropper, interview with author, August 2022.
11. Roby and Schreiber, 95.
12. Roby and Schreiber, 96.
13. Roby and Schreiber, 97.
14. Interview, *Jimi Hendrix, A Selected Press Anthology*.
15. *Jimi Hendrix*, directed by Joe, Boyd, John Head, and Gary Weis (A&E, 1973).
16. Cross, 114.

17. Cross, 115.
18. Roby and Schreiber, 104.
19. Hopkins, 60–61.
20. Roby and Schreiber, 106.
21. Roby and Schreiber, 110.
22. Roby and Schreiber, 109.
23. Roby and Schreiber, 113
24. Roby and Schreiber, 118.
25. Roby and Schreiber, 115.
26. Roby and Schreiber, 115.
27. Roby and Schreiber, 118.
28. Roby and Schreiber, 119.
29. Roby and Schreiber, 119.

Chapter Nine: City Streets

1. James Hendrix, 139–40.
2. Roby and Schreiber, 120.
3. Roby and Schreiber, 120.
4. Cross, 119.
5. Roby and Schreiber, 123.
6. Roby and Schreiber, 123.
7. Curtis Knight, *Jimi: An Intimate Biography of Jimi Hendrix* (Star Books, 1974), 75.
8. Hopkins, 64.
9. Cross, 121.
10. Roby and Schreiber, 126.
11. Roby and Schreiber, 126.
12. Cross, 122.
13. Cross, 122.
14. Roby and Schreiber, 127.
15. Roby and Schreiber, 130.
16. Cross, 124.
17. James Hendrix, 140.
18. Roby and Schreiber, 133–34.
19. Cross, 125.
20. Roby and Schreiber, 139.
21. Roby and Schreiber, 140.
22. Roby and Schreiber, 142.
23. Roby and Schreiber, 143.
24. Hopkins, 65–66.
25. Cross, 126.
26. Roby and Schreiber, 140–41.
27. Cross, 126.
28. Cross, 126.
29. Cross, 127.

30. Roby and Schreiber, 141.
31. Cross, 127.
32. *TIME*, "Night Life: The Roar of the Cheetah, The Look of the Crowd," May 6, 1966.
33. Roby and Schreiber, 144.
34. Roby and Schreiber, 145.
35. Roby and Schreiber, 146–47.
36. Cross, 128.
37. Roby and Schreiber, 147.

Chapter Ten: Discovery and the Village

1. Hopkins, 75.
2. Cross, 131–32.
3. Roby and Schreiber, 148.
4. Cross, 132.
5. Cross, 132.
6. Cross, 133.
7. Cross, 134.
8. Cross, 135.
9. Cross, 135.
10. Cross, 133.
11. *Life*, June 16, 1967.
12. Cross, *A Room Full of Mirrors*, 136.
13. "No Direction Home: Bob Dylan," directed by Martin Scorsese, *American Masters,* (PBS, 2005).
14. Roby and Schreiber, 152.
15. Cross, 137.
16. Cross, 138.
17. Roby and Schreiber, 152.
18. Roby and Schreiber, 152.
19. Roby and Schreiber, 153.
20. Cross, 145.
21. Cross, 145.
22. Roby and Schreiber, 156.
23. Roby and Schreiber, 158.
24. Cross, 138–39.
25. Roby and Schreiber, 161–62.
26. Roby and Schreiber, 162.
27. Roby and Schreiber, 160.
28. Roby and Schreiber, 160.
29. Roby and Schreiber, 164.
30. Cross, 140.
31. Roby and Schreiber, 160.
32. Hopkins, 79–80.
33. Cross, 148.

34. Cross, 149.
35. Hopkins, 81–82.

Chapter Eleven: Ticket to London

1. Cross, 143.
2. Cross, 144.
3. Cross, 146.
4. Cross, 147.
5. Hopkins, 83.
6. Cross, 151.
7. Roby and Schreiber, 172.
8. Cross, 152.
9. Roby and Schreiber, 172.
10. Cross, 152.
11. Hopkins, 85.
12. Cross, 152–53.

Chapter Twelve: Swingin' London

1. Cross, 158.
2. Shawn Levy, *Ready, Steady, Go!: The Smashing Rise and Giddy Fall of Swinging London* (Doubleday, 2002), 43.
3. Levy, 44.
4. Levy, 45.
5. Levy, 45–46.
6. Levy, 69.
7. Levy, 72–73.
8. Levy, 76.
9. Levy, 84.
10. Levy, 85.
11. Levy, 104.
12. Levy, 111.
13. Levy, 205.

Chapter Thirteen: The Experience

1. Hopkins, 88.
2. Hopkins, 88–89.
3. *Jimi Hendrix Experience: Electric Church*, directed by John McDermott (Legacy Recordings, 2015).
4. Cross, 155.
5. Cross, 156.
6. Norman, 101.
7. Cross, 170.
8. Cross, 158.
9. Cross, 160.

10. Cross, 161.
11. Cross, 162.
12. Hopkins, 90.
13. Norman, 104.
14. Cross, 162.
15. Hopkins, 90.
16. Cross, 159.
17. Hopkins, 90.
18. Hopkins, 90.
19. Cross, 160.
20. *Jimi Hendrix Experience.*
21. Cross, 164.
22. Cross, 165.
23. Cross, 166.
24. Hopkins, 93.
25. Cross, 166.
26. Cross, 167.
27. Cross, 167.
28. Cross, 169.
29. Cross, 170.
30. Cross, 171.
31. Cross, 171.
32. Cross, 171.
33. Hopkins, 91.
34. Cross, 172.
35. Hopkins, 95.
36. Cross, 174.
37. Cross, 174–75.
38. Cross, 175.
39. Cross, 176.
40. Cross, 176.
41. Cross, 177–78.
42. Hopkins, 97.
43. Cross, 178.
44. Hopkins, 97–98.
45. Cross, 179.
46. *Jimi Hendrix, A Selected Press Anthology.*
47. Cross, 183.
48. Cross, 183.
49. Cross, 182.
50. Cross, 180.
51. *Jimi Hendrix, A Selected Press Anthology.*
52. Cross, 184.
53. Cross, 184.
54. Cross, 185.

55. Cross, 186.
56. Cross, 187.
57. Cross, 188.
58. Cross, 189.

Chapter Fourteen: America

1. Hopkins, 114–15.
2. Hopkins, 116.
3. Cross, 191.
4. Cross, 192.
5. Cross 192.
6. Cross, 192–93.
7. Cross, 193.
8. *Jimi Hendrix Experience.*
9. Cross, 194.
10. *Jimi Hendrix, A Selected Press Anthology.*
11. Cross, 195.
12. Cross, 195.
13. Hopkins, 121.
14. Cross, 196–97.
15. Hopkins, 123.
16. Cross, 197.
17. Cross, 200.
18. Cross, 199–200.
19. Hopkins, 125.
20. Hopkins, 125.
21. Cross, 202.
22. Cross, 204.
23. *Jimi Hendrix, A Selected Press Anthology.*
24. Cross, 204.
25. Hopkins, 134.
26. Hopkins, 134.
27. *Jimi Hendrix, A Selected Press Anthology.*
28. Cross, 205.
29. Cross, 205.
30. *Jimi Hendrix, A Selected Press Anthology.*
31. Cross, 207.
32. Hendrix, *A Selected Press Anthology.*
33. Noel Redding and Carol Appleby, *Are You Experienced?: The Inside story of the Jimi Hendrix Experience* (Da Capo, 1996), 72.
34. Redding, 75.
35. Hopkins, 137.
36. Hopkins, 143.
37. *Jimi Hendrix, A Selected Press Anthology.*
38. Hopkins, 147.

39. *Jimi Hendrix, A Selected Press Anthology.*
40. Cross, 211.
41. Hopkins, 149.
42. *Jimi Hendrix, A Selected Press Anthology.*

Chapter Fifteen: Cheap Thrills on the Road of Sameness

1. Cross, *A Room Full of Mirrors*, 214–15.
2. Cross, 215.
3. Cross, 214.
4. Cross, 215.
5. Hopkins, 150.
6. *Jimi Hendrix, A Selected Press Anthology.*
7. Cross, 217.
8. Cross, 217–18.
9. Cross, 217–18.
10. Hopkins, 152.
11. Cross, 219.
12. Hopkins, 154–55.
13. Cross, 220.
14. Hopkins, 155.
15. Cross, 221.
16. Cross, 221.
17. Cross, 222.
18. Cross, 222.
19. *Jimi Hendrix, A Selected Press Anthology.*
20. Jimi Hendrix, 68.
21. Cross, 224.
22. Hopkins, 158–59.
23. Hopkins, 162–63.
24. Cross, 225.
25. Hopkins, 161.
26. Hopkins, 161.
27. Cross, 226.
28. Hopkins, 168.
29. Cross, 226.
30. Hopkins, 169.
31. *Jimi Hendrix, A Selected Press Anthology.*
32. *Jimi Hendrix, A Selected Press Anthology.*
33. *Jimi Hendrix, A Selected Press Anthology.*
34. Cross, 230–31.
35. Cross, 228.
36. Cross, 229.
37. Hopkins, 178.
38. Hopkins, 179.
39. Cross, 231.

40. Cross, 232.
41. Faith Hendrix, interview with author, spring 2025.
42. *Jimi Hendrix, A Selected Press Anthology.*
43. Cross, 233–34.
44. Cross, 235–36.
45. Cross, 237.

Chapter Sixteen: At Home with Handel

1. *Jimi Hendrix, A Selected Press Anthology.*
2. Cross, 239.
3. *Jimi Hendrix, A Selected Press Anthology.*
4. Cross, 241–42.
5. Hopkins, 184.
6. Hopkins, 186.
7. Cross, 242–43.
8. Cross, 243.
9. Cross, 244.
10. *Jimi Hendrix, A Selected Press Anthology.*
11. Cross, 244.
12. Cross, 243.
13. Cross, 246–47.
14. *Jimi Hendrix, A Selected Press Anthology.*
15. Cross, 248–49.
16. Cross, 245.
17. Hopkins, 190.
18. Cross, 249–50.
19. *Jimi Hendrix, A Selected Press Anthology.*
20. Cross, 250–51.
21. Cross, 251.
22. Cross, 251–52.

Chapter Seventeen: Bust and Boom

1. Hopkins, 202.
2. Hopkins, 200.
3. *Jimi Hendrix, A Selected Press Anthology.*
4. *Jimi Hendrix, A Selected Press Anthology.*
5. Cross, 255.
6. Cross, 256.
7. Cross, 257–58.
8. Hopkins, 204.
9. Hopkins, 205–6.
10. Hopkins, 206.
11. Hopkins, 207.
12. *Jimi Hendrix, A Selected Press Anthology.*

13. Cross, 246–47.
14. Cross, 259–60.
15. Cross, 259–60.
16. Hopkins, 212–13.
17. Hendrix, *A Selected Press Anthology.*
18. Cross, 262.
19. Hopkins, 219–20.
20. Cross, 264–65.
21. Cross, 266.
22. Hopkins, 222.
23. Norman, 230.

Chapter Eighteen: Woodstock

1. Steven C. Pesant, "Rainy Day, Dream Away: The Jimi Hendrix Experience: Miami Pop Festival," Jimi Hendrix, May 18, 2025, www.jimihendrix.com/editorial/rainy-day-dream-away-the-jimi-hendrix-experience-miami-pop-festival.
2. *Creating Woodstock,* directed by Mick Richards (Virtue Films, 2019).
3. *Creating Woodstock*, Virtue Films, 2019.
4. *Woodstock,* directed by Michael Wadleigh (Warner Bros., 1970).
5. *Woodstock*, Warner Bros., 1970.
6. Cross, 268.
7. Cross, 271.
8. *Jimi Hendrix, A Selected Press Anthology.*
9. Cross, 271.

Chapter Nineteen: Kidnapped and Released

1. Cross, 272–73.
2. Cross, 274.
3. Hendrix, *A Selected Press Anthology.*
4. Cross, 275.
5. Cross, 275–76.
6. Hopkins, 231.
7. Hopkins, 233–34.
8. Hopkins, 237.
9. *Jimi Hendrix, A Selected Press Anthology.*
10. Cross, 277–78.
11. Cross, 278–79.
12. *Jimi Hendrix, A Selected Press Anthology.*
13. Cross, 280.
14. Hopkins, 246–47.
15. Hopkins, 249.
16. Cross, 283–84.
17. Cross, 283.

Chapter Twenty: Playing Good Music

1. Cross, 285.
2. Cross, 285.
3. Cross, 286.
4. Cross, 287–88.
5. Hopkins, 271–72.
6. *Jimi Hendrix, A Selected Press Anthology.*
7. Hopkins, 267–68.
8. Hopkins, 267–68.
9. Bill Graham and Robert Greenfield, *Bill Graham Presents: My Life Inside Rock and Out* (Da Capo, 1992), 107.
10. Hopkins, 256–57.
11. Hopkins, 261.
12. Hopkins, 264.
13. Hopkins, 264–65.
14. *Jimi Hendrix, A Selected Press Anthology.*
15. Cross, 291.
16. Cross, 292.
17. Cross, 292–93.
18. Cross, 295.
19. Cross, 296–97.
20. Cross, 298.
21. Cross, 300–1.
22. Cross, 302.
23. Cross, 303.
24. Cross, 304.

Chapter Twenty-One: An Ending Too Soon

1. Cross, 300.
2. Cross, 307.
3. Cross, 308.
4. Cross, 309–10.
5. Cross, 311.
6. Cross, 312.
7. Hopkins, 286–87.
8. Cross, 313.
9. Cross, 312–13.
10. Hopkins, 288.
11. Cross, 314.
12. *Jimi Hendrix, A Selected Press Anthology.*
13. Cross, 315–16.
14. Cross, 316.
15. Cross, 318.
16. Cross, 320.

17. Cross, 321.
18. *Jimi Hendrix, A Selected Press Anthology.*
19. Cross, 322.
20. Cross, 323.
21. Cross, 323.
22. Cross, 323.
23. Norman, 283.
24. Cross, 323.
25. Cross, 324.
26. *Jimi Hendrix, A Selected Press Anthology.*
27. Cross, 325.
28. Cross, 325.
29. Hopkins, 297.
30. *Jimi Hendrix, A Selected Press Anthology.*
31. Cross, 327.
32. Cross, 327.
33. Cross, 328.
34. Cross, 329.
35. Steve Cropper, interview with author, August 2022.
36. Hopkins, 299.
37. Cross, 330.
38. Cross, 331.
39. Cross, 332.
40. Hopkins, 301–2.
41. Hopkins, 308–9.
42. Nora Hendrix interview, https://www.youtube.com/watch?v=RpIfFKwD034.
43. *Jimi Hendrix, A Selected Press Anthology.*

INDEX

About the Author

Wylie Graham McLallen grew up in Memphis, Tennessee, where his family has deep historical roots. At the University of Tennessee, while obtaining a degree in History and English, he studied Fiction and Composition under a distinguished man of Southern Letters, Professor Robert Drake (a close friend of author Flannery O'Conner) and was able to personally introduce his students to the poet and novelist James Dickey. Wylie worked as a programmer analyst at Malone & Hyde Inc., a wholesale grocery distributor in Memphis, and later owned a small business services center. He currently resides with his wife, Nickey Bayne, in Vancouver, British Columbia, where they have raised two grown children. He continues to write both history and fiction and is the author of *Tigers by the River*, a true story about the early years of pro football in America; and *Hemingway and the Rise of Modern Literature*, a two-volume history of the early years of modern literature. All his work is published by Sunbury Press.